THE LEGEND OF KING AŚOKA

Princeton Library of Asian Translations

JOHN S. STRONG

The Legend of King Aśoka

A Study and Translation of the *Aśokāvadāna*

Princeton University Press, Princeton, N.J.

Published by Princeton University Press, 41 William Street,
Princeton, New Jersey
In the United Kingdom: Princeton University Press,
Guildford, Surrey

Library of Congress Cataloging in Publication Data will be
found on the last printed page of this book

ISBN 0-691-06575-6
ISBN 0-691-01459-0, pbk.

First Princeton Paperback printing, 1989

This book has been composed in Linotron Sabon

Clothbound editions of Princeton University Press books
are printed on acid-free paper, and binding materials are
chosen for strength and durability. Paperbacks, although
satisfactory for personal collections, are not
usually suitable for library rebinding.

Printed in the United States of America by
Princeton University Press, Princeton, New Jersey

For S.M.S. and A.M.S.

Contents

Preface

I have tried, in this book, to be true to a text and to a context. The text is the Sanskrit work known as the *Aśokāvadāna* which tells, from a Buddhist point of view, the story of an Indian emperor of the third century B.C., Aśoka Maurya. A full translation of this legend appears below in Part Two.

The context is somewhat harder to describe. It involves, first of all, the Buddhist milieu of Northwest India where the text, as we now have it, was compiled, probably in the second century of our era. Secondly, it reflects the religious and literary traditions embodied in a number of other popularly oriented Buddhist works, in particular the Sanskrit *avadānas* (legends). Thirdly, and further afield, it includes certain traditions about King Aśoka that took root in other Buddhist centers, especially on the island of Sri Lanka and in Southeast Asia, where Aśoka was long seen as a paradigm of Buddhist kingship. Finally, and most generally, it involves a number of questions that have been of central importance to Buddhists throughout Asia. What is the nature of Buddhist kingship? What is the relationship between the state and the Buddhist monastic community? What role does the king play in this? What is the religious nature of practices such as merit making? What role does devotion play in Buddhism? These, and other questions of context, will be dealt with in the chapters of Part One.

The *Aśokāvadāna* is an interesting work because, ideologically, it stands somewhere between the Buddhist traditions best known to us today: the Pali tradition of Theravāda Buddhism that has prospered in South and Southeast Asia and the fully developed form of the Mahāyāna that was transmitted to China and Japan. Readers more familiar with either one of these traditions will constantly find affinities between the *Aśokāvadāna* and what they know. They should probably not, however, take those affinities too seriously, but allow room for the differences as well. As a product of the Sanskrit Hīnayānist (but non-Theravādin) circles of Northwest India, the *Aśokāvadāna* represents a tradition worthy of consideration in its own right, even though it is now no longer extant in this world.

Thanks and recognition are due here to a number of individuals and institutions: to the late J.A.B. Van Buitenen with whom I first read the *Aśokāvadāna*; to Frank Reynolds who was a constant source of encouragement and advice; to Joseph M. Kitagawa who was a fund of inspiration and support; to Stanley J. Tambiah and A. L. Basham who read and commented on manuscript versions of this work; to Sarah Mehlhop Strong for innumerable suggestions; to Margaret Case and Rita Gentry of Princeton University Press; to the American Council of Learned Societies for a grant-in-aid for 1979-80; and to the Center for the Study of World Religions for use of Harvard University's library facilities during the summer of 1979.

Lewiston, Maine
June, 1982

PART ONE. AŚOKA AND HIS LEGEND

CHAPTER ONE

The Legend and Its Background

When King Aśoka acceded to the Mauryan throne circa 270 B.C., he inherited an empire that extended from Bengal in the East to Afghanistan in the Northwest. His grandfather Candragupta had founded the dynasty, conquering the whole of the Gangetic plain and successfully pushing back the satraps of Alexander the Great. His father Bindusāra had campaigned in the Deccan Plateau, expanding the empire's frontiers as far south as Mysore. It was Aśoka, however, who brought the Mauryan dynasty to its apogee. After conquering the land of the Kalingas in the Southeast, he settled down to almost forty years of rule, in peace and relative prosperity. Under him, for the first time in history, virtually the entire Indian subcontinent was politically unified, with only the southernmost tip of the peninsula remaining outside his domain.

Aśoka is best known today for his royal edicts and rock inscriptions engraved on cliff faces and stone pillars all over his empire. In these he set forth his policies of enlightened rule. In what is, perhaps, the most famous of his edicts, he speaks in touchingly personal terms of his own remorse at the tremendous amount of suffering and loss of life caused by his war against the Kalingas. Henceforth, he states, he will give up violent means of conquest and devote himself entirely to the study, love, and propagation of Dharma.[1]

Precisely what Aśoka meant by Dharma has been the subject of much debate. In Buddhist circles, the word means the Buddha's Teachings—his doctrine—and it is thus widely supposed that this event marked Aśoka's conversion to the Buddhist

[1] N. A. Nikam and Richard McKeon, ed. and tr., *The Edicts of Aśoka* (Chicago: University of Chicago Press, 1959), p. 27. See also Jules Bloch, ed. and tr., *Les inscriptions d' Aśoka* (Paris: Les Belles Lettres, 1950), pp. 125-26.

faith. More generally, however, Dharma can be translated as law, duty, or righteousness, and as such it has many overtones in Indian religion. However he intended it, in his edicts, Aśoka seems to have been obsessed with Dharma. The Aśokan state was to be governed according to Dharma. The people were to follow Dharma. Wars of aggression were to be replaced by peaceful conquests of Dharma. Special royal ministers were charged with the propagation of Dharma. True delight in this world came only with delight in Dharma, and the old royal pleasure-tours and hunts were replaced by Dharma-pilgrimages.[2]

From these and other indications, we may say that Dharma seems to have meant for Aśoka a moral polity of active social concern, religious tolerance, ecological awareness, the observance of common ethical precepts, and the renunciation of war. In Pillar Edict VII, for example, he orders banyan trees and mango groves to be planted, resthouses to be built, and wells to be dug every half-mile along the roads.[3] In Rock Edict I, he establishes an end to the killing and consumption of most animals in the royal kitchens.[4] In Rock Edict II, he orders the provision of medical facilities for men and beasts.[5] In Rock Edict III, he enjoins obedience to mother and father, generosity toward priests and ascetics, and frugality in spending.[6] In Rock Edict V, he commissions officers to work for the welfare and happiness of the poor and aged.[7] In Rock Edict VI, he declares his intention constantly to promote the welfare of all beings so as to pay off his debt to living creatures and to work for their happiness in this world and the next.[8] And in Rock Edict XII, he honors men of all faiths.[9]

[2] Nikam and McKeon, pp. xii-xiii.
[3] Nikam and McKeon, p. 61; Bloch, p. 170.
[4] Nikam and McKeon, p. 55; Bloch, pp. 92-93.
[5] Nikam and McKeon, p. 64; Bloch, p. 94.
[6] Nikam and McKeon, p. 58; Bloch, p. 96.
[7] Nikam and McKeon, p. 59; Bloch, p. 104.
[8] Nikam and McKeon, p. 38; Bloch, p. 109.
[9] Nikam and McKeon, p. 51; Bloch, p. 121.

Because of these and other enlightened policies, students of world history have often spoken admiringly of Aśoka as a ruler. H. G. Wells, for example, finding in the edicts a seemingly modern monarch who appeared to share his own sociopolitical sympathies, declared: "Amidst the tens of thousands of names of monarchs that crowd the columns of history, their majesties and graciousnesses, and serenities and royal highnesses and the like, the name of Aśoka shines, and shines almost alone, a star. From the Volga to Japan, his name is still honoured. China, Tibet, and even India, though it has left his doctrine, preserve the tradition of his greatness. More living men cherish his memory today than ever have heard the names of Constantine or Charlemagne."[10]

There is nothing wrong with such paeans of praise as long as it is clear that they reflect only a personal enthusiasm for the image of Aśoka presented in the edicts. When, however, it is implied that Buddhists the world over—"from the Volga to Japan"—must have admired Aśoka for the same reasons, then an objection must be sounded. Historically speaking, Buddhists the world over have known virtually nothing about the Aśoka-of-the-edicts. Instead, their enthusiasm for Aśoka was based almost entirely on the Buddhist legends that grew up around him, and that form the subject of this book.

The Legends and the Edicts

There is a very simple explanation for the predominance of the legends. Although the edicts were inscribed in the third century B.C., the Brahmi script in which they were written was soon forgotten, and it was only with its decipherment by James Prinsep in 1837 that the Aśoka-of-the-edicts came to the fore once again.[11]

[10] H. G. Wells, *The Outline of History*, 2 vols. (New York: MacMillan Co., 1920) 1:433.

[11] See Romila Thapar, *Aśoka and the Decline of the Mauryas* (London: Oxford University Press, 1961), p. 31.

It is not certain how soon the Brahmi script was forgotten. In the memoirs of his journey to India (629-45), the Chinese pilgrim Hsüan-tsang several times claims to be able to read the inscriptions or, at least, to know what they say. For example, when he visits the site of the Buddha's final nirvāṇa in Kuśinagarī, he reports that the inscription on the Aśoka pillar there recounted the circumstances of the Blessed One's death and adds that, unfortunately, it did not give the day and month of that event.[12] On another occasion, he complains of the deteriorated condition of the script, but claims to be able to make out its meaning anyhow.[13]

Clearly, Hsüan-tsang wants to leave us with the impression that he, or at least someone he met, could actually read the text of the edicts. Unfortunately, the contents he attributes to these inscriptions simply do not correspond to the actual text of known Aśokan edicts. Indeed, in some instances where archaeologists have found the very pillars that Hsüan-tsang must have seen, and read the words he purports to have understood, there is no correspondence between them.[14] Despite his claims, then, it is clear that by his time, and most probably by the time of his predecessor Fa-hsien (whose voyage to India was from 399-414), the Indian script had long been forgotten and the message of the edicts lost.

It is sometimes assumed that, unable to read the inscriptions himself, Hsüan-tsang accepted the word of local monks or guides as to their contents, and that these, unable to read them either, quickly created some interpretation in order to gratify the pilgrim.[15] There may be some truth in this. As we shall see, centuries later, when the Sultan Firuz Shah of Delhi called

[12] Thomas Watters, *On Yuan Chwang's Travels in India*, 2 vols. (orig. pub., 1905; rpt., Delhi: Munshi Ram Manohar Lal, 1961) 2:28.

[13] Ibid., p. 93.

[14] Compare Watters, vol. 2, pp. 6, 17 and 48 with Bloch, pp. 158, 157 and 152.

[15] Radhakumud Mookerji, *Aśoka* (orig. pub. 1928; rpt., Delhi: Motilal Banarsidass, 1972), p. vii. See also V. R. Ramachandra Dikshitar, *The Mauryan Polity* (Madras: The University of Madras, 1932), p. 40.

upon certain Hindu pandits to interpret the inscriptions on an Aśoka pillar, they delivered on the spot a totally fanciful reading in order to please their patron.[16]

But this could hardly be the total explanation for Hsüan-tsang's misreadings of the inscriptions. What are we to make, for example, of the fact that, in one instance at least, he gives us exactly the same reading for a pillar inscription near Pāṭaliputra as his predecessor Fa-hsien did two and a half centuries earlier?[17] It may be, of course, that Hsüan-tsang (who was familiar with Fa-hsien's account of his journey) simply plagiarized his predecessor when he came to the same place, but this would hardly be characteristic of him. It is more likely that they were both told the same thing centuries apart.

Obviously, local guides at pilgrimage sites must have preserved and passed on their own traditions about the meaning of these cryptic inscriptions, however false their interpretations may in fact have been. There is no reason to suspect them of inventing a reading for an inscription out of embarrassment at their inability to read it; they were merely transmitting the oral tradition about what the inscriptions said.

Interestingly, this oral tradition did manage to preserve the knowledge of the connection between the edicts and the person of Aśoka. Even though they could not read the Brahmi inscriptions, nor even get anyone correctly to read them for them, the Chinese pilgrims were told that their author was Aśoka, a king about whom they already knew, of course, from the Buddhist legends. It comes as no surprise, then, that Hsüan-tsang's and Fa-hsien's misinterpretations of the Aśokan inscriptions reflect their knowledge of the Aśokan legends much more than the actual text of the edicts. This is important, for

[16] Shams-i Siraj 'Afif, *Tarikh-i Firoz Shahi*, ed. and tr. John Dowson in *The History of India as Told by its own Historians—The Posthumous Papers of the Late Sir H. M. Elliot*, vol. 3 (orig. pub., 1871; rpt., Allahabad: Kitab Mahal, n.d.), p. 352.

[17] Watters, vol. 2, p. 93; compare James Legge, tr. and ed., *A Record of Buddhistic Kingdoms* (orig. pub., 1886; rpt., New York: Paragon Book Co., 1965), p. 80.

it has long been customary, in scholarly circles, to read and interpret the legends of Aśoka in the light of the edicts. In the history of Buddhism, however, just the opposite happened; the pillars and inscriptions were explained in view of the legends. For example, both pilgrims, familiar with the Chinese versions of the Aśokan story, conceived of the king primarily as a supporter of the Buddhist *sangha* (monastic community) and as a great builder of the stūpas that marked the sites of their pilgrimage route. For them, the pillars were not edicts at all; they did not seek to proclaim a new royal Dharma but simply commemorated an event in the life of the Buddha or in the history of Buddhism and recorded what had happened at that spot. They were ancient signposts piously erected by Aśoka for the benefit of travellers and pilgrims. Thus, as we have seen, according to Hsüan-tsang, the Aśoka pillar at Kuśinagarī merely recounted the circumstances of the Buddha's death. Another pillar not far from there recorded the division of the Buddha's relics among the eight kings. A pillar at Aṭavi told how the Buddha had subdued certain demons there. An inscription at the stūpa of the former Buddha Krakucchanda related the circumstance of his death.[18] In the eyes of the pilgrims, then, Aśoka, much like the modern-day Indian Department of Archaeology, was responsible for marking the important Buddhist sites with signposts.

Now in the Aśokan legends, in both the Sanskrit and Chinese versions, this is precisely one of the things that Aśoka is presented as doing. In fact, prior to his pilgrimage tour with the elder Upagupta, he states his intention to visit all the important sites and to "mark them with signs as a favor to posterity."[19] There is some debate among scholars as to just what these signs were supposed to have been, but it may well be that the Chinese pilgrims and/or their local guides, familiar with the

[18] Watters, vol. 2, pp. 28, 42, 60-61, 6.

[19] Sujitkumar Mukhopadhyaya, ed., *The Aśokāvadāna* (New Delhi: Sahitya Akademi, 1963), p. 81. Compare Jean Przyluski, *La légende de l'empereur Açoka* (Paris: Paul Geuthner, 1923), p. 251.

legends but ignorant of the edicts, assumed that the pillars were just markers intended to commemorate local events.

Another instance of the way that the legends of Aśoka affected the interpretation of the edicts may be found in the pilgrims' account of a pillar edict at a site near Pāṭaliputra. Not too far from the city, Hsüan-tsang declares, "there was a stone pillar above thirty feet high, with an inscription much injured. The sum of the contents of the inscription was that Aśoka, strong in faith, had thrice given Jambudvīpa as a religious offering to the Buddhist order, and thrice redeemed it."[20]

Unfortunately, archaeologists have not found this inscribed pillar, so we have no way of definitely checking Hsüan-tsang's statement. But, as Vincent Smith has pointed out, such an inscription would hardly be in line with the content and character of the known edicts.[21] Hsüan-tsang's misreading of the inscription, however, makes perfect sense to one familiar with the legends of Aśoka. For in the legends, Aśoka is indeed portrayed, several times, as offering the whole world and his own sovereignty to the Buddhist sangha, and on one of these occasions, at the end of his life, he is even said to have made a written inscription recording his gift and testifying to his generosity and devotion.[22] Once again, the Chinese pilgrims may well have been misinterpreting the Aśokan edicts, but they were misinterpreting them in light of what they knew about Aśoka from the legends.

After the demise of Buddhism in India, however, in the twelfth and thirteenth centuries, even the association of the pillars with the name of Aśoka was forgotten. Shams-i Siraj 'Afif, the fourteenth-century chronicler of the reign of the Sultan Firuz Shah of Delhi (1351-88) provides some interesting details about the further fortunes of two of the Aśokan

[20] Watters, vol. 2, p. 93. Compare Legge, p. 80.

[21] Vincent Smith, *Aśoka, the Buddhist Emperor of India* (orig. pub., 1909; rpt., Delhi: S. Chand & Co., 1964), p. 125.

[22] Mukhopadhyaya, p. 132; Przyluski, p. 300.

pillars. According to him, Firuz Shah was "filled with admiration" for two stone columns at Topra and Mirat, and, wishing to have them as trophies and monuments to his glory, he had them transported to Delhi where they still stand today.[23] The account goes on to give details of their transport; they were packed in reeds and animal skins, lifted on to a forty-two-wheel carriage, hauled to the river and then taken by barge to the capital. The writing on the base of the pillars was examined with care. Many Brahmin scholars were asked to decipher it, but none was able. Some, however, declared the inscriptions stated that "no one [w]ould be able to remove the obelisk from its place till there should arise in the latter days a Muhammadan king named Sultan Firoz."[24]

While the pandits puzzled over these Aśokan edicts, however, popular opinion had already made up its mind about the pillars themselves. Again according to Shams-i Siraj, the local tradition was that "these columns of stone had been the walking sticks of the accursed Bhím [Bhīma, one of the Pāṇḍava brothers in the *Mahābhārata*], a man of great stature and size."[25] He goes on to specify that, in those days, beasts were much larger than they are now and that Bhím used these stone pillars as goads while tending his cattle. He and his brothers lived near Delhi, and when he died, these columns were left as memorials to him.[26]

It would be interesting to follow the further fortunes of the Aśokan pillars under Moghul and even British rule. One of the rock edicts, for example, was to become closely associated with a shrine of Śiva, and was the haunt of wild animals.[27] But it is clear that already in the fourteenth century, the in-

[23] Shams-i Sīraj 'Afif, p. 350.

[24] Ibid., p. 352.

[25] Ibid., p. 350.

[26] Ibid. On Aśoka in the *Mahābhārata*, see W. Hopkins, "Two Notes on the *Mahābhārata*—Religious Intolerance," in *Album Kern* (Leiden: E. J. Brill, 1903), pp. 249-51.

[27] See Smith, p. 133, and James M. MacPhail, *Aśoka* (London: Oxford University Press, n.d.), p. 66.

scriptions could not only not be read, but that, in the minds of pandits and populace alike, the pillars themselves had lost all connection with the name of Aśoka.

It is understandable, then, that when James Prinsep deciphered the Brahmi script in 1837 and correctly read the edicts, he did not know whose they were. Misled by Aśoka's use in his inscriptions of the name "Beloved of the Gods" (Devānāmpriya),[28] he claimed the pillars had been erected by King Devānampiya Tissa of Sri Lanka.[29] Shortly thereafter, George Turnour corrected him and rightly attributed the edicts to Aśoka. Interestingly enough, he did this on the basis of his knowledge of the Pali legends that also call Aśoka "Devānampiya."[30] Once again, the legends were influencing the reading of the edicts.

With the identity of the author of the edicts established, however, a new era in the evaluation of the figure of Aśoka began. Basically, two concerns now came to dominate Aśokan scholarship, both determined by the content and character not of the legends but of the epigraphy. First, because the inscriptions contain numerous references to various dates in the reign of Aśoka, there was a great temptation to reconstruct the history, or even more precisely the chronology, of Aśoka's life and rule. In this quest for the historical Aśoka, the edicts were accepted as the historical standard against which all other

[28] The first inscription to mention Aśoka specifically by name, that at Maski in Mysore, was not discovered until 1915 (see Bloch, p. 145).

[29] James Prinsep, "Interpretation of the Most Ancient of the Inscriptions on the Pillar called the Lát of Feroz Shah near Delhi, and of the Allahabad, Radhia, and Mattiah Pillar, or Lát, Inscriptions which Agree Therewith," *Journal of the Asiatic Society of Bengal* 6 (1837): 566. On the various possible interpretations of the epithet "Beloved of the Gods," see Louis de La Vallée Poussin, *L'Inde aux temps des Mauryas* (Paris: E. de Boccard. 1930), p. 79; Sylvain Lévi, "Notes de chronologie indienne—Devānāmpriya, Açoka et Kātyāyana," *Journal asiatique* 18 (1891): 549-53; and F. Kielhorn, "Bhagavat Tatrabhavat, and Devānāmpriya," *Journal of the Royal Asiatic Society*, 1908, pp. 502-550.

[30] George Turnour, "Further Notes on the Inscriptions on the Columns at Delhi, Allahabad, Beliah, etc.," *Journal of the Asiatic Society of Bengal* 6 (1837): 1054; see also La Vallée Poussin, p. 46.

materials were to be measured, and a whole spectrum of attitudes toward the historicity of the legendary traditions emerged. Some scholars were now inclined to dismiss the legends as "downright and absurd mythological accounts."[31] Others held that one could glean from them, especially from the Sinhalese chronicles, some valuable historical materials about Aśoka, although these must "be discredited when found lacking in corroboration from the inscriptions."[32] More liberally, others were willing to accept as historical all those portions of the legends that seemed plausible, some even maintaining that the Buddhist legends preserved "in a large measure a genuine historical tradition."[33]

There may well be something to be gained from these various attempts to read the legends as history or corrupted history, but most of them seem to involve a failure to take seriously into account the literary form and religious intent of the legends qua legends. A graphic example of this may be found in P.H.L. Eggermont's meticulous endeavor to establish an exact chronology for Aśoka's reign by means of a systematic comparison of the edicts and the legendary material. After recognizing that the *Aśokāvadāna*, by itself, is "little or not at all interested in the dating of the events during Aśoka's life,"[34] Eggermont nonetheless goes on to claim that the story of the elder Yaśas hiding the sun with his hand is a reference

[31] Dikshitar, p. 277.

[32] B. M. Barua, *Aśoka and His Inscriptions* (Calcutta: New Age Publishers, 1968) vol. 1, p. vi. See also Emile Sénart, *Les inscriptions de Piyadassi.* (Paris: Imprimerie Nationale, 1881) vol. 2, p. 231; idem., "Un roi de l'Inde au IIIe siècle avant notre ère," *Revue des deux mondes* 92 (1889): 104; T. W. Rhys Davids, *Buddhist India* (orig. pub., 1903; rpt., Calcutta: Susil Gupta, 1959), p. 126. Compare La Vallée Poussin, p. 81.

[33] B. G. Gokhale, *Asoka Maurya* (New York: Twayne Publishers, 1966), p. 172. See also G. M. Bongard-Levin, "The Historicity of the Ancient Indian Avadānas: A Legend about Aśoka's Deposition and the Queen's Edict," *Studies in Ancient India and Central Asia*, Soviet Indology Series, no. 7 (Calcutta: Indian Studies Past and Present, 1971), pp. 123-41.

[34] P.H.L. Eggermont, *The Chronology of the Reign of Asoka Moriya* (Leiden: E. J. Brill, 1956), p. 168.

to the partial solar eclipse that occurred in Northern India on May 4, 249 BC.[35] He seeks thereby to anchor chronologically other events in the legend, and to fit them all into a scheme whose inspiration and basic outline are determined by the edicts. Yaśas's act, however, as we shall see, has nothing to do with chronology at all, and to interpret it as such is grossly to ignore the overall literary and religious context of the legend as a whole.

A second concern of Aśokan scholarship has revolved around the nature of Aśoka's Dharma. Because Dharma was such a central concept in the edicts, it naturally became the focus of much attention and debate. In the process, two trends of thought seem to have emerged.

On the one hand, there are those who have interpreted Aśoka's Dharma in Buddhist terms, emphasizing accordingly the connections between the edicts and the legends. They argue that since Aśoka, in the legends, clearly becomes a Buddhist, the Dharma he propounds in his edicts must be seen as referring, more or less, to the doctrine of the Buddha. Moreover, they point out that in a number of edicts, Aśoka clearly shows his support for the Buddhist cause; he leaves an inscription at Lumbinī to record his pilgrimage to the Buddha's birthplace; he declares his reverence for the Buddha, the Dharma, and the sangha; and, in Rock Edict VIII, he states that, ten years after his coronation, he "left for Sambodhi [complete enlightenment]."[36] Of course, certain Buddhist doctrines, such as nirvāṇa and the Four Noble Truths, are not mentioned in the edicts, but this, we are told, is because, in them, Aśoka was essentially preaching the "Buddhism of the laity."[37] Some scholars have gone even further than this and sought to claim that Aśoka actually became a Buddhist monk,[38] or that, at

[35] Ibid., supplement 4.

[36] Bloch, pp. 112, 154, 157; Nikam and McKeon, pp. 37, 66, 69.

[37] B. G. Gokhale, *Buddhism and Aśoka* (Baroda: Padmaja Publications, 1948), pp. iii, 65; La Vallée Poussin, p. 122.

[38] Smith, p. 35; Sylvain Lévi, "Vyuthena 256," *Journal asiatique* 17 (1911):

least, he held some kind of status between that of a monk and a layperson.[39]

On the other hand, there are those who, for various reasons, have sought to minimize or even deny the Buddhist connections of Aśoka's edicts. They have tended, instead, to read Aśoka's Dharma in the context of the history and development of Indian political science. In particular, they have emphasized its connection or contrast with the most famous of the classical treatises on government, the *Arthaśāstra*, which is traditionally attributed to Kauṭilya, the chief minister of Aśoka's grandfather Candragupta.[40] These scholars recognize that some of the edicts hint at Aśoka's patronage of Buddhism, but they argue that there are really two kinds of Aśokan inscriptions: a few that are specifically addressed to the Buddhist community, and a much larger and more important number that are concerned with maintenance of order in the empire, and are addressed to the general public.[41] The ideas in these edicts, it is claimed, have little to do with Buddhism. As V. R. Ramachandra Dikshitar put it (perhaps out of a sense of Hindu nationalism), they are "in no way new but perfectly characteristic of Brahmanical Hinduism. . . . Aśoka could not have been a Buddhist."[42] What this has meant in terms of the legends is that there has been a tendency by these authors to dismiss them as more or less the fabrications of biased Bud-

---

121; Davids, *Buddhist India*, p. 129. The argument for Aśoka's becoming a monk rests on at least two pieces of evidence: his statement in one of the edicts that one year after becoming a lay follower, he presented himself to the community (see Bloch, p. 146), and the seventh-century Chinese pilgrim I-tsing's claim to have seen an image of Aśoka dressed in monastic robes (see Junjiro Takakusu, tr. *A Record of the Buddhist Religion as Practised in India and the Malay Archipelago (A.D. 671-694)* [orig. pub., 1896; rpt., Delhi: Munshiran Manoharlal, 1966], p. 73).

[39] Mookerji, p. 23; D. R. Bhandarkar, *Aśoka* (Calcutta: University of Calcutta Press, 1925), p. 75.

[40] Dikshitar, pp. 47, 114, 211; Barua, vol. 1, p. 157; Thapar, p. 10.

[41] See Romila Thapar, *A History of India*, vol. 1 (Harmondsworth: Penguin Books, 1966), p. 85.

[42] Dikshitar, pp. 258, 288.

dhists eager to show Aśoka's adherence to their religion. We should not, therefore, take them seriously since they are nothing but the "mendacious fictions of unscrupulous monks"[43] (as though that somehow made them less interesting or important).

The debate on all of these issues has yielded significant insights about the historical figure of Aśoka and the character of his Dharma, but it has done very little to enhance our understanding of the legends as legends. With only a few exceptions, since the decipherment of the Brahmi script, scholars have read the Aśoka legends principally in the light of the edicts.[44] In the sole context of the legends, however, it is quite clear that Aśoka did become a Buddhist, and that his status was that of a Buddhist king. Moreover, as we shall see, in them, the issues of chronology, or historicity, or even political science were not very significant.

It is good to remember that the authors of the Aśoka legends were as much in the dark about the content of Aśoka's inscriptions as we were until James Prinsep deciphered them. In this book, then, we shall deliberately try to return to a time when the edicts were unknown, so as to focus on the traditional significance of the legends of Aśoka which, independent of epigraphy, reflected the religious preoccupations of particular communities, and inspired countless Buddhists throughout Asia for many centuries.

[43] See Barua, vol. 1, pp. 2-3.

[44] The most noteworthy exceptions are Jean Przyluski (on whose work see below) and Eugène Burnouf. In his *Introduction à l'histoire du buddhisme indien*, originally published in 1844, the latter presents the *Aśokāvadāna* not as a potential source of information about the great Mauryan emperor whose edicts had just been deciphered, but simply as a fine example of avadāna literature (p. 319). He, in fact, mentions the edicts only once, in a footnote (p. 330), and although he certainly grants Aśoka his place as the hero of the legend, he seems little concerned with him and the details of his reign. Indeed, in one of his letters to Prinsep (see La Vallée Poussin, p. 46), Burnouf states clearly that, in this, he thought of his role as the explication and interpretation of texts touching on religion, philosophy, and literature.

A Synopsis of the *Aśokāvadāna*

A full consideration of all the legends of Aśoka would be an overwhelming undertaking; there are stories about him not only in Sanskrit but in Pali, Chinese, Tibetan, Japanese, Burmese, Thai, Sinhalese, and other Asian languages as well. We shall primarily be concerned with one text, the Sanskrit work known as the *Aśokāvadāna* presented in translation in Part Two. It might be useful, therefore, to summarize its contents here.

In its present form, our text exists as part of the *Divyāvadāna*, a voluminous Sanskrit anthology of Buddhist legends.[45] However, two Chinese translations of versions of our text, the *A-yü wang chuan* and the *A-yü wang ching*, testify to its independent existence as a separate work.[46] It begins not with the story of Aśoka himself but with that of the elder Upagupta, a Buddhist monk who eventually comes to play a major role in Aśoka's career. It tells first the legend of one of Upagupta's past lives, and then some stories about his birth and youth as the son of a perfume merchant in Mathurā, in Northern India, focussing especially on his encounters with the courtesan Vāsavadattā. It then gives an account of his ordination as a Buddhist monk, of his enlightenment, and finally of his dramatic conversion of Māra, the chief god of the realm of desire (*kāmadhātu*) who plays a somewhat satanic role as a tempter in Buddhism.

Only then does the text switch to the legend of Aśoka per se. Here again, it begins not with Aśoka's birth but with the tale of his previous life as a little boy named Jaya. Jaya is playing by the side of the road when he meets the Buddha,

[45] See P. L. Vaidya, ed., *Divyāvadānam*, Buddhist Sanskrit Texts, no. 20, (Darbhanga, Bihar: Mithila Institute, 1959), pp. 216-82.

[46] The *A-yü wang chuan* (Taishō Tripiṭaka No. 2042) was rendered into Chinese by Fa-ch'in circa 300 A.D. A French translation of it may be found in Przyluski, pp. 225-427. Its Sanskrit title is usually assumed to have been the *Aśokarājāvadāna*. The *A-yü wang ching* (Taishō Tripiṭaka No. 2043) was translated by Sanghabhara in 512 A.D.-Its Sanskrit title is usually given as the *Aśokarājasūtra*.

and promptly offers him a handful of dirt—an act that is to have important karmic consequences for the rest of Aśoka's career. Following this prelude, the text takes us up to the actual time of Aśoka that it repeatedly describes as being one hundred years after the death and *parinirvāṇa* (final nirvāṇa) of the Buddha.

Born as the son of King Bindusāra, Aśoka is, from the start, disliked by his father because of his ugliness. Nonetheless a fortuneteller makes it clear that Aśoka will accede to the throne, and after some clever conniving and the disposal of his stepbrother (the legitimate heir) he does, in fact, do so. He quickly becomes known to his subjects as "Aśoka the Fierce" because of his malicious and impetuous nature. He oppresses the people by building a terrible prison where individuals are randomly tortured and put to death. One day, however, he encounters in this prison a young Buddhist monk who is seemingly immune to all the sufferings inflicted upon him. Tremendously impressed by this (as well as by the other magical feats performed by the monk), Aśoka converts to the Buddhist faith. He destroys the prison and undertakes the greatly meritorious project of building eighty-four thousand *stūpas* (Buddhist reliquary mounds) throughout his empire. Henceforth, he becomes known as Dharma-Aśoka—"Aśoka the Righteous."

There follows a series of stories further demonstrating Aśoka's support for the Buddhist cause. First of all, by clever means, he converts his brother Vītaśoka. Then, he shows Yaśas, one of his ministers, why it is important always to honor the Buddhist monks. Next, he meets the elder Upagupta, and together they go on a grand pilgrimage to all the holy places associated with events in the life of the Buddha. Then, Aśoka proceeds on his own to pay particular respect to the Bodhi tree at Bodhgaya where the Blessed One was enlightened. He also takes it upon himself to entertain the Buddhist monks by holding a great quinquennial festival (*pañcavārṣika*); in the midst of these festivities, he encounters the mysterious figure of Piṇḍola Bhāradvāja, an arhat (enlightened saint) who had known the Buddha personally and who, by means of his supernatural powers, extended his lifespan in order to remain as a living witness to the Buddha's Teachings.

There then intervenes the story of Aśoka's son, Prince Kunāla. In this tragic tale, Kunāla, a handsome and righteous young man much loved by his father, is cruelly blinded while away from the capital, as a result of the contrivances of his evil and jealous stepmother, Queen Tiṣyarakṣitā. In the midst of his torment, however, he realizes the nature of suffering and impermanence, and so attains enlightenment. He then wanders throughout the land as a blind beggar, scraping together a living by singing and playing the vīṇā. Eventually he returns to the capital where, in an emotional scene, he is reunited with his father.

After this somewhat lengthy episode, the text then turns to the story of Aśoka's last days. Terminally ill, Aśoka is caught up in a sudden fever of generosity, and starts using state funds to make donations to the Buddhist monks. His ministers, fearful that he will soon deplete the empire's resources, quickly move to restrict his powers by denying him access to the treasury. Aśoka then starts giving away his own personal fortune, but is soon restricted in this as well. Destitute and powerless, the once great king ends up on his deathbed with nothing but half of a myrobalan fruit. This too he sends to the Buddhist community (sangha) as his final offering. Then, with nothing left, but everything gained, he passes away with a serene mind, having comprehended the vagaries of kingship.

The text then reinforces this lesson in impermanence by ending with the story of King Puṣyamitra, one of Aśoka's descendants, who vehemently persecutes the Buddhist monks and tries to undo everything his forefather accomplished. Nothing, not even the Buddhist religion, will last forever.

The Sanskrit and Pali Recensions of the Legend

Many of the episodes we have just recounted may be found, in somewhat different versions, in a number of other sources in Sanskrit or inspired by the Sanskrit tradition but no longer extant in the original. Chief among these are the several chapters devoted to Aśoka in the *Saṃyuktāgama* (*Tsa a han ching*; Taishō Tripiṭaka No. 99), and in Aśvaghoṣa's *Sūtrālaṃkāra* that was translated into Chinese by Kumārajīva in A.D. 405.[47] Of later date but worth noting are the *Avadānakalpalatā* presenting a number of Aśokan stories reworked by the eleventh-century Kashmiri poet Kṣemendra; the *Aśokāvadānamālā*, a vast and still unedited compendium of Buddhist legends including many about Aśoka; the *Lokapaññatti*, a Pali text based on the Sanskrit tradition whose presentation of the Aśokan story was influential in Burma and Thailand; and Tāranātha's *Chos ḥbyung (History of the Dharma)*, a late sixteenth-century Tibetan work based on earlier Sanskrit sources, some of which are now lost.[48] The *Aśokāvadāna*, however, represents what might be called the basic version of the Sanskrit recension of the Aśoka legend and was popular in Northwest India and, in translation, in Central Asia, China, Korea, Japan, and Tibet.

There also exists, however, a Pali recension of the Aśoka legend that was influential in Sri Lanka, Burma, Thailand, and other parts of Southeast Asia. It is found principally in the fifth-century chronicles of the island of Sri Lanka, the *Mahāvaṃsa* and the *Dīpavaṃsa*, as well as in Buddhaghosa's

[47] On these various sources, see Przyluski, pp. 55ff. See also Edouard Huber, tr., *Aśvaghoṣa Sūtrālaṃkāra* (Paris: E. Leroux, 1908); and idem., "Etudes de littérature bouddhique: trois contes du *Sūtrālaṃkāra* d'Aśvaghoṣa conservés dans le *Divyāvadāna*," *Bulletin de l'Ecole Française d'Extrême-Orient* 4 (1904): 709-26.

[48] See P. L. Vaidya, ed., *Avadāna-Kalpalatā*, 2 vols., Buddhist Sanskrit Texts, nos. 22-23 (Darbhanga, Bihar: Mithila Institute, 1959), especially stories 59, 71, 72, 74. On the *Aśokāvadānamālā,* see Rajendralal Mitra, *The Sanskrit Buddhist Literature of Nepal* (Calcutta; Asiatic Society of Bengal, 1882), pp. 6-17. See also Eugène Denis, ed. and tr., *La Lokapaññatti et les idées cosmologiques du bouddhisme ancien*, 2 vols. (Lille: Atelier Reproduction des thèses, 1977) 1:157-77 (text), 2:141-54 (tr.). For a discussion of Tāranātha's sources in his account of Aśoka, see Tāranātha, *History of Buddhism in India*, trans. Lama Chimpa and Alaka Chattopadhyaya (Simla: Indian Institute of Advanced Study, 1970), pp. 363-66.

commentary on the Vinaya.[49] In addition, interesting variants on a number of episodes of this Pali recension of the legend may be found in the commentary on the *Mahāvaṃsa*; in the *Thūpavaṃsa*, or chronicle of the great Ruvanväli stūpa in Sri Lanka; in the *Mahābodhivaṃsa*, or chronicle of the branch of the Bodhi tree sent from India to Sri Lanka; and, in Thai, in the *Trai Phum Phra Ruang (Three Worlds According to King Ruang)*.[50]

There are many parallels between the Sanskrit and the Pali recensions[51] of the Aśoka legend, and these have often been emphasized by scholars studying these traditions. For exam-

[49] Wilhelm Geiger, ed., *The Mahāvaṃsa* (orig. pub. 1908; rpt., London: Luzac and Co., 1958), see esp. ch. 5; compare Wilhelm Geiger, tr., *The Mahāvaṃsa or the Great Chronicle of Ceylon* (London: Pali Text Society, 1912), ch. 5; B. C. Law, ed. and tr., *The Dīpavaṃsa, Ceylon Historical Journal* 7 (1957-58), pp. 49ff. and 172ff.; N. A. Jayawickrama, ed. and tr., *The Inception of Discipline and the Vinaya Nidana*, Sacred Books of the Buddhists, 21 (London: Luzac and Co., 1962), pp. 37-55, 165-80.

[50] G. P. Malalasekera, ed., *Mahāvaṃsa-ṭīkā*, 2 vols. (London: Pali Text Society, 1935-36), 1:125ff; N. A. Jayawickrama, ed. and tr., *The Chronicle of the Thūpa and the Thūpavaṃsa*, Sacred Books of the Buddhists, 28 (London: Luzac and Co., 1971), pp. 47-55, 184-90; S. Arthur Strong, ed., *Mahābodhivaṃsa* (London: Pali Text Society, 1891), 98-111; and Frank E. Reynolds and Mani B. Reynolds, tr., *Three Worlds According to King Ruang*, Berkeley Buddhist Studies Series, vol. 4 (Berkeley: Asian Humanities Press, 1982), pp. 172-88.

[51] I am by no means satisfied with the use of these two terms, but it should be clear that by "Sanskrit" I do not mean Mahāyāna nor Theravāda by "Pali." Such a classification according to schools would make little sense in the context of these popular traditions. There was moreover some overlap between the two linguistic traditions. In Burma, for example, the Aśoka legends contained in the Pali text, the *Lokapaññatti*, are clearly based on the Sanskrit tradition. See Eugène Denis, "La *Lokapaññatti* et la légende birmane d'Aśoka," *Journal asiatique* 264 (1976): 97-116. In China, on the other hand, we find the Pali version of the Aśoka story translated in the Chinese rendition of Buddhaghosa's Commentary on the Vinaya. See Hubert Durt, "La version chinoise de l'introduction historique de la Samantapāsādikā," 3 vols. (Ph.D. Dissertation, Université Catholique de Louvain, Institut Orientaliste, 1970), and P. V. Bapat and Akira Hirakawa, trs., *Shan-Chien-P'i-P'o-Sha: A Chinese Version by Saṅghabhadra of the Samantapāsādikā*, Bhandarkar Oriental Series, No. 10 (Poona: Bhandarkar Oriental Research Institute, 1970), pp. 20-32.

ple, both tell the story of Aśoka's previous life, of his birth as the son of King Bindusāra, of his somewhat violent accession to the throne, of his conversion by a young Buddhist monk, of his construction of eighty-four thousand stūpas (or *vihāras* [monasteries] in the *Mahāvaṃsa*), of his donations to the Buddhist community, of his worship of the Bodhi tree.

Despite these immediate similarities, however, what is perhaps more striking in the long run are the differences between the two recensions. Taking the *Aśokāvadāna* and the *Mahāvaṃsa* as the two most representative texts of the two traditions, we may usefully take note of some of these differences here. The first concerns an apparently minor discrepancy, but one that has been the subject of much discussion. In the *Aśokāvadāna*, Aśoka is said to have been born one hundred years after the parinirvāṇa of the Buddha; in the *Mahāvaṃsa*, however, he is said to have been consecrated king 218 years after the parinirvāṇa. Scholars interested in chronological problems have spent much energy trying to deal with this discrepancy. Some have even argued that the *Aśokāvadāna* has here confused the figure of the great emperor Aśoka with that of his reputed forefather, King Kālāśoka, who is unknown in the Sanskrit tradition, but who, according to the *Mahāvaṃsa*, was reigning at the time of the Second Buddhist Council at Vaiśālī a century after the death of the Buddha.[52]

There is, however, little reason to believe that the *Aśokāvadāna*'s declaration that Aśoka lived one hundred years after the parinirvāṇa was intended as a chronological statement at all. On the one hand, it contradicts the text's own indication that there were eleven generations of kings between the Buddha's contemporary, King Bimbisāra, and Aśoka; eleven generations can hardly fit into a single century. On the other hand, as we shall see, the designation "one hundred years"

[52] Barua, vol. 1, p. 41. See also Jean Filliozat, "Les deux Aśoka et les conciles bouddhiques," *Journal asiatique* 236 (1948): 189-95. For a summary discussion of Kālāśoka, see Etienne Lamotte, *Histoire du bouddhisme indien* (Louvain: Institut Orientaliste, 1958), p. 105.

was simply a traditional way of stating that Aśoka was living at a time when there was no one still alive who had actually known the Buddha personally.

What we are dealing with here, then, is not a chronological issue, but something reflecting a much greater difference in the whole outlook of these two texts; while the *Mahāvaṃsa* as a *vaṃsa* (a chronicle) is naturally concerned with history and lineage, the *Aśokāvadāna*, as an *avadāna* (a legend) is not; its focus is on the religious and psychological setting of its story.

The importance of this difference in literary genre cannot be overestimated. An avadāna is a narrative of the religious deeds of an individual and is primarily intended to illustrate the workings of karma and the values of faith and devotion. It can often be moralistic in tone but at the same time there is no denying that it has a certain entertainment value. The avadānas were and still are used by Buddhist preachers in popular sermons, and as such have often been compared to the *jātakas* (stories of the Buddha's previous lives). Unlike the jātakas, however, the main protagonist of the avadāna is usually not the Buddha himself, but a more ordinary individual, often a layman.[53] As an avadāna, then, the *Aśoka-avadāna* emphasizes the karmic deeds of Aśoka and of his family—in this and in past lives. Most especially it focusses on his acts of merit and on his relationship as a Buddhist king to the Buddha and to the members of the sangha.

A vaṃsa, on the other hand, is a lineage or chronicle. It is primarily concerned with giving the sacred pedigree of a country (such as Sri Lanka), or of a particular Buddhist sect, or of

[53] For discussions and descriptions of avadāna literature, see Maurice Winternitz, *A History of Indian Literature*, trans. S. Ketkar (Calcutta: University of Calcutta Press, 1933), vol. 2, pp. 277-94; W. G. Weeraratne, "Avadāna," *Encyclopedia of Buddhism*, ed., G. P. Malalasekera (Colombo: Government Publications, 1966); Ratna Handurukande, ed. and tr., *Maṇicūḍāvadāna and Lokānanda*, Sacred Books of the Buddhists, 24, (London: Luzac and Co., 1967), pp. xix-xxiii; and J. A. Nilakantha Sastri, *Gleanings on Social Life from the Avadānas* (Calcutta: Indian Research Institute, 1945).

a holy object. Its overall emphasis is on tracing the line of descent from the time of the Buddha down to the time of the author of the text. In terms of the Aśoka legends, this has meant that the *Mahāvaṃsa* has been primarily interested in Aśoka as an important link in the chain of legitimacy connecting the Buddhists of Sri Lanka (and in particular the kings of that island) with the Buddhists of ancient India, and ultimately with the Buddha himself.[54]

Given these basic differences in literary genre and in the orientation of the two texts, it now becomes easier to assess some of the specific divergences between them. For example, one of the important stories in the *Mahāvaṃsa* that is absent in the *Aśokāvadāna* tells how Aśoka convenes and participates in the Third Buddhist Council at Pāṭaliputra. As a result of Aśoka's great munificence, we are told, the Buddhist community in India has come to enjoy unprecedented prosperity. Therefore, many heretics, seeking a life of relative ease, have donned the yellow robe and entered the sangha while still continuing to maintain their heretical views. The strict Theravādins, however, refuse to carry out the bimonthly ceremony of confession with them, since its celebration demands the purity of all members of the community. The situation worsens until Aśoka, after some initial unsuccessful attempts to resolve the issue, enlists the help of the great elder Moggaliputta Tissa. Together, the king and the elder examine all the monks as to their beliefs, and purge the ranks of the community, defrocking no less than sixty thousand adherents of false views. Only those monks who accept the Vibhajja doctrine, that is, the orthodox Theravāda beliefs, are allowed to remain in the sangha. Then, under Aśoka's sponsorship, a

[54] For discussions of the form and function of the Sinhalese chronicles, see Heinz Bechert, "The Beginnings of Buddhist Historiography: *Mahāvaṃsa* and Political Thinking," in *Religion and Legitimation of Power in Sri Lanka*, ed. Bardwell L. Smith (Chambersburg, Pa.: Anima Books, 1978), pp. 1-12; and Bardwell L. Smith, "The Ideal Social Order as Portrayed in the Chronicles of Ceylon," ibid., pp. 48-72.

great council is held by the Theravādins who come together and recite the true Dharma.[55]

Obviously, the whole thrust of this account is to associate the great king Aśoka with the specific sect of the Theravādins favored by the authors of the *Mahāvaṃsa* and, by implication, by the island of Sri Lanka in general. In the *Aśokāvadāna*, however, there is no mention at all either of the elder Moggaliputta Tissa or of this Third Council.

Some have argued that, in the Sanskrit tradition, the elder Upagupta plays the role of Tissa and must therefore be identified with him, but, as we shall see, there are difficulties with this parallelism.[56] As to the Third Council, the closest the *Aśokāvadāna* gets to it, perhaps, is its account of Aśoka's great quinquennial festival, but that too is really quite a different tradition. As one might expect in an avadāna, it is primarily concerned with illustrating Aśoka's great meritorious deeds; it involves no purification of the doctrine, no purge of unorthodox monks, and the similarities between it and the Third Council do not extend much further than the fact that they are both large assemblies of monks.[57]

Following the account of the Third Council in the *Mahāvaṃsa*, there is another episode that does not figure at all in

[55] Geiger, tr. pp. 45ff. See also André Bareau, *Les premiers conciles bouddhiques*, Annales du Musée Guimet, vol. 60 (Paris: 1955), pp. 112-33. For several different comparisons of the chronicles and the edicts on the matter of schisms in the sangha, see Heinz Bechert, "Aśokas 'Schismenedikt' und der Begriff Sanghabheda," *Wiener Zeitschrift für die Kunde Süd-und Ostasiens* 5 (1961): 18-52; N. A. Jayawickrama, "A Reference to the Third Council in Aśoka's Edicts?" *University of Ceylon Review* 17 (1959): 61-72; and Ludwig Alsdorf, "Aśoka's Schismen-Edikt und das dritte Konzil," *Indo-Iranian Journal* 3 (1959): 161-74.

[56] L. A. Waddell, "Upagupta, the Fourth Buddhist Patriarch, and High Priest of Açoka," *Journal of the Asiatic Society of Bengal* 66 (1897): 76-84; idem, "Identity of Upagupta, the High-priest of Açoka with Moggaliputta Tisso," in *Proceedings of the Asiatic Society of Bengal* 1899, pp. 70-75; Vincent Smith, "Aśoka's Father Confessor," *Indian Antiquary* 32 (1903): 365-66. For more balanced accounts of both the parallels and differences between the legends of these two elders, see Przyluski, p. 112 and Lamotte, p. 225.

[57] See Mukhopadhyaya, pp. 100ff.

the *Aśokāvadāna*: the dispatch of missionaries to spread the Buddhist faith. For example, the elder Majjhantika, we are told, is sent to Kashmir and Gandhāra, the elder Majjhima to the Himālayas, Mahādhammarakkhita to Mahāraṣtra, and Soṇa and Uttara to Suvaṇṇabhūmi in Southeast Asia. Finally, and most importantly for the *Mahāvaṃsa*, Aśoka's own son, the elder Mahinda, is sent to Sri Lanka.[58]

There may well be some truth to this whole episode concerning the missionaries. The relics of some of the elders mentioned in the *Mahāvaṃsa* have been uncovered by archaeologists at Sāñchī, and to this day, Buddhists in all the countries referred to commonly trace the arrival of the faith in their land to these Aśokan envoys.[59] At the same time, however, the story of Mahinda, which is given in more detail than the others, is clearly governed, once again, by the desire of the author of the *Mahāvaṃsa* to enhance the prestige of the Theravādins of Sri Lanka and emphasize the intimate family connection between their founding father Mahinda and the great emperor Aśoka.

In the *Aśokāvadāna*, on the other hand, there is no reference to this tradition, and no mention at all of the elder Mahinda. In much later Sanskrit sources, there are references to an elder Mahendra who is perhaps identifiable with Mahinda and is variously portrayed as a disciple of Ānanda, a contemporary of the Buddha, or a younger brother of Aśoka.[60] But in the *Aśokāvadāna*, as we have seen, Aśoka's son is called Kunāla, and his story serves to point out the workings of karma in the lives of both the prince and the father.

One more illustration of this basic difference in outlook

[58] Geiger, tr., pp. 82ff.

[59] For a summary account of all of the missions, see Lamotte, pp. 320ff. For a discussion of the historicity of one of them, see Erich Frauwallner, "Die ceylonesischen Chroniken und die erste buddhistische Mission nach Hinterindien," in *Actes du IVe Congrès International des Sciences Anthropologiques* (Vienna, 1955), vol. 2. pp. 192-97.

[60] See Sylvain Lévi, ed. and tr., *Mahākarmavibhaṅga et Karmavibhaṅgopadeśa* (Paris: E. Leroux, 1932), pp. 63, 131; Watters, vol. 2, pp. 93, 230, 234; Lamotte, p. 332.

between the *Mahāvaṃsa* and the *Aśokāvadāna* should be given here. The dissimilarity in their world views resulted not only in their emphasis on different stories about Aśoka, it also led to radically different treatments of one and the same legend. For example, both texts relate the story of Aśoka's wicked queen, Tiṣyarakṣitā (Pali, Tissarakkhā) and her use of black magic on the Bodhi tree at Bodhgaya. In the *Mahāvaṃsa*, she seeks to injure the tree soon after Aśoka sends one of its branches to Sri Lanka for transplanting, and her endeavor meets with success when the original tree withers and dies.[61] The implication is, of course, clear: Sri Lanka is now in sole possession of the living tree of enlightenment; what has died in India still thrives on the island. In the *Aśokāvadāna*, however, Tiṣyarakṣitā is not successful. She does not carry through with her plan, and the Bodhi tree, instead of perishing, recovers through Aśoka's devoted care.[62]

The World of the *Aśokāvadanā*

There are many other divergences and discrepancies between the *Mahāvaṃsa* and the *Aśokāvadāna*'s account of the Aśoka legend,[63] and we shall be examining some of them in detail in the course of the chapters that follow. At this point, however, we should turn to consider the milieu in which the *Aśokāvadāna* itself took form.

We do not know who composed the text of the *Aśokāvadāna*, nor indeed whether it can be considered the work of a single author. Its first translation into Chinese in A.D. 300 sets its annus ante quem; its reference to the gold coin *dīnāra* puts

[61] Geiger, tr., p. 136.

[62] Mukhopadhyaya, pp. 93ff.

[63] In addition to the differences mentioned, there are several episodes in the *Aśokāvadāna* which do not figure at all in the *Mahāvaṃsa* and with which we shall deal during the course of our discussion: the story of Aśoka and his minister Yaśas, the tale of Aśoka's pilgrimage with the elder Upagupta, the episode of his encounter with the great arhat Piṇḍola Bhāradvāja, and the tragic account of Aśoka's final gift to the sangha of half a myrobalan.

at least part of it after the first century A.D., so we probably would not err too much in assigning it, in its present form, to the second century A.D.[64] The legends themselves, however, are clearly several centuries older than that. Some of them have been represented on the bas-reliefs of the stūpa at Sāñchī (second-first centuries B.C.), and it is likely that at least some Aśoka stories, in one form or another, were current in Buddhist oral tradition shortly after Aśoka's death.[65]

We do know more or less, however, where the *Aśokāvadāna* was composed. Jean Przyluski, in his *Légende de l'empereur Açoka*, claims to have detected several layers of tradition in the text. He traces the journey of the Aśoka legend as it moved westward from Aśoka's old capital of Pāṭaliputra (modern-day Patna) to Kauśāmbī (near the confluence of the Jumna and the Ganges), and thence on to Mathurā. At each stage along the way, it accumulated new motifs and featured new stories about a local abbot. Thus, in the first stratum of the text, we find stories concerning Yaśas, the elder of the Kukkuṭārāma Monastery near Pāṭaliputra, while in the Kauśāmbī phase, the arhat Piṇḍola is featured.[66] But it is on the figure of Upagupta and the community of Mathurā that Przyluski fixes his attention. The Mathurans, he claims, were responsible for the basic recension of the text, and throughout the work sought to promote the interests of the community and the fame of their favorite son. Przyluski is quite dogmatic about this: "The wish to glorify Mathurā, its saints and its monasteries . . . comes out in every part of the *Aśokāvadāna*. The work could be entitled 'The Legend of Upagupta,' with the subtitle: 'A praise and glorification of the Church at Mathurā.' Never have local influences been more rigorous in determining the contents of a religious work. This Māhātmya

[64] Mukhopadhyaya, p. ix.

[65] John Marshall, *A Guide to Sāñchī*, 3rd ed. (Calcutta: Government of India Press, 1955), pp. 50-68. See also Przyluski, pp. 92ff., and Winternitz, p. 288.

[66] Przyluski, p. 118.

could only have been compiled by a writer from the land of Mathurā."[67]

Although there are a number of problems with this point of view (for example, Upagupta is not as consistently related to the city of Mathurā as Przyluski would have us believe),[68] it is probably true that the *Aśokāvadāna* in its present form should be seen as a product of the Buddhist Sanskrit community of Mathurā or, more generally, of Northwest India as a whole.

This enables us, then, to gain a better understanding of the religious milieu that formed our text. From the time of its first establishment in the fifth century B.C., Buddhism was a missionary religion. From the region of the Middle Ganges where the Buddha himself had lived, preached, and died, it spread within a few generations throughout most of India. Early on, the region of Mathurā, an important center on the Jumna River, must have received the attention of the Buddhist missionaries.

In fact, in the *Vinaya of the Mūlasarvāstivādins*, a Northwestern Indian Sanskrit text compiled later than the *Aśokāvadāna* but with close affinities to it,[69] there is a story that would have us believe the Buddha himself visited Mathurā. It records, however, his rather negative impression of the city. "Monks," he declared, "there are five bad things about Mathurā. What five? The ground is uneven, it is covered with stumps and thorns, there are a lot of stones, grit and gravel, people eat at night, and there are too many women."[70] Much

[67] Ibid., p. 8.

[68] See on this John Strong, "The Buddhist Avadānists and the Elder Upagupta," in *Tantric and Taoist Studies in Honour of R. A. Stein*, ed. Michel Strickmann, *Mélanges chinois et bouddhiques*, vols. 20-22 (forthcoming).

[69] See Edouard Huber, "Les sources du Divyāvadāna," *Bulletin de l'Ecole Française d'Extrême-Orient* 6 (1906): 1-37; Sylvain Lévi, "Eléments de formation du Divyāvadāna," *T'oung pao* 8 (1908): 105-22; and Vaidya, *Divyāvadānam*, pp. viii, 548.

[70] Nalinaksha Dutt, ed. *Gilgit Manuscripts*, vol. 3, pt. 1 (Srinagar: Research Department, 1947), pp. 14-15; see also Watters, vol. 1, p. 312; Nalinaksha Dutt and Krishna Datta Bajpai, *Development of Buddhism in Uttar Pradesh*

the same statement can be found in the Pali *Aṅguttara Nikāya* where we are told that, in Mathurā, "[the ground] is uneven; there is much dust; there are fierce dogs; bestial yakkhas [demons]; and alms are got with difficulty."[71]

In spite of these drawbacks, however, Buddhism soon became established in the region. The *Vinaya of the Mūlasarvāstivadins*, in fact, also tells of the rather quick conversion of a learned Brahmin from Mathurā named Nīlabhūti. The story is interesting in its own right; the Brahmins of Mathurā, unhappy about the fact that the Buddha is preaching the purity of all four castes, ask their teacher, Nīlabhūti, publicly to revile the Blessed One. Nīlabhūti, however, has a tongue that will only speak the truth; it reviles what deserves to be reviled, and praises what is worthy of praise. Thus, when together with the most venerable Brahmins of Mathurā, he goes to encounter the Buddha, instead of condemning him, he breaks out, willy-nilly, into no less than forty stanzas in praise of the Blessed One and his teachings. He then converts, is instructed in the Dharma, and soon attains enlightenment.[72]

Another story of an important conversion—that of the king of Mathurā named Avantiputta (Skt., Avantiputra)—may be found in the *Majjhima Nikāya* in the relatively short "Madhurā Sutta." This sutta (Skt., sūtra) is set quite frankly after the death of the Buddha. King Avantiputta visits Mahākaccāna (Skt., Mahākātyāyana), a disciple of the Buddha, and inquires about caste. The Brahmins, he says, claim that they are the highest, fairest, and purest of all castes; what do the Buddhists say? Mahākaccāna answers with various arguments designed to show the insignificance of all caste distinctions,

---

(Lucknow: Government of Uttar Pradesh Publication Bureau, 1956), p. 261; and, more generally, Jean Przyluski, "Le Nord-ouest de l'Inde dans le Vinaya des Mūlasarvāstivādin et les textes apparentés," *Journal asiatique* 4 (1914): 493-568.

[71] F. L. Woodward and E. M. Hare, trs., *The Book of the Gradual Sayings (Aṅguttara Nikāya)*, 5 vols., Pali Text Society Translation Series, nos. 22, 24-27 (London: Pali Text Society, 1932-36) 3: 188.

[72] Dutt, pp. 8-14.

and, convinced by his reasoning and much impressed, the king decides to become a Buddhist layman and seeks to take refuge in Mahākaccāna himself. The latter, however, promptly protests: "Do not, sire, go for refuge to me. You must go for refuge only to that Lord [the Buddha] to whom I have gone for refuge." There is, however, a problem with this: the Buddha is no longer alive. He has attained final nirvāṇa and has passed beyond this world. How then, wonders the king, can he take refuge in him? The sutta does not really resolve this issue, but seeks to bypass it by use of an analogy. If, it says, we should hear that the Lord were ten, twenty, thirty, forty, fifty, even a hundred leagues away, we would go those hundred leagues to see him. Just so, though the Lord is absent in final nirvāṇa, we should still go to him for refuge. And this is precisely what king Avantiputta does.[73]

Buddhism in Mathurā and Beyond

Although it is not exactly clear from these stories just what form of Buddhism these Mathurans were being converted to, the city itself came to be known as an important center of the Buddhist Sanskrit tradition, and more specifically of the Sarvāstivāda school.[74]

Buddhism, like most founded religions, quickly broke up into numerous sects following the death of its founder. Even before the formal separation of the Hīnayāna and Mahāyāna schools, the Hīnayāna itself reputedly split up into no less than eighteen different sects. The Sarvāstivādins, along with the Mahāsāṃghikas (forerunners of the Mahāyāna), and the Theravādins (who eventually were established in Sri Lanka and Southeast Asia), were among the most important early filiations to emerge.

[73] I. B. Horner, tr., *The Middle Length Sayings (Majjhima-Nikāya)*, 3 vols., Pali Text Society Translation Series, nos. 29-31 (London: Luzac and Co., 1954-59), 2:278.

[74] Lamotte, p. 364.

Philosophically, the Sarvāstivādins were famous for their doctrine of "pan-realism" that asserted the existence of all elements of reality (*dharmas*) in the three modes of time—past, present, and future.[75] Just how this view worked itself out in terms of legends such as the *Aśokāvadāna*, however, is very difficult to assess. More important for our purposes perhaps, is the fact that the Sarvāstivādins were the first to introduce the use of the Sanskrit language for the writing of Buddhist texts. Living in a land where there were many educated Brahmins versed in the Vedas, and where the prestige of Sanskrit was commonly recognized, they reworked the Buddhist tradition into that language so as to propagate it more effectively.[76] In so doing, they were quite willing to add more materials to their "canon." These included many of the stories in the *Divyāvadāna*, as well as texts such as the *Avadānaśataka*, an anthology of one hundred Buddhist legends compiled in the Northwest at approximately the same time as the *Aśokāvadāna*, and referring, in fact, to the Aśoka story in its last chapter.[77]

At the same time, Northwest India as a whole began to see the emergence of individual Buddhist authors whose works, also in Sanskrit, were closely related to the *Aśokāvadāna* in purpose and in world view. The most famous of these writers was Aśvaghoṣa (second century A.D.?), whose *Sūtrālaṃkāra* contains several direct parallels to episodes in the *Aśokāvadāna*.[78] Others included Āryaśūra, whose *Jātakamālā*, a "gar-

[75] See Edward Conze, *Buddhist Thought in India* (Ann Arbor: University of Michigan Press, 1962), pp. 138-42.

[76] Lamotte, p. 364.

[77] P. L. Vaidya, ed., *Avadāna-śatakam*, Buddhist Sanskrit Texts, no. 19 (Darbhanga, Bihar: Mithila Institute, 1958), p. 262. Compare Léon Feer, tr., *Avadāna-çataka: cent légendes (bouddhiques)*, Annales du Musée Guimet, vol. 18 (Paris: E. Leroux, 1891), p. 434. On the inclusion of these and other materials in the Sarvāstivāda canon, see A. K. Warder, *Indian Buddhism* (Delhi: Motilal Banarsidass, 1970), p. 341; and E. J. Thomas, "Avadāna and Apadāna," *Indian Historical Quarterly* 9 (1933): 33.

[78] Huber, "Etudes," pp. 709ff. See also Huber, tr., *Aśvaghoṣa Sūtrālaṃkāra*, pp. 90-96, 138-45, 263-73.

land" of thirty-four birth stories of the Buddha, is also related to our text;[79] Dhārmika Subhūti whom Tāranātha confuses with Aśvaghoṣa and Āryaśūra;[80] Kumāralāta, whose *Kalpanāmaṇḍitikā* is both in style and in contents closely akin to the *Sūtralaṃkāra*;[81] and Mātṛceṭa, a junior contemporary of Aśvaghoṣa, noted for his devotional hymns in praise of the Buddha.[82] Stylistically, the works of these men are sometimes rather different from the *Aśokāvadāna*, but they share with our text a basic outlook and certain specific religious concerns that are well worth examining here.

First of all, the authors of these texts, like those of the Sanskrit avadānas, were not so much composers of original works as reworkers of old legends and oral traditions. Their role was not to create but to retell in a better way the Buddhist stories that they had either read or heard. This improvement on tradition could take the form of poetic embellishment as in Aśvaghoṣa's masterpiece, the *Buddhacarita*, a work that eloquently recounts in verse the already well-known legend

[79] P. L. Vaidya, ed., *Jātaka-mālā by Ārya Śūra*, Buddhist Sanskrit Texts, no. 21 (Darbhanga, Bihar: Mithila Institute, 1959). Compare J. S. Speyer, tr., *Ārya Śūra's Jātakamālā*, Sacred Books of the Buddhists, vol. 1 (London: Henry Frowde, 1895).

[80] Tāranātha, p. 131; see also Paul Mus, *La lumière sur les six voies*, Travaux et mémoires de l'Institut d'Ethnologie, no. 35 (Paris: Institut d'Ethnologie, 1939), p. 186.

[81] Johannes Nobel, "Kumāralāta und sein Werk," *Nachrichten von der königlichen Gesellschaft der Wissenschaften, Göttingen, Philol-histor. Klasse*, 1928, pp. 295ff. See also Heinrich Lüders, *Bruchstücke der Kalpanāmaṇḍitikā des Kumāralāta*, Kleinere Sanskrittexte aus den Turfanfunden, no. 2 (Leipzig, 1926).

[82] For editions and translations of these, see D. R. Shackleton-Bailey, "The Varṇārhavarṇa Stotra of Mātṛceṭa," *Bulletin of the School of Oriental and African Studies* 13 (1950): 671-810, 947-1003; idem, *The Śatapañcaśatka of Mātṛceṭa* (Cambridge: University Press, 1951); P. Python, "Le Sugatapañcatriṃśatstotra de Mātṛceṭa (Louange des trente-cinq Sugata)," *Etudes tibétaines dédiées à la mémoire de Marcelle Lalou* (Paris: Adrien Maisonneuve, 1971), pp. 402-10. For a more thorough discussion of the connections of the works of all these authors to the *Aśokāvadāna*, see John Strong, "Making Merit in the *Aśokāvadāna*," (Ph.D. dissertation, University of Chicago, 1977), ch. 1.

of the Buddha,[83] or in Dhārmika Subhūti's stanzas on the six realms of rebirth that may be viewed as a formalization of the oral explanations of the Wheels of Life traditionally depicted in monastery gates and explicated by monks stationed there for that purpose.[84] Alternatively, improvement could involve the judicious selection of certain stories to be retold, as in Āryaśūra's *Jātakamālā* that puts into verse thirty-four of the almost countless birth stories of the Buddha; or again, it could consist of the systematic arrangement of disparate legends, as in the *Avadānaśataka*, a work that anthologizes one hundred avadānas, in ten chapters of ten tales, each organized according to the various karmic destinies of its main protagonists. Similarly, as we shall see, the *Aśokāvadāna*, in setting forth the old legends concerning Aśoka and his family, is not without a system of its own.

Secondly, one of the purposes of these authors in retelling and embellishing popular stories, was to preach and to proselytize. Like the storytellers and monks who, in the context of Buddhist oral tradition, freely employed the jātakas and avadānas as an essential part of their sermons, these writers used their literary skills actively to promote and to reinforce the spread of Buddhism. It is important to remember that none of them operated in a context that was exclusively Buddhistic. Their works tended not to be heavily doctrinal but were designed to attract potential converts or maintain the faith of previous converts. They address the situation of the layman more than that of the monk or meditator.

Aśvaghoṣa, himself a convert to Buddhism, is quite explicit about this. At the end of his *Saundarananda* (a poetic epic about the conversion of the Buddha's half-brother), he tells us that he has rewritten this popular tale so as to make it

[83] E. H. Johnston, ed. and tr., *The Buddhacarita or Acts of the Buddha* (orig. pub., 1936; rpt., Delhi: Motilal Banarsidass, 1976), p. xxvi.

[84] For a translation of the stanzas, see Mus, pp. 216-93; for a description of the origin of the Wheel of Life and the oral explanations accompanying it, see Vaidya, *Divyāvadānam*, p. 185.

attractive to non-Buddhists and to win them over to the faith.[85] Similarly, we are told that Māṭrceṭa rewrote his hymns in praise of the Buddha in the form of dramatic performances to be staged by troops of actors, and that in this way he contributed much to the spread of Buddhism and converted many persons.[86] His hymns themselves were so admired that eventually they were included as part of the elementary curriculum to be memorized by new converts at the Buddhist University of Nālanda.[87] The Aśoka legends too, as we shall see, reflect a certain desire to spread the faith in their portrayal of Aśoka and his family, and in their emphasis on their conversion to Buddhism and subsequent support of the Buddhist community.

Thirdly, in this evangelistic enterprise, these authors were concerned with emphasizing a number of themes. One of these, as already mentioned, was the doctrine of karma and the context of rebirth. Seeking to inculcate a sense of moral action, the *Avadānaśataka* and the *Divyāvadāna*, for example, tell us almost *ad nauseum* that good deeds will result in reaping good rewards in a future life, while bad deeds will have negative effects. At the same time, these good and bad deeds are defined primarily in terms of one's relationship to the Buddha. The other traditional refuges or devotional foci of Buddhism—the Dharma and the sangha—do play some role in this as well, but the emphasis is on faith (*śraddhā*) and devotion (*bhakti*) to the person of the Buddha. As W. G. Weeraratne has pointed out, in these avadānas, it is bhakti that defines what good karma is. Any act which expresses one's devotion to the Buddha, or to his relics, or to some other object of veneration

[85] E. H. Johnston, ed. and tr., *The Saundarananda of Aśvaghoṣa* (Lahore: 1928; rpt., Delhi: Motilal Banarsidass, 1975), p. 141. For further examples of Aśvaghoṣa's efforts at conversion, see Sylvain Lévi, "Encore Aśvaghoṣa," *Journal asiatique* 213 (1928): 192-216, esp. 199-200, and idem, "Sur la récitation primitive des textes bouddhiques," *Journal asiatique* 5 (1915): 401-47, esp. 433.

[86] Tāranātha, p.134.

[87] Takakusu, pp. 154, 156.

associated with his person, is an act which is likely to have good karmic consequences.[88]

Even though he is "gone beyond" in parinirvāṇa and so no longer of this world, it is the Buddha who governs the religious emotions of the authors of these texts, and it is the Buddha who is meant to inspire religious feelings in the hearts of potential converts. Thus the chief purpose of Mātṛceṭa's hymns was to exalt the Buddha with fervent praise, and, in Aśvaghoṣa's works, there may be found this same glowing fervor of personal devotion.[89] It will come as no surprise, then, to find exhibited in the *Aśokāvadāna* an almost constant preoccupation with the person of the Buddha. We shall, in fact, devote the whole of Chapter Four to this subject; suffice it to say now that it is ultimately the desire for a closer relationship with the Buddha that inspires Aśoka's acts of merit and religious life.

Finally, mention should be made here of one last aim in the works of many of these authors: their purpose is not only to convert and maintain the faith, but also to stress the importance of material support for the Buddhist religion. In some instances, this has simply meant an advocacy of the merits of *dāna* (giving) to the Buddhist community. This is the case in many of the avadānas, and the message is found in the *Aśokāvadāna* as well. In other cases, it has meant an interest in the powers and potentials of the state—in particular the institution of kingship and its relationship to the Buddhist religion. Thus Aśvaghoṣa was not only a popular poet and preacher; he was also associated either historically or legendarily with the court of the great Kushan emperor Kaniṣka. He is even said by some to have been Kaniṣka's Buddhist "advisor."[90] Likewise, Mātṛceṭa is reputed to have written a

[88] Weeraratne, p. 397.

[89] Johnston, *Buddhacarita*, p. xxvi.

[90] Ibid., p. xv. This issue is related to the notoriously difficult problem of the dating of Kaniṣka's reign; see A. L. Basham, ed., *Papers on the Date of Kaniṣka* (Leiden: E. J. Brill, 1968).

letter full of advice to King Kaniṣka II, urging support for the Buddhist cause.[91]

Though not specifically addressed to any monarch, the *Aśokāvadāna*, of course, in its portrayal of Aśoka is concerned with kingship and the role it can play in support of the Buddhist religion. At the same time, as we shall see in Chapter Two, its attitude toward this institution is not without its own ambiguities.

Conclusion

The Sarvāstivādins clearly played an important role in the spread and popularization of Buddhism in Mathurā and throughout the Northwest, but we should not be too quick to conclude that the region was the exclusive domain of that one sect. Northwest India as a whole, and Mathurā in particular, was rather a patchwork of different Hīnayānist and, later, Mahāyānist schools. At the same time, non-Buddhist groups—orthodox Brahmins and Jains in particular—remained strong forces in the region.

It is useful to consider the testimony of the Chinese pilgrim, Hsüan-tsang, who visited the area on his trip to India. Though writing in the seventh century, he describes a religious pluralism that was perhaps not atypical of the time of the formation of the *Aśokāvadāna*. In the region of Mathurā, he tells us, "there are about twenty *sanghārāmas* [monasteries] with 2000 priests or so. They study equally the Great and the Little Vehicles. There are five Déva temples, in which sectaries of all kinds live. There are three *stūpas* built by Aśokarāja. There are very many traces of the four past Buddhas here. There are also *stūpas* to commemorate the remains of the holy followers of Śākya Tathāgata."[92] To further complicate things, the Bud-

[91] Lamotte, p. 656. For a translation of the letter, see F. W. Thomas, "Maharajakanikalekha," *Indian Antiquary*, 1903, pp. 345ff.

[92] Samuel Beal, tr., *Si-Yu-Ki: Buddhist Records of the Western World*, 2 vols. (rpt., New York: Paragon Book Reprint Corp., 1968) 1:180.

dhists themselves were divided into many groups, at times regardless of sectarian lines, each of which worshipped its own patron saint:

> Those who study the *Abhidharma* honor Śāriputra; those who practise meditation honor Mudgalaputra; those who recite the *sūtras* honor Pūrṇamaitrāyāniputra; those who study the *Vinaya* reverence Upāli. All the Bhikshuṇīs [nuns] honor Ānanda, the Śrāmaṇeras [novices] honor Rāhula; those who study the Great Vehicle reverence the Bodhisattvas. On these days they honor the *stūpas* with offerings. They display their jewelled banners; the precious parasols are crowded together as a network; the smoke of incense rises in clouds; and flowers are scattered in every direction like rain. . . . The king of the country and the great ministers apply themselves to these religious duties with zeal.[93]

Clearly, we are dealing here with a situation that is rather complex, not only in sectarian terms but along other divisional lines as well. We should not, then, too readily characterize Mathurā or Northwest India—the milieu in which the *Áśokāvadāna* took form—as the bastion of any one sect or school. Although our text is certainly a Hīnayānist and probably a Sarvāstivādin work, it also, as we shall see, reflects the many influences of its pluralistic setting, including that of the proto-Mahāyānists. However, as a popular legend broadly oriented to the whole Northwest Indian Sanskritic world, the *Aśokāvadāna* is little concerned with scoring sectarian points. This does not mean that it is devoid of doctrinal stands. As we shall see, it takes definite positions on questions such as faith, kingship, devotion to the Buddha, donations to the sangha, and the nature of suffering and how to overcome it. But its stance is assumed rather than explicit, and is embedded in the telling of the legend itself. Our task in the chapters that follow will thus be primarily an exegetical one.

[93] Ibid., pp.180-81.

CHAPTER TWO

Dirt and Dharma: Kingship in the *Aśokāvadāna*

The study of Buddhist conceptions of kingship has come a long way since Max Weber, in 1916, declared that early Buddhism was a classic example of other worldly mysticism divorced from any real involvement in political rule or in worldly economic activities.[1] Today, this Weberian viewpoint has been fundamentally undermined, and a number of important works have established a new context for discussing a genuinely Buddhist polity and theory of kingship.[2] Paul Mus, culminating a trend in French buddhology, has stressed the prime importance of royal symbolism and cosmology in the development of Buddhist ideology and iconography.[3] Balkrishna Gokhale and Frank Reynolds have both clarified the notion of the Two Wheels of the Buddha's Teachings and have made obvious the need to examine the complementarity in Theravāda Buddhism of the monastic and royal spheres.[4] More recently, Stanley Tambiah has artfully combined historical and structural perspectives in order to describe the development of Buddhist kingship, in both India and Thailand, in terms of a pulsating galactic or maṇḍala model.[5]

[1] Max Weber, *The Religion of India*, tr. Hans H. Gerth and Don Martindale (New York: The Free Press, 1958), p. 213.

[2] For a discussion of one aspect of this discrediting of Weber, see Heinz Bechert, *Buddhismus, Staat, und Gesellschaft in den Ländern des Theravāda-Buddhismus*, 3 vols. (Wiesbaden: Otto Harrasowitz, 1966-73), 1:115.

[3] Paul Mus, *Barabuḍur: Esquisse d'une histoire du bouddhisme fondée sur la critique archéologique des textes*, 2 vols. (Hanoi: Imprimerie d'Extrême-Orient, 1935).

[4] B. G. Gokhale, "Early Buddhist Kingship," *Journal of Asian Studies* 26 (1966): 15-22; Frank E. Reynolds, "The Two Wheels of Dhamma: A Study of Early Buddhism," in *The Two Wheels of Dhamma*, ed. Bardwell L. Smith (Chambersburg, Pa.: American Academy of Religion, 1972), pp. 6-30.

[5] Stanley J. Tambiah, *World Conqueror and World Renouncer* (Cambridge: University Press, 1976).

In this chapter, I would like to use some of the insights of these scholars, as well as some of the Buddhist sources that they have elucidated, to examine as specifically as possible the view of kingship reflected in the *Aśokāvadāna*.

Throughout Buddhist Asia, the figure of Aśoka has played a major role in concretizing conceptions of kingship and general attitudes toward rulers and government. Buddhists everywhere have looked back upon the Aśoka-of-the-legends as an ideal king. In Theravāda countries such as Sri Lanka, Thailand, Laos, and Burma, he was and still is portrayed as a paradigmatic ruler, a model to be proudly recalled and emulated.[6] Likewise, in China, Korea, and Japan, his legend inspired and guided a number of Buddhist emperors who consciously patterned their rule on his.[7]

[6] For specific examples of the way that the legend of Aśoka has functioned as a model in these countries, see, for Sri Lanka: Bardwell L. Smith, "The Ideal Social Order as Portrayed in the Chronicles of Ceylon," in *Religion and Legitimation of Power in Sri Lanka*, ed. Bardwell L. Smith (Chambersburg, Pa.: Anima Books, 1978), pp. 73-95; for Thailand: Barbara Watson Andaya, "Statecraft in the Reign of Lü Tai of Sukhodaya," in *Religion and Legitimation of Power in Thailand, Laos, and Burma*, ed. Bardwell L. Smith (Chambersburg, Pa.: Anima Books, 1978), p. 4, and Frank E. Reynolds, "Sacral Kingship and National Development: The Case of Thailand," in ibid., p. 105; for Laos: Frank E. Reynolds, "Ritual and Social Hierarchy: An Aspect of Traditional Religion in Buddhist Laos," in ibid., p. 170, and Charles Archaimbault, "La fête du T'at à Luong P'răbang," in *Essays Offered to G. H. Luce*, 2 vols. ed. Ba Shin, Jean Boisselier and A. B. Griswold (Ascona: Artibus Asiae, 1966), 1:22; for Burma: John P. Ferguson, "The Quest for Legitimation by Burmese Monks and Kings: The Case of the Shwegyin Sect (19th-20th Centuries)," in *Religion and Legitimation of Power in Thailand, Laos, and Burma*, p. 66, and E. Sarkisyanz,"Buddhist Backgrounds of Burmese Socialism," in ibid., pp. 87-89.

[7] See Kenneth K. S. Ch'en, *Buddhism in China* (Princeton: University Press, 1964), pp. 125, 200; Arthur Wright, "The Formation of Sui Ideology, 581-604," in *Chinese Thought and Institutions*, ed. John K. Fairbank (Chicago: University Press, 1957), pp. 98-102; Peter H. Lee, *Lives of Eminent Korean Monks*, Harvard-Yenching Institute Studies, 25 (Cambridge: Harvard University Press, 1969), p. 66; Shundo Tachibana,"Prince Shōtoku, King Aśoka of Japan," *Studies on Buddhism in Japan* 4 (1942): 103-09. For the curious legends connecting Aśoka and the kingdom of Nanchao in Yünnan, in Southwestern China, see Paul Pelliot, "Deux itinéraires de Chine en Inde à la fin du VIIIe siècle," *Bulletin de l'Ecole Française d'Extrême-Orient* 4 (1904): 167ff., and M. Carthew, "The History of the Thai in Yunnan," *Journal of*

Yet, as we shall see, the image of Aśoka in the legends (or at least in the *Aśokāvadāna*) is more complex than this. For one thing, it is fraught with inconsistencies. Not only is Aśoka revered as an ideal king; he is also feared, maligned, and ridiculed as an all-too-real figure who sometimes does not live up to the ideal. In what follows, then, these different and sometimes paradoxical attitudes will have to be explained.

Aśoka the Fierce

Readers principally familiar with the image of Aśoka presented in the *Mahāvaṃsa* may be surprised to find that his portrayal in the *Aśokāvadāna* is not always as bright and glorious as it is in the Sinhalese chronicle. In fact he is, in the text, presented as being physically ugly. His father cannot stand the sight of him; his skin is rough and harsh; and the young women in his harem refuse to sleep with him because of his repugnant appearance.[8]

Hendrik Kern, who was very familiar with the Sanskrit legends we are concerned with, once stated that these "give the worst idea of Aśoka. If we knew him only by the[se] Buddhist sources, we should have to conclude that he was a sovereign of exceptional insignificance, remarkable only in that he was half-monster, half-idiot."[9] Kern, it is true, seems to have had some special bias against Aśoka and presents here a very lopsided opinion, but it is well worth examining some of the stories that may have led him to have such a view.

There are, in fact, several such episodes in the *Aśokāvadāna*. In the first chapter, for example, Aśoka does not hesitate to trick and kill his elder brother in order to usurp the throne,

---

the Siam Society, Selected Articles, 10 vols. (Bangkok: The Siam Society, 1954-61), 3:135-37.

[8] Sujitkumar Mukhopadhyaya, ed. *The Aśokāvadāna* (New Delhi: Sahitya Akademi, pp. 37, 43.

[9] Hendrik Kern, *Histoire du Bouddhisme indien*, 2 vols, tr. J. Huet (Paris: E. Leroux, 1901-1903), 2:335.

and he does this in a dastardly manner by enticing him into a pit filled with live coals. Later, he builds a state prison and torture chamber, where hundreds are put to death, that comes to be known as "Aśoka's hell." Also, he tests his ministers by giving them an absurd order, and then summarily decapitates five hundred of them whom he finds lacking in loyalty. Moreover, when his royal dignity is insulted by some of the women in his harem, he flies into a fury and has them burned at the stake.[10]

Scholars have generally argued that these stories are featured in the legend because they were meant to emphasize Aśoka's cruel and impetuous temperament before his conversion to Buddhism and so magnify the greatness of his change of heart. There is some degree of truth in this. All of the episodes mentioned so far do indeed occur before Aśoka becomes a Buddhist, and they earn him the appellation "Aśoka the Fierce" (Caṇḍāśoka). After his conversion, when he comes to be known as "Dharma-Aśoka," the implication is that such ferocious acts cease. If we look at the rest of the legend, however, we find that in fact they do not. For example, immediately after his conversion experience, when one would suppose that he would be highly moved by his newly found ethic, Aśoka shows no mercy toward Caṇḍagirika, his former executioner-in-chief, and has him tortured to death. Or again, later on, he flies into a fury and has eighteen thousand heretics killed as a punishment for the misdeed of one of them. In a related episode, he locks a Jain layman and his family inside their home, sets the place on fire, and then launches a veritable pogrom against the Jains, setting a bounty on the head of any heretic. Still later, he announces with relish all the tortures he is going to inflict on his wife Tiṣyarakṣitā, and carries through with her execution, despite the repeated pleas of his son Kuṇāla—a Buddhist saint—for leniency toward her.[11]

Other examples along these lines could be given, but they

[10] Mukhopadhyaya, pp. 42, 43, 45.
[11] Ibid., pp. 52, 67, 68, 122.

all raise an important question: why have these terrible acts—even after Aśoka's conversion to Buddhism—been retained in the story of his life and passed on as among the legendary deeds of the greatest Buddhist king in history? The answer is rather complex, but, at least initially, I would suggest that the inclusion of these acts reflects an underlying Buddhist apprehension toward the institution of kingship as inherently, perhaps inevitably, prone to such actions.

Gokhale has pointed out that there can be found in many Buddhist texts a distinct attitude toward kingship of "disquiet bordering on fear."[12] In the semi-canonical *Questions of King Milinda*, for example, when the elder Nāgasena is asked to discuss the fine points of Buddhist philosophy with the king, he refuses to do so if Milinda insists on discussing them as a king rather than as a scholar, for "when a king discusses a matter and advances a point, if any one differ from him on that point, he is apt to fine him saying: 'Inflict such and such a punishment upon that fellow.' "[13] Nāgasena is simply being practical here: he does not want to suffer torture or imprisonment. He is well aware that even though Milinda has expressed a desire to learn about and follow the Buddhist Dharma, he is still a king, and while kings can be benevolent, they can also be dangerously preoccupied with their own prestige and power.

It is important to remember that Buddhists in ancient India did not live in a political vacuum, and that one of the several notions of government being propounded at that time was that which received perhaps its fullest expression in Kauṭilya's *Arthaśāstra*. This treatise has often been labeled Machiavellian in its principles, and does not hesitate to recommend rather ruthless expedients to consolidate further the king's

[12] Gokhale,"Early Buddhist Kingship," p. 15.

[13] T. W. Rhys Davids, tr. *The Questions of King Milinda*, 2 vols. Sacred Books of the East, nos. 35-36 (orig. pub. 1890-94; rpt., New York: Dover, 1963), 1:46.

position.[14] For Kauṭilya, *daṇḍa* (literally the use of a "stick" or punishment) was an accepted and necessary means to an end which might eventually be the establishment of Dharma, but which more immediately assured the king's prestige and power.

Some of the episodes just referred to in the *Aśokāvadāna* might readily be interpreted along Kauṭilyan lines. Aśoka, as a king interested in maintaining his power, systematically disposes of those who oppose him; he does not hesitate to punish disloyal ministers and unfaithful wives, and deals summarily with those who are against his adopted faith of Buddhism. All of this becomes even more relevant, perhaps, when we recall the tradition that Kauṭilya himself was reputedly the prime minister and chief political theorist of Aśoka's grandfather, Candragupta Maurya. Thus the very empire that Aśoka inherited was presumably based on and built up along Arthaśāstric principles.[15]

It is important to remember, however, that these actions do not represent the Buddhist view of kingship, at least not at the theoretical level. As Stanley Tambiah has pointed out, the Buddhist tradition of kingship as a whole rejects "that brand of arthashastric thought that recommends the objective of maximum advantage to the ruler and his polity."[16] Indeed, our text, when it stands back and comments, roundly condemns Aśoka's violent acts. But Buddhist kings do not always act in Buddhist ways, and some of the stories retained even in the legend of the great Aśoka seem to be a reflection as well as a reminder of that fact.

[14] For a balanced discussion of the Machiavelli-Kauṭilya comparison, see Charles Drekmeier, *Kingship and Community in Early India* (Stanford: Stanford University Press, 1962), pp. 204ff.

[15] See M. V. Krishna Rao, *Studies in Kautilya* (Delhi: Munshi Ram Manohar Lal, 1958), p. 13; R. P. Kangle, *The Kauṭilīya Arthaśāstra*, 3 vols. (Bombay: University of Bombay, 1963-65) 3:280. See also Drekmeier, p. 290.

[16] Tambiah, p. 32.

The Myth of the Cakravartin

All of this, however, represents only one part of the *Aśokāvadāna's* depiction of kingship. These basically negative perspectives occur side by side with presentations of Aśoka as a brilliant and prosperous king, a paradigm of royalty, a righteous ruler (*dharmarāja*), a wheel-turning monarch who rules the world (*cakravartin*), and a wise sovereign. His legend is thus paradoxical in its attitude, reflecting at the same time two distinct Buddhist reactions to the institution of kingship: wariness and criticism on the one hand, admiration and respect on the other.

To understand the positive side of this presentation, we must turn to the Buddhist mythological tradition about kingship. There are two principal Buddhist myths of the origin and nature of kings and their rule. The first of these, which is of only marginal importance for our text, is the myth of King Mahāsammata, the "Great Elect," classically found in the "Aggañña Sutta" of the *Dīgha Nikāya*.[17] The "Aggañña Sutta" begins by portraying an ideal paradisial time, an Illud Tempus (to use Mircea Eliade's term) of natural, effortless existence. Ethereal, self-luminescent beings live in bliss and know no discrimination between polar opposites such as male and female, good and evil, rich and poor, ruler and subject. The earth itself is made of a delightful soft edible substance that looks like butter and is as sweet as honey. Gradually,

[17] See T. W. Rhys Davids, tr., *Dialogues of the Buddha*, 3 vols. Sacred Books of the Buddhists, nos. 2-4. (London: Pali Text Society, 1899-1921), 3:79-94. For the Pali text, see J. Estlin Carpenter, ed. *Dīgha Nikāya*, 3 vols. (London: Pali Text Society, 1911), 3:80-98. For other versions of this important Buddhist myth, see Pe Maung Tin, tr. *The Path of Purity*, 2 vols., Pali Text Society Translation Series, nos. 11, 17 (London: Pali Text Society, 1923), 2:484-86; W. Woodville Rockhill, *The Life of the Buddha* (London: Kegan Paul, Trench, Trübner and Co., 1907), pp. 1-8; J. J. Jones, tr. *The Mahāvastu*, 3 vols., Sacred Books of the Buddhists, nos. 16, 18-19 (London: Pali Text Society, 1949-56), 1:285-301; Louis de La Vallée Poussin, tr. *L'Abhidharmakośa de Vasubandhu*, 6 vols. (Paris: Paul Geuthner, 1923-31), 3: 203-06.

however, because of karma remaining from a previous world cycle, this Golden Age is lost. During a long period of decline that might, perhaps, best be described as a hardening (in the literal and metaphorical sense) of the world and the beings in it, greed, grasping, sex, theft, violence, and murder all come into the world. Finally, sheer anarchy prevails, and in order to put an end to it, the beings get together to select from among their ranks a king to rule over them and maintain order. This is Mahāsammata, the Great Elect, and in return for fulfilling his functions as a monarch, the beings each agree to pay him a portion of their rice.[18]

The second myth of kingship is the myth of the cakravartin, or "wheel-turning" king, and is of more direct relevance to our text. A basic version of it appears in the *Dīgha Nikāya*'s "Cakkavatti Sīhanāda Sutta," which features a cakravartin named Daḷhanemi.[19] It, too, begins with an account of the Illud Tempus at the start of this world cycle. It describes a Golden Age when beings had beautiful bodies, life-spans of eighty thousand years, and led wonderful, effortless existences. This time, however, the king—the cakravartin Daḷhanemi—is present from the start. He is, in fact, very much a part of the Golden Age for his presence is instrumental in

[18] Carpenter, vol. 3, pp. 85-93; Davids, *Dialogues,* 3:82-88. The notion of a monarch being selected to rule in return for payment of the rice tax is, of course, not unique to Buddhism. It has close parallels, for example, with the Hindu story of the election of Manu as the first king. Manu, the father of mankind, "at first refused to assume royalty, owing to the sinful nature of man," but finally agreed to his enthronement when the people consented to give him a percentage of their income. (See Jan Gonda, *Ancient Indian Kingship from the Religious Point of View* [Leiden: E. J. Brill, 1966], p. 132.) The myth, which has been incorporated into the *Mahābhārata*, is also mentioned in the *Arthaśāstra*. "When," we are told, "people were oppressed by the law of fishes (matsyanyāya) they made Manu, the son of Vivasvat, the king. They fixed one sixth part of the grain and one tenth of their goods and money as his share." See Kangle, vol. 2, p. 31 and vol. 3, p. 116. See also Drekmeier, pp. 137-38.

[19] Carpenter, vol. 3, pp. 58-79; Davids, *Dialogues*, 3:59-76. For related versions of the myth, see the "Mahāsudassana Sutta," (Carpenter, vol. 2, pp. 169-99; Davids, *Dialogues*, 2:199-232). See also Tambiah, pp. 42-47.

maintaining the paradisial state. Because he knows what is good and rules through Dharma, poverty, ill-will, violence, and wrongdoing are all absent from his kingdom.[20]

Traditionally, the cakravartin is portrayed in quite extraordinary terms. He is said to exhibit the thirty-two bodily marks of the Great Man (Mahāpuruṣa), and to be endowed with the seven jewels or emblems of sovereignty, the most important of which is the wheel.[21] In the "Cakkavatti Sīhanāda Sutta," this magnificent wheel appears in mid-air before Daḷhanemi at the beginning of his reign as a sign of his righteousness. It then leads him in a great cosmic conquest of the four continents. It takes him East, South, West, and North as far as the great ocean, and, wherever it rolls, he encounters no resistance; the power of his Dharma, symbolized by his wheel, is such that local kings immediately submit to him. Finally, his wheel leads him back to his capital at the center of the world, and there it remains, miraculously suspended in mid-air over the royal palace, as an emblem of his sovereignty.[22]

[20] In addition to the descriptions of the cakravartin's rule in the sources cited in n. 19, see F. L. Woodward and E. M. Hare, tr., *The Book of the Gradual Sayings (Aṅguttara Nikāya)*, 5 vols., Pali Text Society Translation Series, nos. 22, 24-27 (London: Pali Text Society, 1932-36), 1:71, and 3: 113ff.

[21] The seven emblems of sovereignty are, besides the wheel, the elephant, the horse, the woman, the gem, the treasurer, and the minister. The thirty-two physiognomic marks of the Great Man are (according to one list): (1) feet with level tread, (2) designs of wheels on the soles of the feet, (3) long toes and fingers, (4) broad and projecting heels, (5) sharply arched feet, (6) legs like the antelope's, (7) a divinely straight body, (8) hands that touch the knees while standing erect, (9) a male organ encased in a sheath, (10) a body proportioned like the banyan tree, (11) soft and tender hands and feet, (12) hands and feet that are webbed, (13) a perfectly formed body, (14) down on the body that grows in single hairs, one to each pore, (15) down on the body that grows straight up, (16) smooth skin, (17) soft [?] skin, (18) the gait of a swan, (19) no hollow between the shoulder-blades, (20) a body with seven convex surfaces, (21) an excellent sense of taste, (22) skin the color of gold, (23) the bust of a lion, (24) regular teeth, (25) perfectly white eye-teeth, (26) a bust that is equally rounded, (27) a long and slender tongue, (28) a voice like Brahmā's, (29) blue eyes, (30) eyelashes like those of a cow, (31) a hairy mole (ūrṇā) between the eyebrows, and (32) a head shaped like a royal turban (uṣṇīṣa). See Jones, tr. *Mahāvastu* 2:26.

[22] Davids, *Dialogues*, 3:62-64.

After many years of reigning in peace over a contented and prosperous empire, however, Daḷhanemi's Wheel of Dharma begins to sink. This is a sign of the approaching end of his reign, and when the wheel disappears altogether into the earth, the wise king entrusts his throne to his son and retires from this world to lead an ascetic forest-dwelling life.[23]

It is important to note that the Wheel of Dharma is not automatically passed on from one cakravartin to the next. Daḷhanemi's son must, in his turn, merit his own wheel by calling it forth with his own righteousness. This fact sets the scene for the rest of the myth, which, like the story in the "Aggañña Sutta," traces the gradual degradation of this world and the beings in it. After a long series of rules by the successors of Daḷhanemi who are perfect cakravartins, there comes a king who fails to follow Dharma, and for whom the wheel does not appear. Consequently, there is resistance to his rule; friction develops, the people fail to prosper, the king fails to support them, and one thing leads to another: "From goods not being bestowed on the destitute poverty grew rife; from poverty growing rife stealing increased, from the spread of stealing violence grew apace, from the growth of violence the destruction of life became common, from the frequency of murder, both the span of life in those beings and their comeliness also wasted away."[24]

The myth then goes on to trace the further decline in the quality and span of life until a state of virtual anarchy is reached.[25] In this, then, the myth of the cakravartin is quite similar to that of the Great Elect. In terms of its understanding of kingship, however, it presents a somewhat different view. In the "Aggañña Sutta," the Great Elect is called upon only

[23] Ibid., p. 64.

[24] Ibid., pp. 67-68.

[25] From this nadir, things slowly get better again. People change their ways and the span of their lives gradually lengthens. The myth as we have it in the "Cakkavatti-Sīhanāda Sutta," then goes on to tell of the arrival of a new righteous cakravartin, Śankha, whose reign is connected to the advent of the future Buddha Maitreya. See Carpenter, vol. 3, pp. 75-77, and Davids, *Dialogues*, 3:72-74.

when the need for him arises. He functions as a stopgap against further anarchy, but the Golden Age itself requires and knows no king at all. In the cakravartin myth, on the other hand, the king is a crucial part of the Golden Age. By his very presence and by his proper rule, he ensures a peaceful, prosperous, idyllic existence for all, and he will continue to do so as long as he is righteous enough to merit the Wheel of Dharma, that is as long as he truly is a wheel-turning cakravartin king.

Scholars have much debated the origin of this notion of the cakravartin. Indeed, it has a long and complex history with many interwoven strands, and we can hardly hope to untangle them all here.[26] In India, the concept goes back at least to the tenth century B.C.,[27] and although Buddhism was to give it its own special significance, the idea of the cakravartin was retained in non-Buddhist circles as well. The *Maitri Upaniṣad*, for example, refers to a number of specific cakravartins,[28] and politically oriented works such as the *Arthaśāstra* speak of the hypothetical territory of the ideal king (extending from the Himālayas to the sea) as the *cakravartikṣetra*, the "field of the cakravartin."[29] Moreover, the general notion of an ideal monarch who is instrumental in maintaining an ideal kingdom is found in such well-known texts as the *Mahābhārata*'s myth of Pṛthu. Unlike Manu, who, in the manner of the Great Elect, was called upon to put an end to a period of anarchy, Pṛthu presides over a Golden Age of abundance, fertility, and prosperity. Under his rule, the earth yields fruit of its own accord, the cows give milk whenever it is desired, and every lotus-bud

[26] K. A. Nilakanta Sastri, "Cakravartin," *New Indian Antiquary* 3 (1940): 307. By no means were all these strands necessarily Indian; indeed several scholars have pointed to the ancient Near East as a possible source for the cakravartin ideology. See ibid., p. 311, and Jean Przyluski, "La ville du cakravartin: influences babyloniennes sur la civilization de l'inde," *Rocznik Orjentalistyczny* 5 (1927): 165-85.

[27] Drekmeier, p. 203; see also Gonda, p. 123.

[28] S. Radhakrishnan, ed. and tr. *The Principal Upaniṣads* (New York: Harper and Brothers, 1953), p. 797.

[29] Kangle, vol. 2, p. 471. Kauṭilya's ideal ruler is known as the "world conqueror" (*vijigīṣu*).

is filled with honey. All beings proclaim Pṛthu their king and savior, and live seemingly endless lives of happiness and plenty.[30]

What is different about the Buddhist cakravartin myth, however, is that it does not stop at this Golden Age, but goes on to describe in no uncertain terms what happens when a king does not live up to the ideal. The suggestion is made, therefore, that there are really two possible types of rulers. One—a full-fledged cakravartin—is righteous and rules according to Dharma, and so, like Pṛthu or Daḷhanemi, ensures a Golden Age. The other—perhaps not truly worthy to be called a cakravartin—is not so righteous, fails to rule according to Dharma, and so is responsible for a cosmic catastrophe, the degradation of the world.

Aśoka and the Cakravartin Ideal

How does this mythic view of kingship relate to the figure of Aśoka as he is depicted in the *Aśokāvadāna*? It is clear from what we have just seen that the cakravartin myth presented Buddhists with the problem of a rather inflexible ideal of kingship. The figure of the cakravartin was, as Melford Spiro has pointed out, too ideal, too "mythical" for actual historical Buddhist kings to be identified with it.[31] Either a king possessed the thirty-two marks of the Great Man, in which case he was a cakravartin, or he did not. Either he ruled the entire universe, perfectly, according to Dharma, or he did not. Either the wheel appeared at the start of his reign or it did not. Either his was a Golden Age, or he was responsible for the degradation of the cosmos. In practical terms, this

[30] Gonda, p. 129. A variant of the myth in the Purāṇas does place this glorious rule immediately following the time of anarchy and tyranny. See ibid., p. 131.

[31] See Melford Spiro's review of *World Conqueror and World Renouncer* in *Journal of Asian Studies* 36 (1977): 789-91, as well as his "Reply to Professor Tambiah," ibid. 37 (1978): 809-12. See also Stanley J. Tambiah,"The Buddhist Conception of Kingship and its Historical Manifestations: A Reply to Spiro," ibid., pp. 801-9.

meant that there was very little middle ground for would-be cakravartins to stand on.

To some extent, the "Aggañña Sutta" might have provided a solution to this dilemma in that the Great Elect is not a king for the Golden Age but a this-worldly monarch for an imperfect time much like our own. The difficulty, however, is that by himself, the Great Elect was perhaps too down-to-earth. He was an important figure, of course, a *primus inter pares*, but he lacked the prestige and aura that surrounded the cakravartin. What was needed, in a sense, was a combination of the two figures: a cakravartin who could rule an imperfect world.

It is my understanding that this is precisely what the *Aśokāvadāna* provides. In the process, however, it calls on several theories that distinguish different types of cakravartins and so allow for a compromise of the mythic ideal.

In the *Aśokāvadāna*, Aśoka is seldom simply called a "*cakravartin*." Instead he is called a "*caturbhāga-cakravartin*," that is, a "ruler over one of the four continents,"[32] or, alternatively, a "*balacakravartin*," a term which I suspect should be translated as "armed cakravartin" or "cakravartin who has to use or threaten physical force to become the ruler of his cosmos."[33] Related to these appellations is yet another epithet; in the Chinese translation of the *Aśokāvadāna*, Aśoka is called "a king of the Iron Wheel ruling over Jambudvīpa."[34] All of these notions merit further investigation.

[32] Eugène Burnouf (*Introduction à l'histoire du buddhisme indien*, [Paris: Adrien Maisonneuve, 1876], p. 356), interprets this term as meaning one who rules over all four continents, but he is clearly wrong. See Mukhopadhyaya, p. 166 and Jean Przyluski, *La légende de l'empereur Açoka* (Paris: Paul Geuthner, 1923), p. 228.

[33] Other translations that have been offered for this term include "ruler of armies" (see Hendrik Kern, tr., *Saddharma-Puṇḍarīka or the Lotus of the True Law*, Sacred Books of the East, no. 21 [Oxford: Clarendon Press, 1884], pp. 7, 20), and "mighty ruler of the world." (See J. Ensink, tr. *The Questions of Rāṣṭrapāla* [Zwolle, 1952], p. 51.)

[34] Przyluski, *Légende*, p. 219; James Legge, tr. and ed., *A Record of Buddhistic Kingdoms* (orig. pub., 1886; rpt. New York: Paragon Book Co., 1965), p. 90 (text), p. 31 (tr.).

The concept of the iron-wheeled king is found most prominently in a schema for categorizing cakravartins according to the material used to make their wheel, and according to the number of continents of the universe (in the classic Indian cosmological system) over which they ruled. Perhaps the clearest presentation of this scheme is that found in Vasubandhu's *Abhidharmakośa*, a relatively late work but one that systematized many of the major tenets of the Sanskrit Buddhist tradition.

According to Vasubandhu, there are four possible types of cakravartin:[35] (1) The cakravartin with the golden wheel (*suvarṇacakravartin*) who rules all four continents: Uttarakuru in the North, Purvavideha in the East, Jambudvīpa in the South, and Apara Godaniya in the West. (2) The silver-wheeled cakravartin (*rūpyacakravartin*) who rules three continents (all the above except Uttarakuru). (3) The copper-wheeled cakravartin (*tāmracakravartin*) whose sovereignty extends to two continents (Jambudvīpa and Purvavideha); and (4) the iron-wheeled cakravartin (*ayaścakravartin*) who rules only Jambudvīpa.[36]

These various cakravartins achieve the conquest of their territory in different ways. The golden-wheeled cakravartin who rules all four continents conquers them, like Daḷhanemi in the myth, simply by his "own going forth" (*svayamyāna*); his personal presence is enough to cause all the minor kings to submit to him spontaneously. The silver-wheeled cakravartin's victory comes after some sort of encounter (*pratyudyāna*) with the petty kings in three continents. It is not exactly clear what this means, except that the submission of the minor kings does not appear to be quite as spontaneous as in the

[35] This fourfold classification appears not to be known in the Pali tradition. Instead, we find there, a threefold distinction between (a) cakkavāḷa-cakkavatti who rule over four continents, (b) dīpa-cakkavatti who rule over one, and (c) padesa-cakkavatti who rule over only a portion of one. See R. C. Childers, *Dictionary of the Pali Language* (London: Trübner and Co., 1875) s.v. "cakkavatti." This curiously resembles the classification scheme of the *Lotus Sūtra*, on which, see below.

[36] La Vallée Poussin, *Abhidharmakośa*, 3:197.

case of the golden-wheeled cakravartin. The copper-wheeled king is "victorious after a quarrelsome confrontation" (*kalahajita*). In this case the petty kings show some initial sign of resistance to the cakravartin but then are brought to submission, probably after some sort of argument or struggle that, however, does not involve weapons. Finally, the iron-wheeled cakravartin is "victorious by means of the sword" (*śastrajita*). Vasubandhu, as though wishing to safeguard the ideal image of the cakravartin, quickly adds that no one is killed in the confrontation. Nevertheless it would seem that we have here a situation approaching traditional warfare.[37]

In any case, it is clear from the overall scheme that there is now room for compromise of the mythic ideal set forth in the "Cakkavatti Sīhanāda Sutta." Not all cakravartins were necessarily like Daḷhanemi, with charisma sufficient enough to conquer the cosmos; some seem in fact, to have had to have used physical force (or the threat thereof) to achieve their position. Moreover, not all cakravartins necessarily ruled over all four continents. Some, indeed, conquered only one of them—Jambudvīpa—and were thus rulers over one fourth of the cosmos (caturbhāga-cakravartins).

Obviously, this image of an iron-wheeled king who rules over Jambudvīpa, that is, India, which he has conquered by the sword or threat of the sword, perfectly fits the figure of Aśoka in the legends, as well as in the edicts. At the same

[37] Ibid., pp. 197, 202. I am following here the order given in that late but great encyclopedia of Buddhism, the *Mahāvyutpatti*. (See Ryōzaburo Sakaki, ed. *Mahāvyutpatti*, Kyoto University, Department of Literature, publication 3 [Kyoto: 1916] p. 250.) La Vallée Poussin, following the *Abhidharmakośa*, reverses the order of svayamyāna and pratyudyāna, translating the latter as "spontaneous surrender" (reddition spontanée) which hardly does justice to the sense of "meeting" or "encounter" implicit in the term. For a discussion of the ways in which this four-fold classification of cakravartins was reinterpreted in China, see Antonino Forte, *Political Propaganda and Ideology in China at the End of the Seventh Century* (Naples: Istituto Universitario Orientale, 1976), pp. 139ff. For Southeast Asia, see Eugène Denis, ed. and trans., *La Lokapaññatti et les idées cosmologiques du bouddhisme ancien*, 2 vols. (Lille: Atelier Reproduction des thèses, 1977), 1:xliv.

time, it helps to explain a rather bizarre passage in the *Aśokāvadāna*. When, before he actually becomes king, Aśoka is sent to subdue an uprising in the city of Takṣaśilā, his father Bindusāra fails to provide him and his army with any weapons. Aśoka's men are worried about this. "Prince," they say to him, "we do not have any weapons of war; how and with what shall we do battle?" Aśoka's response is to declare: "If my merit is such that I am to become king, may weapons of war appear before me," and immediately the earth opens up and various deities bring forth weapons and arm both Aśoka and his troops.[38] At first glance, this story appears to be rather strange, especially when it turns out that Aśoka does not actually use the weapons at all; as soon as the Takṣaśilāns see him and his army approaching, they immediately submit to him. But, as an iron-wheeled cakravartin, Aśoka is by definition armed and able to threaten force, and this passage seems to emphasize that. The same point is made in the very next episode. After conquering Takṣaśilā, Aśoka hires two great warriors; with them he marches throughout the whole earth as far as the ocean, and everywhere he goes, they proclaim: "Aśoka is to become a cakravartin ruler over one of the four continents: no one is to oppose him!"[39]

The notion of an iron-wheeled monarch who rules over one of the four continents is also related to the other epithet Aśoka is given in the *Aśokāvadāna*—that of "armed cakravartin" (balacakravartin). This concept belongs to two somewhat different systems of categorizing kings. They are found most prominently in our text and in the *Lotus Sūtra*.

In the *Aśokāvadāna*'s account of the Buddha's smile (which we shall consider in greater detail below) different types of beings in the cosmos (gods, humans, animals, kings, etc.) are symbolically made to correspond to different parts of the body of the Buddha. In the hierarchical schema that is thus established we find reference to two sorts of cakravartin: the bala-

[38] Mukhopadhyaya, p. 39.
[39] Ibid., p. 40.

cakravartin who is associated with the Buddha's left hand, and the cakravartin (with no epithet) who is associated with his right hand and is thereby somewhat superior to him.[40]

In the *Lotus Sūtra*, a slightly different distinction occurs. In its listings of the many sorts of beings who commonly make up the congregation of the Buddha, mention is routinely made of three kinds of kings: (1) *caturdvīpakacakravartin*, that is, rulers over all four continents; these are also sometimes called simply cakravartin (without epithet), (2) balacakravartin, and (3) *maṇḍalin*, that is, kings who govern only a minor region.[41]

Altogether then, we are dealing with three different schemes of classifying cakravartin: Vasubandhu's four-fold system, the two-fold system in the account of the Buddha's smile that simply contrasts cakravartin and balacakravartin, and the three-fold system of the *Lotus Sūtra*. It is not difficult to see where the overlap occurs. The silver-wheeled and copper-wheeled monarchs do not seem to have played very important roles. Instead, the significant categories are the iron-wheeled king (who would appear to be the same as the balacakravartin of the *Aśokāvadāna* and the *Lotus*) and the golden-wheeled king (who seems to correspond to the cakravartin without epithet of the *Aśokāvadāna* and the caturdvīpaka-cakravartin of the *Lotus*). (See Table 1)

While this golden-wheeled monarch preserved the full mythic ideal of the cakravartin and may thus be identified with the figure of Daḷhanemi, the iron-wheeled king is a ruler who, though still a cakravartin, can also be fully involved in this imperfect world. He corresponds to Aśoka.

Lest any of these distinctions be drawn too rigidly, however,

[40] Ibid., p. 33. The same schema of the smile may also be found in the *Avadānaśataka*. See Léon Feer, tr., *Avadāna-çataka: cent légendes (bouddhiques)*, Annales du Musée Guimet, vol. 18 (Paris: E. Leroux, 1891), pp. 10-12; P. L. Vaidya, ed., *Avadāna-śatakam*, Buddhist Sanskrit Texts, no. 19 (Darbhanga, Bihar: Mithila Institute, 1958), pp. 297-98.

[41] Hendrik Kern and Bunyu Nanjio, ed., *Saddharmapuṇḍarīka Sūtra*, Bibliotheca Buddhica, no. 10 (St. Petersburg, 1912), pp. 6, 20, 363; compare Kern, *Lotus*, pp. 7, 20, 343.

TABLE 1. CORRESPONDENCES BETWEEN THE DIFFERENT CLASSIFICATIONS OF CAKRAVARTIN

Vasubandhu's *Abhidharmakośa*	*Lotus Sūtra*	Pali Tradition (see n. 35)	*Aśokāvadāna*	Legendary Traditions
suvarṇacakravartin (golden-wheeled, 4 continents)	caturdvīpaka-cakravartin	cakkavāḷa-cakkavatti	cakravartin	Daḷhanemi
rūpyacakravartin (silver-wheeled, 3 continents)				
tāmracakravartin (copper-wheeled, 2 continents)				
ayaścakravartin (iron-wheeled, 1 continent)	balacakravartin	dīpacakkavatti	balacakra-vartin (= caturbhāga-cakravartin)	Aśoka
	maṇḍalin (petty ruler)	padesacakkavatti		

we must hasten to add that both of these basic types of cakravartin belong at the same time to a broader, more inclusive Buddhist category of kingship: that of the dharma-king (dharmarāja). Indeed, one of the other epithets given to Aśoka in the *Aśokāvadāna* is "dharmika dharmarāja" (righteous dharma-king),[42] and the same title was later used in Buddhist tradition to designate other Buddhist kings who were known to be balacakravartins.[43] At the same time, however, it was also one of the stock appellations of the full-fledged cakravartin who ruled over all four continents.[44]

It is thus apparent that all cakravartins, no matter what their type, were dharmarājas. As such they ruled with justice and impartiality. They may not all have reigned over four continents conquered by their charismatic presence, but, as the *Aṅguttara Nikāya* put it, they were familiar with the purpose of rule, with the measure for justice and taxation, with the proper time for various types of action, and with the social groupings with which they had to deal.[45] At the same time, they at least nominally relied on Dharma, honored, revered, and esteemed Dharma, had Dharma as their standard, Dharma as their banner, and Dharma as their mandate.[46]

The Gift of Dirt

We have seen so far that the *Aśokāvadāna* reflects several different Buddhist views of kingship, and is marked therefore by an ambiguity of attitude toward the figure of Aśoka. He fits, on the one hand, the image of an impetuous monarch to

[42] Mukhopadhyaya, p. 34.

[43] See Tambiah, *World Conqueror*, p. 81, for a Burmese example.

[44] Carpenter, vol. 2, p. 16; Davids, *Dialogues*, 2:13.

[45] Woodward and Hare, vol. 3, p. 113. See also B. G. Gokhale, "Dhammiko Dhammarājā: A Study in Buddhist Constitutional Concepts," in *Indica*, The Indian Historical Research Institute Silver Jubilee Commemoration Volume (Bombay: St. Xavier's College, 1953), p. 162.

[46] Woodward and Hare, vol. 1, p. 94; Richard Morris, ed. *The Aṅguttara-Nikāya* (London: Pali Text Society, 1885) 1: 109-10.

be feared or maligned. On the other hand, he also recalls in his person the mythical ideal of the cakravartin. This ambiguity needs to be taken seriously and not glossed over if we are to interpret correctly a number of passages in the text itself. In the remainder of this chapter, I would like to illustrate this more specifically by examining the story of Aśoka's gift of dirt. At the same time, this should help shed new light on our text's overall valuation of kingship.

Aśoka's gift of dirt to the Buddha is one of the most famous episodes in the whole *Aśokāvadāna*. As has been mentioned, it was actually made by Aśoka not in this but in a previous lifetime. He was then not a great king but simply a little boy named Jaya who happened to see the Buddha one day, while playing in the dirt of the road, and quite spontaneously decided to make him an offering of food. Conceiving, in his child's world of make-believe, of one of his piles of dirt as a heap of ground grain, he scooped up a handful of it and put it into the Buddha's begging bowl.[47]

In the Buddhist tradition, any good deed, especially any act of offering to the Buddha, the Dharma or the sangha, is thought of as making merit that will, according to the laws of karma, bring about beneficial rewards for its doer in this or a future life. In avadāna literature, the Buddha in particular is seen as a vast and fertile field of merit (*puṇyakṣetra*) where devotees can "plant" their meritorious deeds. Thus any good (or bad) action directed toward him, no matter how petty it may seem, can have positive (or negative) karmic results beyond all expectations. The actual theory of karma is, of course, more complex than this, and seeks to take into consideration a whole web of interdependent causes and effects. But in popular Buddhist literature—the avadānas and other stories meant to illustrate the workings of karma—the complexity of the system is much simplified. The focus is often on a single significant act that then sets a theme for the whole story of

[47] Mukhopadhyaya, p. 31.

the person's subsequent lifetime and the development of his or her character.

For example, in the *Avadānaśataka*, we are told of a householder who once burned incense in front of the stūpa of the past Buddha Vipaśyī, and annointed it with sandalwood paste and other perfumes. Then, with a heart full of faith and devotion, he firmly resolved to attain arhatship in a future lifetime. When, eventually he dies and is reborn, his whole being is defined by the rewards of this act of merit: he is called Sugandhi ("sweet-smelling"), his mouth exhales the odor of incense and perfumes, and his body smells delightfully of sandalwood. After becoming a monk, he quickly attains arhatship.[48]

This very simple example of how one act can define a person's character, even the nature of his physical body, is typical of many avadāna stories. Generally speaking, the physical act of offering is also accompanied by a mental and verbal formulation of a resolute wish, a *praṇidhāna*. This is a formal vow, a statement of intent to use the merit that has just been gained in order to attain some kind of enlightenment.[49]

In Mahāyāna texts, of course, praṇidhānas are a well-known and important feature of a *bodhisattva*'s (future Buddha's) career. Often, as in the case of Amitābha in the Pure Land sūtras, they can become quite complex and involve many specific conditions whose fulfillment is promised. In avadāna literature, however, as well as in present-day Theravāda practice,[50] praṇidhānas remain rather simple and stereotyped. In the *Avadānaśataka*, for example, we find the story of a gardener who offers a lotus to the Buddha and then simply states his resolve to become a Buddha himself.[51] In another story

[48] Vaidya, *Avadānaśatakam*, pp. 257-59; Feer, pp. 238-40.

[49] Har Dayal, *The Bodhisattva Doctrine in Buddhist Sanskrit Literature*, (orig. pub., 1932; rpt., Delhi: Motilal Banarsidass, 1975), pp. 64-67.

[50] Richard Gombrich, *Precept and Practice. Traditional Buddhism in the Rural Highlands of Ceylon* (Oxford: Clarendon Press, 1971), pp. 217-26.

[51] Vaidya, *Avadānaśatakam*, p. 18; Feer, p. 42.

another gardener, who is to become a *pratyekabuddha* (a Buddha who keeps his enlightenment for himself), offers a toothstick to the Buddha, and then full of faith, formally states: "May I, by this root of merit, experience *pratyekabodhi*" (the enlightenment of a pratyekabuddha).[52] Similarly, in the story we have just looked at, Sugandhi, after making his offering of various perfumes to the stūpa of the Buddha Vipaśyī, makes a praṇidhāna to be reborn and attain arhatship under a teacher with qualities similar to those of Vipaśyī (i.e., under another Buddha).[53]

The case of Aśoka is just as straightforward. After making his gift of dirt to the Buddha, he then proceeds to formulate his praṇidhāna: "By this root of merit," he declares, "I would become king, and, after placing the earth under a single umbrella of sovereignty, I would pay homage to the Blessed Buddha."[54]

The significance of this moment is then marked in the story by two closely related events: the Buddha's smile, and his prediction (*vyākaraṇa*) pertaining to Aśoka. Having accepted the offering of dirt, the Buddha first displays his smile. This is, of course, no ordinary grin; as our text makes clear, it is nothing less than a revelation of the entire cosmos and an indication of Aśoka's future place in the scheme of things. Rays of light of different color shoot out in all directions from the Buddha's lips. Some illuminate the hells, where they bring relief to the suffering hell-beings, others penetrate the heavens where they proclaim to the deities the impermanence inherent in their blissful state, but all the rays eventually return and are reabsorbed into the Buddha's body. The point where they reenter the Buddha, however, can differ according to circumstances. If the Buddha wants to announce some individual's future Buddhahood, for example, the rays will disappear into his *uṣṇīṣa* (the protuberance on top of the Buddha's head). If

[52] Vaidya, *Avadānaśatakam*, p. 73; Feer, p. 109.
[53] Vaidya, *Avadānaśatakam*, p. 258; Feer, p. 239.
[54] Mukhopadhyaya, p. 31.

he wishes to announce someone's future pratyekabuddhahood, they will disappear unto his *ūrṇā* (the whorl of hair between his brows). If someone is to become an arhat, they will vanish into his mouth. If a person is to become a god, then the rays will enter the Buddha's navel; if a cakravartin, then into his right palm; if a balacakravartin, then into his left palm; if a human being, then into his knees; if an animal, or a hungry ghost, then into his heels or toes; and finally, if the Buddha wants to announce someone's rebirth in hell, then the rays will disappear into the soles of his feet. A whole hierarchy of possible destinies is thus established and made to correspond to various points on this "cosmic body" of the Buddha (see Table 2).[55] In the case of Aśoka, the rays reenter the Buddha's left-palm signifying he is to become a balacakravartin.

The Buddha's smile and the revelation it entails are intimately connected with the formal prediction (vyākaraṇa) the Buddha then makes about Aśoka. "Ānanda," he says to his

TABLE 2. HIERARCHY OF BEINGS AND THEIR RELATION TO THE BUDDHA'S BODY

Buddha's body		*Type of being*	
uṣṇīṣa		Buddha	
ūrṇā		pratyekabuddha	
mouth		arhat	
navel		deity	
right hand	left hand	cakravartin	balacakravartin
knees		human	
heel	toe	animal	hungry ghost
soles		hell-being	

[55] For a study of the Buddha's smile, see Paul Mus, "Le sourire d'Angkor: art, foi et politique bouddhiques sous Jayavarman VII," *Artibus Asiae* 24 (1961): 363-81; and idem, "Où finit Puruṣa?" *Mélanges d'indianisme à la mémoire de Louis Renou* (Paris: E. de Boccard, 1968), pp. 539-63. See also John Strong, "The Transforming Gift," *History of Religions* 18 (1979): 235-37.

favorite disciple who is with him on this occasion, "do you see that boy who threw a handful of dirt into the Tathāgata's bowl?" "Yes, Bhadanta." "Because of that meritous deed, Ānanda, one hundred years after the Tathāgatha has attained parinirvāṇa, that boy will become a king named Aśoka in the city of Pāṭaliputra. He will be a righteous dharmarāja, a cakravartin who rules over one of the four continents, and he will distribute my bodily relics far and wide and build eighty-four thousand dharmarājikās [stūpas]. This he will undertake for the well-being of many people."[56]

We have then here a full disclosure of the principal themes of young Jaya's future life, all as a result of his having made a praṇidhāna and offered the Buddha a handful of dirt.

If this description of Aśoka's gift of dirt has been given in some detail, it is because, when viewed in the context of the structurally similar acts of offering that abound in avadāna literature, two things about it stand out which are of significance for our understanding of Aśoka's kingship. The first of these is that it is not usual in avadāna literature to find people making vows (praṇidhānas) to become kings. If we look again at the stories in relatively early avadāna anthologies such as the *Avadānaśataka* and *Divyāvadāna*, we can find vows for various types of enlightenment—for Buddhahood, or arhatship, or even pratyekabuddhahood—but none for kingship. In the *Aśokāvadāna*, however, the praṇidhāna is associated with the attainment of kingship, more specifically of Aśoka's balacakravartinhood. We should not take this as somehow belittling Aśoka's vow. Rather, it suggests that, in our text, Aśoka's kingship is treated as though it were a form of enlightenment. To put it more simply, cakravartinhood is for Aśoka what Buddhahood is for a Buddha.

The connecting link between them, of course, is the element of Dharma. As we shall see later on, the Buddha and the cakravartin and Aśoka are all dharmarājas—kings of Dharma—

[56] Mukhopadhyaya, p. 34.

and the attainment of their status is, in all cases, what might be called a "dharmalogical achievement."

But perhaps this notion should be expanded. From the account of the Buddha's smile, it would seem that not only is cakravartinhood for Aśoka what Buddhahood is for the Buddha; it is also what arhatship is for the arhat, divinity for the god, humanity for men, animality for the beasts and so on. In the account of the Buddha's smile, all of these various destinies are brought together; the only difference between them is their relative position in the cosmological hierarchy revealed by the various places of entry of the rays of light on the Buddha's body. This is an important point for there has long been a tendency, especially among Western scholars focussing on Theravāda Buddhism, to think of the various types of beings in the cosmos as radically distinct from each other in dharmalogical terms, that is, according to whether or not they are enlightened; an arhat is enlightened, an animal or a *preta* (hungry ghost) is not. As we shall see, there are real difficulties with such a view. Even Theravādins, of course, admit that Buddhas, pratyekabuddhas, and arhats have all achieved the same enlightenment and differ rather according to their lifestyles and the manner in which their enlightened state was attained; but this principle of differentiation is not then extended to the other types of beings—the kings, deities, animals, and so on. In a sense, it will be up to Mahāyāna Buddhism to do this explicitly, with its doctrine that all beings, no matter what their status, are fundamentally enlightened; it is just that some have developed their Buddha nature more than others. Yet it is already clear from the *Aśokāvadāna* and its account of the Buddha's smile, that a dog and an arhat, or, more pertinently, a cakravartin and a Buddha, differ not so much in terms of their dharmalogical nature as in terms of their cosmological scope or field. The Buddha, at the top of the hierarchy, has the greatest cosmological field; his enlightenment extends further than that of any other being and is, in fact, infinite in time and space. The denizen of hell, at the bottom of the hierarchy has almost no cosmological field; he lives in constant darkness so that he is not even aware of the beings around him and totally preoccupied with his own intense physical suffering. Kings, in the middle of the hierarchy, have an intermediate cosmological scope; specifically, in the case of a balacakravartin like Aśoka, it extends throughout the one continent of Jambudvīpa. The gift of dirt, then, as well as Aśoka's praṇidhāna and the smile of the Buddha, not only brings about Aśoka's kingship, it also delimits and sets precisely for Aśoka his dharmalogical potential: that of being the dharmic ruler over one of the four continents.

At this point, it might be helpful to make a second comment about the originality of Aśoka's gift of dirt. Just as it is not usual, in avadāna literature, for persons to make vows to become kings, so too it is not usual to find people presenting to the Buddha offerings of dirt—an impure substance. Aśoka is sometimes excused for this on the grounds that he was a little boy and so did not know any better, but even so dirt is in no case a fit offering for a Buddha or a monk, especially when it is placed in their begging bowl. Once again, if we look at the avadāna stories in the *Avadānaśataka*, we can find offerings of flowers, jewels, lights, umbrellas, or food, but never dirt. In this Aśoka's act is virtually unique.

In the *Aśokāvadāna*, this dirt is viewed in at least two ways. On the one hand, it is symbolic of the earth. As a little boy, Aśoka offers a handful of dirt to the Buddha; in his next lifetime, as a great cakravartin king, he offers the whole earth. As one scholar put it, "the gift of the child announces the gift of the entire world."[57] In terms of merit making, however, the gift of dirt is not merely a symbolic act, it also, through the processes of karma, results in Aśoka's sovereignty over the earth. Our text makes this clear several times and marvels that such a simple, lowly, impure offering could have led to so great a reward as the attainment of kingship. Thus, when

[57] Mus, *Barabuḍur* 2:290.

the elder Upagupta tells King Aśoka (for, of course, he could not himself remember his previous life) about his offering of dirt to the Buddha and how it resulted in his present royal splendor, Aśoka is utterly amazed and exclaims to his ministers:

> I was rewarded with the kingship of a balacakravartin
> simply because of a gift of dirt!
> You should spare no effort, sirs,
> in honoring the Blessed One.[58]

Later texts were to comment on this. For example, the *Mahākarmavibhaṅga*, a relatively late treatise on the workings of karma, marvels at the fact that Aśoka's gift of dirt could have led him to the throne of a cakravartin, and seeks to explain this phenomenon (which it calls "incredible") by emphasizing the greatness and power of the Buddha as a field of merit.[59] Other sources stress the purity of intent that accompanies Aśoka's gift, but there too the emphasis is still on the fact that such a simple offering should have such magnificent karmic effects.[60]

On the other hand, the gift of dirt is also seen, in the *Aśokāvadāna*, as having rather unfortunate results. Aśoka's physical ugliness and rough skin, for example, are attributed to the fact that he offered dirt to the Buddha in his past life.

[58] Mukhopadhyaya, p. 81. See also Appendix No. 12, below, for the story of the young monk who remarks that all of Aśoka's magnificence resulted from having put a handful of dirt into the Buddha's bowl.

[59] Sylvain Lévi, ed. and tr., *Mahākarmavibhaṅga et Karmavibhaṅgopadeśa* (Paris: E. Leroux, 1932), p. 170.

[60] This is the case, for example, in the *Sūtrālaṃkāra* (Edouard Huber, tr. *Aśvaghoṣa Sūtrālaṃkāra* [Paris: E. Leroux, 1908], p. 122), and in the *Jātakamālā* where we are told that "even a gift of dirt made by people of childlike minds is a good gift." See P. L. Vaidya, ed. *Jātakamālā by Arya Śūra*, Buddhist Sanskrit Texts, no. 21. (Darbhanga, Bihar: Mithila Institute, 1959), p. 19. In translating this passage, J. S. Speyer (*Ārya Śūra's Jātakamālā*, Sacred Books of the Buddhists, vol. 1 [London: Henry Frowde, 1895]) mistakenly assumes that pāṃśu ("dirt" or "dust") means pāṃśukūla (dust-heap robes), but see Franklin Edgerton, *Buddhist Hybrid Sanskrit Dictionary* (New Haven: Yale University Press, 1953) s.v. "pāṃśu-kūla."

Thus, when Aśoka notices that the elder Upagupta's limbs are smooth and his skin "like Benares silk," while his own limbs are "hard and coarse and his rough skin unpleasant to touch," Upagupta tells him rather bluntly: "That is because the gift I gave to that peerless Person was very pure and pleasing. I did not offer the Tathāgata a gift of dirt like you!"[61]

Dirt is an impure substance, and to offer it to the Buddha (even with great purity of intention) necessarily entails impure karmic consequences. It is not insignificant that, in the story itself, the Buddha takes Aśoka's offering and asks Ānanda to mix it with some cowdung and spread it on his meditation walkway. Cowdung, in India, universally purifies. Aśoka's dirt thus must be purified before it can finally be accepted by the Buddha.[62]

Some later traditions, in fact, even refused to admit that a gift of dirt could have led to Aśoka's royal splendor. Thus, in a late Chinese life of the Buddha (Pao Ch'eng's *Shih-chia ju-lai ying-hua lu*), there occurs an interesting sequel to our story. After the Buddha makes his prediction that the little boy who has just given him the dirt will be reborn as the great king Aśoka and build "an infinite number of stūpas," Ānanda is said to ask: "Is it possible that the offering of a little dust will result in the glory of erecting so many stūpas?" And the Buddha, significantly, is made to answer in the negative: "No, another prior act of merit will result in that glory," and he goes on to tell Ānanda a different previous life-story of Aśoka as a king who made a vast number of statues of the Tathāgata at the time of the past Buddha Puṣya.[63] In other words, here, the gift of dirt is specifically dissociated from Aśoka's later greatness, and another more believable story (which to my knowledge is found nowhere else) has been inserted to explain it.

[61] Mukhopadhyaya, p. 80.

[62] Ibid., p. 34.

[63] Léon Wieger, ed. and tr. *Les vies chinoises du Bouddha* (Shanghai, 1913; reprint ed., Paris: Cathasia, 1951), p. 183.

The Gift of Dirt and the Gift of Honey

Clearly, the story of the gift of dirt was a focal point for the feelings of ambiguity about Aśoka. On the one hand it expressed the rudeness of his character—the physicality and roughness of his person and kingship. On the other hand it pointed to his future greatness and to his dedication, as king of the whole earth, to the Buddha, the Dharma, and the sangha. In this regard, it is interesting to compare the episode of the gift of dirt in the *Aśokāvadāna* with a somewhat similar story in the *Mahāvaṃsa*. In the Sinhalese chronicle, Aśoka in his previous life is no longer portrayed as a little boy who offered dirt to the Buddha but as a merchant who gave some honey to a pratyekabuddha:

> A certain paccekabuddha [Skt. *pratyekabuddha*] was sick of a wound; and another paccekabuddha, who, for his sake, wished for honey, came even then to the city on his usual way for seeking alms. A maiden, who was going for water to the river-bank, saw him. When she knew, from questioning him, that he wished for honey, she pointed with hand outstretched and said: 'Yonder is a honey-store sir, go thither.'
>
> When the paccekabuddha came there, the trader, with believing heart, gave him a bowlful of honey, so that it ran over the edge. As he saw the honey filling the bowl and flowing over the edge, and streaming down to the ground, he, full of faith, wished: 'May I, for this gift, come by the undivided sovereignty of Jambudipa, and may my command reach forth a yojana upward into the air and downward under the earth. . . .' Asoka was he who gave the honey.[64]

Paul Mus is one of the few scholars who has sought to compare the *Mahāvaṃsa*'s "gift of honey" with the *Aśokā-*

[64] Wilhelm Geiger, tr., *The Mahāvaṃsa or the Great Chronicle of Ceylon* (London: Pali Text Society, 1912), p. 30, slightly altered.

vadāna's "gift of dirt." For him the two offerings can be equated as both being symbolic offerings of the whole cosmos:

> The bowl of the Buddha, just like the stūpa (of which it is the mystical equivalent) represents the cosmic vault. According to one of the most ancient of Indian conceptions, the world may be compared to a cup or a set of cups full of soma, the sacred liquid which represents the very essence of the world. On the other hand, it should be noted that "honey" (madhu) is one of the most common Vedic words for soma. By filling up the Buddha's bowl with honey, to the point of overflowing, the merchant in the *Mahāvaṃsa* was thus making an offering of all things in their essence. So too was the child [in the *Aśokāvadāna*] with his handful of earth—an Earth which, later on as king, he would dedicate to the Buddha in the more condensed form of a stūpa.[65]

Mus's interpretation is interesting and suggestive, but in the final analysis it remains rather tortuous. In my view, he assumes far too readily that bowls used in begging can be viewed as stūpas, that honey in this context recalls vedic cups of soma, so that to put a handful of dirt in a bowl is comparable to filling it to the brim with honey as well as to constructing a stūpa and offering in essence the cosmos. More importantly, however, he fails to note along with this positive symbolism the negative and impure connotations implicit in the notion of a gift of dirt. Hence he does not see the ambiguity of the episode in the *Aśokāvadāna*.

It is clear that, in the *Mahāvaṃsa*, with the substance of the gift changed to honey (a delicious foodstuff), much of this ambiguity has been lost. As one might expect, in the Sinhalese chronicle, most of the negative side of Aśoka's personality has been dropped. No mention is made of his ugliness or of his rough skin; rather he stands high above his brothers "in valour, splendour, might, and wondrous powers."[66] Nor is any

[65] Mus, *Barabuḍur*, 2:289.
[66] Geiger, tr., *Mahāvaṃsa*, p. 27.

reference made to his torturing people in a prison built for the purpose, but instead (apart from a quickly mentioned fratricide prior to his conversion) he is consistently presented as a magnificent, pious monarch.

The comparison of these two stories of the gift of honey and the gift of dirt is, however, also interesting for another reason. It must not be forgotten that things put into the begging bowl of a Buddha (or for that matter of any Buddhist monk) are meant to be eaten. Obviously, in the background of all the negative symbolism implicit in Aśoka's gift in the *Aśokāvadāna* is the fact that people do not eat dirt, at least not in this day and age. There was, however, a time when they did.

It is curious that no one seems to have connected the gift of dirt with the myth of Mahāsammata, "the Great Elect," that we looked at earlier in this chapter. In that text, the primordial paradisial time—a time without kings—is portrayed as one when the earth itself is edible. Dirt was then not simply "dirt," but a delightful soft substance that looked like butter, and, significantly in light of the *Mahāvamṣa* version of our story, was as sweet as honey. It was only later, with the loss of the Golden Age, that the earth hardened, that plants grew, and that "dirt" became dirty.

In many of his works, Mircea Eliade has emphasized the way that ritual actions and myths can return one to the Illud Tempus and reaffirm the basic structures at the beginning of time.[67] In his childish play in the *Aśokāvadāna*, Jaya, in a sense, does just that; he makes believe that dirt can be eaten and thereby recalls the Golden Age when, in fact, this was the case. Interestingly, that Golden Age was also a time without kings. Kingship, in the story of the Great Elect, appears only long after the hardening of the earth has occurred and the Golden Age has been lost. It is appropriate therefore that the gift of dirt should be made by Jaya, a little boy. As a king,

[67] Mircea Eliade, *Cosmos and History*, trans. Willard H. Trask (New York: Harper and Row, 1959), pp. 51ff.

as Aśoka, he can no longer offer dirt to the Buddha, not simply because he knows better, nor just because he has more to give, but also because, in the mythic dimension, the time when dirt can be eaten is a time when there are no kings.

It is now possible to see how involved the interpretation of the gift of dirt becomes. We have already noted that it has both negative and positive karmic results. Here, in the notion that the gift itself symbolically recalls an ideal age, we find a reinforcement of its positive overtones, yet, at the same time, in terms of kingship, these connotations are called into question because that ideal age was, by definition, a time without kings. Once again then, we are left with ambiguity.

Conclusion

We have, in this chapter, examined a number of different Buddhist views and attitudes toward kingship. On the one hand, we have seen that Buddhists in India never lost a certain amount of apprehension for the powers and potential dangers of the king. On the other hand, they never rejected the monarchical system per se. They applauded it as the recognized mode of government and, in fact, maintained a rather positive image and ideal of kingship in their myth of the cakravartin. At the same time, in the myth of the Great Elect, they maintained an image of an ideal time without kings while recognizing the need for them for maintaining order in this day and age.

In the figure of Aśoka, the iron-wheeled balacakravartin, as well as in the account of his gift of dirt, we have an attempted synthesis of these various elements. Aśoka is both an impetuous ruler caught up in a web of worldly passions and a paradigmatic monarch recalling an ideal mythic king or, paradoxically, an ideal kingless age. It is precisely in this combination, I would suggest, that the power and appeal of his example lie. In the legendary Aśoka, Buddhists had a mythical but down-to-earth monarch in whom they could give vent to or find expressed their own feelings of fear, disdain, and fervent admiration for the figure of the king. Aśoka was, in other words, the full embodiment of their own ambiguous attitudes toward kingship.

CHAPTER THREE

King and Layman: Aśoka's Relationship to the Buddhist Community

The question of kingship in the *Aśokāvadāna* is intimately bound up with the equally important matter of Aśoka's relationship to the Buddhist community of monks, the sangha. Students of Buddhism have long been fascinated by this topic. They have quite rightly seen in Aśoka and his dealings with the sangha a model that later Buddhist kings in Burma, Thailand, Sri Lanka, and elsewhere sought to emulate. The model is often described in terms of the "Two Wheels" of Buddhism. On the one hand, there is the "Wheel of Dharma" (*dharmacakra*; Pali, *dhammacakka*), also called the *śāsanacakra* (Pali, *sāsanacakka*), that refers to the sphere of the Buddhist order. It consists of the three traditional refuges of Buddhism: the Buddha, his Teachings (Dharma), and the community of his monks (sangha). On the other hand, there is the "Wheel of State" or "Sphere of Command" (*ājñācakra*; Pali, *āṇācakka*). It consists of the Buddhist king (paradigmatically Aśoka), his royal Dharma, and the Buddhist state.[1]

Buddhist tradition traces this parallelism right back to the time of the Buddha. According to Buddhaghosa's *Commentary on the Vinaya*, when King Ajātasattu agreed to the holding of the First Buddhist Council shortly after the Blessed One's death, he told the elders: "Mine is the Wheel of Command (āṇācakka), let yours be the Wheel of the Dhamma!"[2]

[1] Frank E. Reynolds, "The Two Wheels of Dhamma: A Study of Early Buddhism," in *The Two Wheels of Dhamma*, ed. Bardwell L. Smith (Chambersburg, Pa.: American Academy of Religion, 1972), pp. 6-30; see also Stanley J. Tambiah, *World Conqueror and World Renouncer* (Cambridge: University Press, 1976), p. 42.

[2] N. A. Jayawickrama, ed. and tr., *The Inception of Discipline and the Vinaya Nidana*, Sacred Books of the Buddhists, 21 (London: Luzac and Co., 1962), p. 143 (text), p. 8 (tr.); see also B. G. Gokhale, "Early Buddhist Kingship," *Journal of Asian Studies* 26 (1966): 22.

It is only with the figure of Aśoka and the legends about him, however, that we find a full development and propagation of this paradigm.

It is sometimes claimed that the actual relationship between the two wheels of the Buddhist tradition was a simple symbiotic one. The king, through his sponsorship in the form of donations and protection, materially supported the sangha in exchange for its Dharma—its sermons, advice, and ethical backing.[3] In fact, the relationship between these two wheels was somewhat more complex than this. We are not dealing here with a church's involvement with a secular state, but with the full correlation of two poles of a single religious structure. The Buddha and the king embody distinct yet complexly interwoven notions of Dharma. At the same time, they both serve as paradigms for the religious life, the one for that of the monks (*bhikṣus*), the other for that of the laity. Thus the relationship between the two wheels is not only one of complementarity; it involves an overlap of function as well.[4]

It will be one of the purposes of this chapter to sort out the various roles Aśoka is involved in in the context of this scheme. As a dharmarāja, he clearly corresponds (within the Wheel of the State) to the Buddha. At the same time, however, he is also just an ordinary Buddhist layman and, as such, he relates in another fashion to Buddhist monks.

It is important, in turn, to remember that within the sangha, there are various sorts of monks including abbots, elders, charismatic saints, ordinary bhikṣus, and novices. Aśoka does not treat all of these individuals in the same way. Before generalizing, then, about Aśoka's relationship to the Buddhist order as a whole, we shall have to examine closely his personal relationships with the variety of monks with whom he deals. Specifically, we shall consider his encounter with four different monks: Samudra (who converts him to Buddhism), Upagupta (with whom he goes on pilgrimage), Piṇḍola Bhāradvāja (a

[3] Melford Spiro, *Buddhism and Society* (New York: Harper and Row, 1970), p. 379.

[4] Reynolds, pp. 29-30.

rather mysterious enlightened arhat), and Yaśas (the abbot of the Kukkuṭārāma Monastery). As we shall see, Aśoka relates differently to the first three of these figures than he does to the last one.

Aśoka and Samudra

According to the *Aśokāvadāna*, Samudra is the son of a merchant of Śrāvastī. When his father falls victim to a band of brigands, he joins the Buddhist sangha and becomes a wandering monk. One day he inadvertently enters the prison Aśoka had built in Pāṭaliputra and from which no one was allowed to leave. Seized by Caṇḍagirika, the executioner-in-chief, he is told he will soon be killed. First, however, he witnesses the tortures being inflicted on the other prisoners, and contemplating them he comes to realize the Buddhist truth of suffering and attains arhatship. The next day, when it is his turn to be boiled alive in a cauldron, he enters into a meditative trance and is unaffected by the futile efforts of his would-be tormentors. He simply sits cross-legged on a lotus blossom that has miraculously sprung from the bottom of the pot. King Aśoka is then called to come and see this marvel, and so begins his relationship with Samudra. Realizing that the time is ripe for Aśoka's conversion to Buddhism, Samudra performs the magical feat of suspending himself in mid-air while half of his body is on fire and the other half raining down water. Aśoka is impressed by this, and enquires as to Samudra's identity. The monk tells him he is a disciple of the Buddha and a follower of Dharma, and reprimands him for having built the torture chamber. Instead, Aśoka should guarantee the security of all beings and fulfill the Buddha's prophecy by building the eighty-four thousand stūpas. Aśoka then confesses his evil deeds and takes refuge in the Buddha and the Dharma.[5]

This story of Aśoka's initial conversion to Buddhism be-

[5] Sujitkumar Mukhopadhyaya, ed., *The Aśokāvadāna* (New Delhi: Sahitya Akademi, 1963), pp. 46-52; compare Jean Przyluski, *La légende de l'empereur Açoka* (Paris: Paul Geuthner, 1923), pp. 120-56, 237-41.

came well known throughout the Northern Buddhist world.[6] In China, there are several versions of the episode including one in which Samudra is replaced by an aged monk named Suprabuddha.[7] In Tibet, much the same tale is told except that Samudra is now represented as an incarnation of the great Indo-Tibetan saint Padmasambhava who is thus credited with Aśoka's conversion.[8] In India itself, the site of the prison, known as "Aśoka's Hell," became a popular place of pilgrimage near Pāṭaliputra; both Fa-hsien and Hsüan-tsang reported visiting it and used the occasion to recount the tale of Samudra in slightly different versions.[9]

In all of these versions of the story it is interesting to note the emphasis placed on Samudra's magical powers. It was commonly felt, in ancient India, that powers such as levitation, the divine eye, and mastery over the various elements of nature, developed naturally from the practice of yoga and marked the attainment of certain advanced meditative stages. Buddhist tradition, however, was of two minds about the display of such supernatural powers. On the one hand, it was clearly fascinated by them and relished telling stories about the great miraculous feats of the Buddha or of his disciples. Often these feats were performed in a contest of magical powers between Buddhists and heretics, and were clearly intended to show to all the superiority of the Buddhist monks over their rivals. As a line attributed to the Buddha in the *Divyāvadāna* puts it:

[6] The Pali counterpart of this episode is the story of Aśoka and Nigrodha that we shall consider below. See Wilhelm Geiger, tr., *The Mahāvaṃsa* (orig. pub. 1908; rpt. London: Luzac and Co., 1958), pp. 29-32.

[7] Przyluski, *Légende*, pp. 215-18.

[8] Yeshe Tsogyal, *The Life and Liberation of Padmasambhava*, tr. Kenneth Douglas and Gwendolyn Bays, 2 vols. (Emeryville, Cal.: Dharma Publishing, 1978), 1:280-82; compare W. Y. Evans-Wentz, ed., *The Tibetan Book of the Great Liberation* (London: Oxford University Press, 1954), pp. 153-54.

[9] James Legge, tr. and ed., *A Record of Buddhistic Kingdoms* (orig. pub., 1886; rpt., New York: Paragon Book Co., 1965), pp. 90-92; Thomas Watters, *On Yuan Chwang's Travels in India*, 2 vols. (orig. pub., 1905; rpt. Delhi: Munshi Ram Manohar Lal, 1961), 2:88-90.

"A magical feat quickly converts an ordinary person."[10] On the other hand, these magical powers were also seen as distracting rather than attracting the faith of the masses. They were not thought to be conducive to enlightenment, and their display by monks in front of the laity was seen as a violation of the Vinaya rule specifically forbidding the practice.[11]

That the Buddhists never really resolved this basic ambivalence toward magical powers is perhaps best illustrated by a well-known story in the *Dhammapada Commentary*. The Buddha himself, after accepting a challenge to a tournament of supernatural powers with some heretics, is asked "Have you not laid down a precept forbidding the performance of miracles?" "I have not," the Buddha answers, "laid down a precept for myself; the precept was intended only to apply to my disciples," and he then proceeds to perform the most famous magical feat of his career, the twin miracle of Śrāvastī.[12]

In the story of the conversion of King Aśoka, Samudra clearly has no qualms about displaying his supernatural powers, and it is these, in fact, which cause Aśoka to turn to the Dharma and take refuge in the Buddha. This point, as we shall see, is of some importance. What initially attracts Aśoka to Buddhism is not the profundity of its doctrine nor (as in the Aśokan edicts) his remorse at his own misdeeds, but the personality of its monks. Similarly, what stimulated him, in his past life as a little boy, to make his offering of dirt, was not the preaching of the Buddha but his charismatic presence.

[10] P. L. Vaidya, ed., *Divyāvadāna*, Buddhist Sanskrit Texts, no. 20 (Darbhanga, Bihar: Mithila Institute, 1959), p. 118.

[11] For the Pali Vinaya account, see T. W. Rhys Davids and Hermann Oldenberg, trs., *Vinaya Texts*, 3 vols., Sacred Books of the East, nos. 13, 17, 20 (orig. pub. 1882-85; rpt., Delhi: Motilal Banarsidass, 1975), 3:78-81. For other Vinaya interdictions in this regard, see Sylvain Lévi and Edouard Chavannes, "Les seize arhat protecteurs de la loi," *Journal asiatique* 8 (1916): 235-47.

[12] H. C. Norman, ed., *The Commentary on the Dhammapada*, 3 vols. (London: Pali Text Society, 1912), 3:204; compare E. W. Burlingame, tr., *Buddhist Legends*, 3 vols., Harvard Oriental Series, nos. 28-30 (orig. pub. 1921; rpt., London: Luzac and Co., 1969), 3:39.

It is interesting to compare this episode of Samudra with its counterpart in the Pali tradition: the *Mahāvaṃsa*'s story of Aśoka and the young monk Nigrodha. Nigrodha is an ascetically inclined Buddhist novice of peaceful demeanor who happens to pass by Aśoka's window; the king invites him in and asks him to sit down. The monk seats himself on the royal throne. Aśoka is impressed by his noble bearing and asks him what doctrine his master, the Buddha, taught. Nigrodha answers by preaching the Appamādavagga (a part of *Samyutta Nikāya*), and Aśoka, upon hearing this, is won over to the doctrine of the Blessed One.[13] There is thus, in the *Mahāvaṃsa*'s account of Aśoka's conversion, no reference either to the infernal prison or to a display of supernatural powers, but only to the more common situation of a monk preaching a sermon. Nonetheless it is clear that both Samudra and Nigrodha share the element of personal charisma, and that this is fundamental in effecting Aśoka's change of heart. In the *Aśokāvadāna*, this charisma manifests itself in the form of miraculous displays,[14] while in the *Mahāvaṃsa* it is reflected in Nigrodha's noble and peaceful bearing.

Aśoka and Upagupta

After initially converting Aśoka to Buddhism, Samudra flies off by means of his supernatural powers and never returns again. The further development of the king-monk relationship he initiated is left to the story of Aśoka's dealings with the Elder Upagupta.

Upagupta, in a sense, embodies even more fully the charismatic qualities of Samudra. Quite apart from his association with Aśoka, he is famous in his own right as the subject of several legends. A number of these have been incorporated

[13] Geiger, tr., *Mahāvaṃsa*, p. 31.

[14] On the connections between miracles and charisma, see S. N. Eisenstadt, *Max Weber on Charisma and Institution Building* (Chicago: University of Chicago Press, 1968), p. 22.

into the *Aśokāvadāna* as we now have it. In a previous life, on Mount Urumuṇḍa, Upagupta is said to have been the leader of a band of monkeys who converted five hundred Brahmanical ascetics by imitating in front of them the meditative postures of Buddhist monks.[15] In this lifetime, he has been born as the son of a perfume merchant of Mathurā; he helps his father in the store and is renown for doing business "according to Dharma." It is then that he has his encounter with Vasavadattā, the most famous courtesan of Mathurā. She becomes enamored of him and attempts to seduce him, but he withstands all her advances. Only later, when she has come on hard times, does he go to her, help her in her suffering, and preach the Dharma.[16]

Upagupta is best known, however, as the converter of Māra, the Evil One of Buddhist mythology. Māra, who functions in Buddhism as a sort of satanic tempter, had been successfully resisted by the Buddha at Bodhgaya, but he had not actually been defeated. Hence he was still abroad in the world and tempting saintly monks and nuns. Upagupta's encounter with him comes early in his preaching career at Mathurā. Māra is interfering with Upagupta's sermons there by showering pearls and gold down on his audience, thus totally distracting his listeners. When, the next day, he stages a magical show of dancing girls and musicians, Upagupta decides the time has come to act. He takes several corpses, momentarily metamorphoses them into a garland of flowers, and pretending to honor Māra, places them around his neck. Māra, soon real-

[15] Mukhopadhyaya, p. 3. The same story is found in the *Vinaya of the Mūlasarvāstivādins*. See Nalinaksha Dutt, ed., *Gilgit Manuscripts*, vol. 3, pt. 1 (Srinagar: Research Department, 1947), pp. 4-7.

[16] Ibid., pp. 8-14. For parallel versions of the Vasavadattā story, see Edouard Huber, tr., *Aśvaghoṣa Sūtrālaṃkāra* (Paris: E. Leroux, 1908), p. 110, and P. L. Vaidya, ed., *Avadāna-kalpalatā*, 2 vols., Buddhist Sanskrit Texts, nos. 22-23 (Darbhanga, Bihar: Mithila Institute, 1959), 2:449-51. See also Przyluski, *Légende*, pp. 349-352. The Sanskrit text was used as the basis for a short story by Rabindranath Tagore. See Rabindranath Tagore, *The Collected Poems and Plays* (New York: MacMillan Co., 1937), pp. 154-55.

izing that these are not flowers but dead bodies, desperately tries to remove them, but he cannot counter Upagupta's magical powers. Thus bound, he is forced to recognize the superiority of the Buddha and his disciple, and he is soon converted to the good Dharma.[17]

Having tamed Māra, Upagupta then asks him a favor. By virtue of his own enlightenment, he says, he has seen the *dharmakāya* (doctrinal body) of the Buddha many times, but he has never seen his *rūpakāya* (his physical form). Would Māra be willing to take on the appearance of the Buddha, by means of his magical powers, and show it to him? Māra, who, of course, had personally known the Buddha, agrees to do so. He magically appears before Upagupta in the magnificent guise of the Blessed One, and Upagupta, thinking he is actually seeing the Buddha, gets carried away in an excess of devotion and falls down and worships Māra. Māra, who himself has just come to recognize the greatness of the Buddha, is rather taken aback by this, and he quickly puts an end to what he thinks of as Upagupta's idolatry. The latter, however, justifies his act by claiming it is really just the same as paying *pūjā* (ritually worshiping) to an image of the Blessed One.[18]

[17] Mukhopadhyaya, pp. 16-22; compare Przyluski, *Légende*, pp. 353-62. See also the translation of the Sanskrit text in Ernst Windisch, *Māra und Buddha* (Leipzig: S. Hirzel, 1895), pp. 161-76. For other versions of the Upagupta-Māra story, see Huber, *Sūtrālaṃkāra*, pp. 263-273; Charles Duroiselle, "Upagutta et Māra," *Bulletin de l'Ecole française d'Extrême-Orient* 4 (1904): 414-28; Vaidya, *Avadāna-kalpalatā*, 2:451-53; Tāranātha, *History of Buddhism in India*, trans. Lama Chimpa and Alaka Chattopadhyaya (Simla: Indian Institute of Advanced Study, 1970), pp. 35ff.; Sylvain Lévi; "La Dṛṣṭāntapaṅkti et son auteur," *Journal asiatique* 211 (1927): 119-22. For a recent interpretation of this legend, see Lowell W. Bloss, "The Taming of Māra, Witnessing to the Buddha's Virtues," *History of Religions* 18 (1979): 156-76.

[18] Mukhopadhyaya, pp. 23-27. There are other dimensions to the legend of Upagupta that we cannot explore here. In the Northern Buddhist tradition, he is counted as the fifth of the Great Masters of the Law, and as such is sometimes mistakenly identified with Moggaliputta Tissa, the fifth Master of the *Vinaya* in the Pali tradition, whom the *Mahāvaṃsa* portrays as Aśoka's chief spiritual advisor and president of the Third Buddhist Council. (See Etienne Lamotte, *Histoire du bouddhisme indien* [Louvain: Institut Orientaliste, 1958], pp. 226-30, 773; Geiger, tr., *Mahāvaṃsa*, pp. 34-39; and L. A.

Soon after this episode, Upagupta moves to a forest hermitage on Mount Urumuṇḍa not far from Mathurā, and it is there that he is living when King Aśoka first finds out about him. Aśoka quite naturally immediately wishes to meet him, but since he is far away in Pāṭaliputra this desire raises an interesting question of protocol. Who should defer to whom? Should Aśoka as a layman honor Upagupta by going to visit him, or should he as king summon Upagupta to come to the capital? Aśoka himself, with his newly found faith, is personally willing to go to Mount Urumuṇḍa and even starts making preparations toward that end. His ministers, however, object. They maintain that Aśoka ought instead to send a messenger to Upagupta and ask him to come to the king.[19]

This role of the ministers of state is an important one in any consideration of a king's relationship to the sangha. These officials are the persons who are constantly concerned with matters of royal prestige and protocol, even when the king himself may not be. In another passage of the *Aśokāvadāna*, for example, it is the minister Yaśas (not to be confused with the elder Yaśas) who tells Aśoka he really should not publicly prostrate himself before the Buddhist monks because some of them come from low castes.[20] And at the end of his life, when Aśoka starts giving away everything to the sangha, including his personal possessions, it is his ministers who put a stop to

---

Waddell, "Upagupta, the Fourth Buddhist Patriarch, and High Priest of Açoka," *Journal of the Asiatic Society of Bengal* 66 [1897]:76-84.) In India, Upagupta also came to be seen as the preserver *par excellence* of popular Buddhist stories, and often figures as the narrator of whole avadāna texts. (See John Strong, "The Buddhist Avadānists and the Elder Upagupta," in *Tantric and Taoist Studies in Honour of R. A. Stein*, ed. Michel Strickmann, *Mélanges chinois et bouddhiques*, vols. 20-22, forthcoming.) Finally in Thailand and Burma, up to this day, he is still the object of a popular cult and is connected to rain and fertility rituals. (See Stanley J. Tambiah, *Buddhism and the Spirit Cults in North-East Thailand* [Cambridge: University Press, 1970], pp. 168-78; Maung Kin, "The Legend of Upagupta," *Buddhism* [Rangoon] 1 [1903]: 219-42, and Eugène Denis, ed. and trans., *La Lokapaññatti et les idées cosmologiques du bouddhisme ancien*, 2 vols. [Lille: Atelier Reproduction des thèses, 1977], 1:liii-lxv.)

[19] Mukhopadhyaya, pp. 75-76.

[20] Ibid., p. 71.

his fit of dāna, fearful for the well-being of the state.[21] In all of these stories, the ministers represent the harness of state that checks the enthusiasm of a Buddhist king who, carried away by religious devotion, may be inclined to forsake his kingship.

In the present story, Aśoka wants to defy his ministers, but even so he does this by countering their objections on their own terms. Upagupta, he points out, is an enlightened arhat and so has an indestructible, adamantine body; if therefore he were to refuse an order to come to the capital, there would be little that could be done about it in the way of punishing him, and this would cause a tremendous loss of royal face. Thus, Aśoka argues, he had better go himself to see Upagupta.[22]

The ministers are not comfortable with this but, fortunately for them, their dilemma is soon solved when Upagupta decides to go to the capital. If Aśoka were to come to Mount Urumuṇḍa, he reasons, it would be difficult to find provisions for the large number of men in his retinue. Aśoka then arranges for the elder's passage by boat, and, as a favor to him, Upagupta condescends to take the ferry thus provided.[23] This rather complex protocol thus ends more or less at equality, with both the king and the elder showing themselves generous by deferring to each other.

There then follows, however, the actual meeting of Aśoka and Upagupta with the new question of who is to bow down to whom. The issue was not without controversy in the history of king-monk relations and was to be hotly debated (in Chinese Buddhist circles, for example) for a long time.[24] The *Aśokāvadāna*, however, at least initially, leaves no doubt as to what

[21] Ibid., p. 128.
[22] Ibid., p. 77.
[23] Ibid.
[24] See, for example, Leon Hurvitz, " 'Render unto Caesar' in Early Chinese Buddhism," *Liebenthal Festschrift*, ed. Kshitis Roy (Santiniketan: Visvabharati, 1957), pp. 80-114.

position it takes on the matter: the king is to defer to the monk. Most likely to his ministers' distress, Aśoka does not wait in the city for Upagupta's arrival, but personally goes down to the river to welcome him. Then, after helping him off the boat, he prostrates himself fully in front of the elder and kisses his feet. His joy at meeting the elder, he claims, is greater than it was when he gained full control of his empire, for Upagupta represents the Buddha in this world, now that the Blessed One is in parinirvāṇa.[25]

In formally paying pūjā to a monk, Aśoka is, of course, reaffirming a long Indian and Buddhist tradition of kings ritually honoring members of the sangha. In the "Sāmaññaphala Sutta" of the *Dīgha Nikāya*, for example, King Ajātasattu resolves positively the even more extreme case of whether a monarch should honor one of his former slaves who has become a monk: "We should," he says, "greet him with reverence, and rise up from our seat out of deference towards him, and press him to be seated. And we should have robes and a bowl, and a lodging place, and medicine for the sick—all the requisites of a recluse—made ready, and beg him to accept them."[26]

Even more important, however, than this notion of ritual subservience is the fact that, in this situation, Upagupta reminds Aśoka of the Buddha. Upagupta, in fact, is called a "Buddha without the marks" (*alakṣaṇakabuddha*)[27] and is repeatedly said to fulfill the role of the Blessed One. Aśoka himself has this fact formally proclaimed throughout his king-

[25] Mukhopadhyaya, p. 78.

[26] T. W. Rhys Davids, tr., *Dialogues of the Buddha*, 3 vols., Sacred Books of the Buddhists, nos. 2-4 (London: Pali Text Society, 1899-1921),1:77.

[27] "Alakṣaṇaka Buddha" was an epithet commonly applied to Upagupta. The implication is that he is like the Buddha in that he is enlightened and preaches sermons, but unlike him in that he does not possess the thirty-two major and eighty minor bodily marks of the Great Man (Mahāpuruṣa). The best discussion of the term is still that of Eugène Burnouf, *Introduction à l'histoire du buddhisme indien* (Paris: Adrien Maisonneuve, 1876), p. 337, n. 1.

dom, and he has his crier announce the arrival of Upagupta in Pāṭaliputra as follows:

> If you never saw the foremost of men
> the greatly compassionate self-existent Master,
> go and see the elder Upagupta who is like the Master,
> a bright light in this Triple World.[28]

We have arrived here at one of the crucial aspects of Aśoka's relationship to the Buddhist community. For him, Buddhist monks, especially enlightened ones such as Upagupta, are not simply spiritual followers of the Buddha's Teachings, they, in a sense, play the role of the Buddha in his absence and are his legitimate heirs.

Paul Mus has pointed out that in ancient India, the notion of inheritance should be considered primarily as taking over one's father's position and identity, rather than as taking over his possessions. As he put it in his succinct manner: "One does not inherit *from* one's father; instead, one inherits *one's father*."[29] We should not hesitate to apply this notion to the filiation of Buddhist monks. As "sons of Śākyamuni" (Śākyaputra) and "heirs of the Dharma" (*dharmadāyada*), Buddhist monks (or at least some of them) were more than Buddhists; they were also, in a sense, Buddhas.[30] It is at least in this context that we should view Aśoka's emotions at meeting Upagupta, and his exclamation on that occasion that: "Looking at you today, I see in you the Incomparable Self-Existent Pure One, even though he is gone beyond."[31]

At the same time, in being reminded of the Buddha, Aśoka is also reminded of his own special status as a balacakravartin. As we have seen, it is Upagupta who tells Aśoka that his gift

[28] Mukhopadhyaya, p. 78.

[29] Paul Mus, *Barabuḍur*, 2 vols. (Hanoi: Imprimerie d'Extrême-Orient, 1935), 1:12.

[30] Ibid. See also, in this regard, the discussion, in the last chapter, of enlightenment and cosmic hierarchy in terms of the smile of the Buddha.

[31] Mukhopadhyaya, p. 79.

of dirt, that is, his own personal encounter with the Buddha, resulted in his great royal status. Moreover, Upagupta also proclaims at the time of his encounter with Aśoka that both he and Aśoka are joint inheritors of the Buddha's Teaching and that together they have been entrusted with the safekeeping and promotion of the religion.[32] In some sense, then, Aśoka too represents the Buddha in this world, or at least he does so in so far as he acts as a cakravartin.

We shall explore the full meaning of Aśoka's relationship to the Buddha in our next chapter. For the moment, one particular aspect of that question concerns us, namely that in relating to Upagupta, Aśoka is not only relating to a monk but also, through that monk, to the Buddha who has gone beyond.

Aśoka and Piṇḍola Bhāradvāja

Much of the same theme sets the tone for the subsequent relationship of Aśoka and another great monk, the arhat Piṇḍola Bhāradvāja. When Aśoka first meets Piṇḍola, he in fact repeats the same actions and even the same words that marked his initial meeting with Upagupta; he prostrates himself fully in front of the elder, kisses his feet, makes an *añjali* (respectful salutation), and declares that Piṇḍola's presence gives him greater joy than he had even when he gained control of his empire. Moreover, he adds, "by looking at you, I can, even today, see the Tathāgata."[33]

In this regard, the Piṇḍola-Aśoka meeting is but a replica of the one between Upagupta and Aśoka. As an individual, however, Piṇḍola is an even more charismatic and mysterious figure than Upagupta. In the *Aṅguttara Nikāya*, he is designated by the Buddha as the "foremost of lion-roarers," an epithet that has spawned several stories of his previous birth as a lion, but that actually refers to his "shout of exultation"

[32] Ibid., p. 79.
[33] Ibid., p. 97.

upon attaining enlightenment.[34] Generally speaking, however, in the Pali commentaries, he is presented as a rather gluttonous person who initially joins the sangha because he has heard that Buddhist monks get lots of food. In due course he becomes an arhat endowed with supernatural powers. When, however, he displays these gratuitously in front of the laity, he is reprimanded by the Buddha, exiled from Jambudvīpa, and (in some versions of the story) condemned not to enter parinirvāṇa until the coming of the future Buddha Maitreya. As a result of this, he remains alive and occasionally, as in our text, appears as a living witness to events in the Buddha's life.[35]

In the *Aśokāvadāna*, when Aśoka meets with Piṇḍola, it is this connection with the time and the figure of the Buddha that is most emphasized. Not only does Piṇḍola, in his person, remind Aśoka of the Buddha, he becomes, for the king, a living witness to the charisma of the Blessed One. "Lifting up his long eyebrows and looking straight at the king," he tells of the times he saw face to face

that great incomparable sage
whose brilliance matched that of the best polished gold
whose body bore the thirty-two marks
whose face was like the autumn moon
whose voice carried more authority than Brahmā's
who dwelt ever free from passion.[36]

[34] See John Strong, "The Legend of the Lion-Roarer: A Study of the Buddhist Arhat Piṇḍola Bhāradvāja," *Numen* 26 (1979): 68-71.

[35] Ibid., 76-78. These features of Piṇḍola's legend also figure prominently in the Buddhist tradition of the Sixteen (or Eighteen) Great Arhats (Chinese, *lo-han*). Piṇḍola, in fact, is the leader of this group of saints who were asked by the Buddha magically to extend their lifespans and look after his Teaching until the end of this world cycle. In China and Japan, Piṇḍola also became famous as the patron saint of monastic refectories and, as such, was the subject of a rather elaborate cult. See Lévi and Chavannes, pp. 6-24, 205-75; and Marinus Willem De Visser, "The Arhats in China and Japan," *Ostasiatische Zeitschrift* 10 (1922-23): 60-64.

[36] Mukhopadhyaya, p. 97. See also, for this last episode, Tsurumatsu Tokiwai, *Studien zum Sumāgadhāvadāna* (Darmstadt: G. Ottos, 1898), pp. 17-63.

He saw the Buddha, he recalls, right after he had attained enlightenment and was spending the rains retreat (the months of the monsoon season when monks refrain from traveling) in Rājagṛha. Then again, he saw him when he performed the great miracle at Śrāvastī in order to defeat the heretics. Then, when the Buddha came down from the Trāyastriṃśa Heaven (the heaven of Indra, the chief of the gods) where he had spent a rains retreat preaching the Dharma to his mother, Piṇḍola was right there. And also when the Blessed One flew to Puṇḍavardhana by means of his magical powers, Piṇḍola did so too, and on that occasion the Buddha forbade him to enter parinirvāṇa until the disappearance of the Dharma.[37] But the most interesting occasion when Piṇḍola saw the Buddha is one much closer to the king's heart; Piṇḍola claims to have been "right there, when, long ago as a child, you [Aśoka] threw a handful of dirt into the bowl of the Blessed One . . . thinking you would offer him some ground meal."[38]

Piṇḍola has occasionally been compared to the figure of the Wandering Jew who, in Christian legend, was condemned by Jesus on his way to Golgotha to remain in this world until the Second Coming. He therefore did not die but roamed for centuries throughout Christendom, appearing mysteriously and recalling for the faithful the events of the Christian Holy Week.[39] In the Buddhist context of karma and rebirth, Piṇḍola can fill the same function even more specifically; he recalls for Aśoka not only the recognized glories of the Buddha, but the particular time in a past life when he, Aśoka, was with the Buddha, and when he, Aśoka, planted the seeds of merit that was to result in his balacakravartinhood. He thus functions in quite a personal way not only as a living charismatic link with the Buddha who is in nirvāṇa, but as a witness to the origin of Aśoka's own personal identity as king. In this he acts in much

[37] Ibid., pp. 98-99.

[38] Ibid., p. 99.

[39] Kumagusu Minakata, "The Wandering Jew," *Notes and Queries* 4 (1899): 123.

the same way as Samudra and Upagupta who, as we have seen, also recall for Aśoka the time of his gift of dirt.

More generally, then, the stories of Aśoka's encounters with these three monks all represent variations on a theme; they all show how Aśoka, in relating to them as members of the sangha, is reminded graphically first of the person of the Buddha, and secondly of his own personal status vis-à-vis the Buddha; and this inspires in him religious emotions of a devotional, almost ecstatic nature.

Aśoka and Yaśas

Not all of Aśoka's personal relationships with members of the sangha follow this pattern, however. In order to arrive at a more balanced view of this topic, we must consider his encounter with yet another Buddhist monk, the elder Yaśas.

Piṇḍola, Upagupta, and Samudra are all rather extraordinary figures. None of them is really what might be called a regular member of the sangha with whom Aśoka might deal on a day to day institutional basis. It is not insignificant, for example, that none of these monks resides in an ordinary nearby monastery; Samudra does not remain in the capital but flies off we know not where, while Piṇḍola and Upagupta live on far away semimythical mountain tops, the former on Mount Gandhamādana (which can be reached only by magical flight) and the latter on Mount Urumuṇḍa. To varying degrees, these figures represent a particular kind of charismatic Buddhist saint, and it is as such that they relate to Aśoka.

The case of the elder Yaśas, however, is somewhat different. He routinely appears, again and again, throughout the *Aśokāvadāna*, as the abbot of the Kukkuṭārāma monastery, in the capital of Pāṭaliputra. According to Buddhist tradition, the Kukkuṭārāma was founded by Aśoka. It was the central royal monastery, in many ways Aśoka's own personal monastery, and was, in fact, sometimes called the Aśokārāma.[40]

[40] Watters, vol. 2, pp. 98-99.

Yaśas, the abbot of this institution, was thus always available, not far away, to meet the needs of the king or the royal family.

Thus it is to Yaśas that Aśoka's brother Vītaśoka goes when he seeks ordination, and Yaśas who, quite properly tells him that he will initiate him only after he gets the permission of the king. It is also Yaśas who instructs Aśoka's son Kunāla in the basics of Buddhist meditation. Aśoka himself goes to Yaśas whenever he has a question he cannot answer. He tells Aśoka about Upagupta when the king asks whether the Buddha ever made any prediction about anyone else akin to the one he had made about him. He tells Aśoka about Piṇḍola when he asks about the seat of honor in the great quinquennial assembly. Furthermore, it is Yaśas who tells Aśoka how to make merit, and who instructs him how to wait correctly upon the Buddhist community. Finally, it is Yaśas who accepts on behalf of the sangha Aśoka's last gift of half a myrobalan.[41]

On all these occasions, Yaśas is presented as a wise, insightful, kindly abbot, but there is little really extraordinary about him. Although he is said to be endowed with the six supernatural faculties, he is never pictured as flying through the air, or making flames leap out from half of his body while water pours down from the other. He does seem able to divine the future, and he does demonstrate his magical powers when he signals the completion of the construction of the eighty-four thousand stūpas by eclipsing the sun, but Aśoka does not seem to react to this as something extraordinary. It is just an explanation for a natural phenomenon.

In the figure of Yaśas, I would argue, we have a different sort of representative of the sangha than Piṇḍola or Upagupta. He is much more thickly involved in the business of royalty, and is the prototype perhaps, of the *sangharāja* (supreme patriarch) who in some Theravāda countries, was appointed by the king to head the Buddhist community. With Yaśas, Aśoka can pursue an ongoing, routine, symbiotic relationship. He is

[41] Mukhopadhyaya, pp. 62, 106, 75, 96, 102, 130.

an elder whose charisma rests in his office rather than in his person. He is a city monk, if it is possible to draw for India the Theravāda distinction between city-dwelling and forest-dwelling monks. But most of all, he is an abbot who does the things abbots do: he preaches to the laity, ordains new monks, gives advice to the king, presides over the community, and, of course, he accepts donations. Aśoka's relations with him, then, are quite different from his relationships with the other personalities we have considered.

From what has been said so far, it is clear that in the *Aśokāvadāna* as a whole Aśoka's dealings with the sangha involve him in relations with at least two types of monks: saintly figures such as Samudra, Upagupta, and Piṇḍola, and abbots such as Yaśas with whom he deals on a more regular basis. In Weberian terms, the "saints" might be said to appeal to Aśoka because of their personal charisma, or perhaps rather because of their personal embodiment of the Buddha's charisma. The mere sight of them is enough to inspire in Aśoka feelings of ecstasy and devotion. They remind him, either directly or indirectly, of his relationship to the Buddha and consequently of his own status of balacakravartin.

The appeal of the "abbots," on the other hand, might be said to be based on a charisma that has become routinized and institutionalized. Yaśas is the head of the monastic organization in the capital. He is never said to remind Aśoka directly of the figure of the Buddha. Instead, Aśoka and his family associate with him routinely, with courtesy and respect, but without fainting from an excess of religious emotion. In his presence, the king seems more to take on the role of a layman, still royal, of course, but seeking advice, listening to sermons, and making offerings.

Thus parallel to the polarity between saints and abbots, we find a polarity in how Aśoka relates to the sangha as a whole. As a balacakravartin his relationship with the person of the Buddha through the monks is emphasized; as a royal layman, it is his relationship through them with the sangha as an institution that is stressed.

Aśoka's Offerings to the Sangha

There is, of course, a great deal of overlap between Aśoka's two roles as a balacakravartin and as a royal layman (just as there is between the roles of abbot and saint). Aśoka, in the end, must be seen as both king and layman, but for purposes of analyzing his relationship with the monks, it seems useful to set up this polarity. In particular, it is helpful in analyzing the various acts of dāna (donation) that Aśoka carries out toward the sangha. Three of these (recounted in the *Aśokāvadāna*) might profitably be examined here. In the first (Aśoka's offering of food and robes to the community) the king's role as layman is stressed. In the second (his sponsorship of a great quinquennial festival) his role as dharmarāja-balacakravartin is emphasized. Finally, in the third (his gift of half a myrobalan fruit to the sangha at the end of his life) we will find a combination of these two roles.

Aśoka's offering of food and robes to the sangha is, significantly, featured in the context of his relationship with the abbot Yaśas. After Aśoka makes clear his willingness to entertain the sangha, Yaśas announces that the monks are assembled and ready to be waited upon "in the correct manner." Apparently this means the donor should personally serve the food to the monks with his own hand—something that Aśoka proceeds to do, starting with the most senior elders in the assembly and working his way down to the most junior novices.

The emphasis placed here on Aśoka's personally serving the bhikṣus, that is, on the physical contact between the king and the monks, is significant. As in many ancient cultures, it was not customary, in the Buddhist world, for kings to come into immediate contact with ordinary people. Kings were sacred persons, more akin to the gods than to men, and touching them was taboo. Indeed, as Jean Filliozat has pointed out, in Buddhaghosa's commentary on the Vinaya, there is a story (similar to that told above of Aśoka's meeting with Upagupta), in which King Aśoka welcomes the elder Moggaliputta Tissa, and touches him with his hand. Immediately, the king's guards draw their swords and declare they will cut off the elder's head; for to come into contact with the king—even his hand—is a crime punishable by death. Aśoka, however, restrains them; in this situation, he is no longer a "king," but has become an ordinary person, a common layman who is free to touch and be touched by a monk.[42]

The routine nature of the serving of the food is stressed in the *Aśokāvadāna*. As soon as Aśoka has finished his rounds, Yaśas asks him whether, while serving the monks, he saw anything that raised doubts in his mind about the worthiness of the sangha itself. Aśoka replies that when he got to the end of the line, he saw two young novices who did not appear to be paying attention but were playing games in which they ritually offered each other little cakes and sweetmeats. There could hardly be a better way to emphasize the commonplace character of this occasion of dāna than to have two little *śrāmaṇeras* (novices) misbehaving while the "great" Aśoka serves the sangha.[43]

[42] Jean Filliozat, "Les deva d'Aśoka: dieux ou divines majestés," *Journal asiatique* 237 (1949): 225-47. For further discussion of this theme, see John Strong, "Aśoka's Quinquennial Festival and Other Great Acts of Dāna: An Essay on the Nature of Buddhist Giving," (unpublished ms., Lewiston, Maine, 1982).

[43] To do this passage justice, it should be pointed out that Yaśas quickly denies that these little boys are misbehaving by stating that actually, despite appearances, they are both fully enlightened and disciplined arhats. The whole episode is made even more complex by the fact that these two novices also appear to remind Aśoka of his own past life in which he made an offering of dirt to the Buddha. "These novices," he tells Yaśas, "were playing at games of ground meal just as young boys play at building houses in the dirt." Might there be some reminder here of Aśoka's special relationship to the Buddha, even though he is acting as an ordinary layman?

Aśoka then proceeds to make a further offering of undyed cloth to the community; it is accepted (by the two novices in question), colored and made into robes. What we have here, of course, is simply an account of a perfectly proper and ordinary kaṭhina ceremony—the traditional gift of cloth (*kaṭhina*) for robes as it was performed in India and is practiced by Buddhist laymen in South and Southeast Asia to this day.[44] Once again, in this, Aśoka can be seen engaging in a routine relationship with the monks. There is nothing particularly royal or "dharmarājic" about his actions. In fact, here, he has clearly become less of a great cakravartin monarch and more of a regular layman.

The Great Quinquennial Festival

Aśoka's gifts to the sangha, however, are not always of a routine nature. He is, after all, Lord of Jambudvīpa, a bala-cakravartin, and though at times he might act like an ordinary layman, he enjoys a special position with regard to the monks. Accordingly his duty of dāna and of materially supporting the sangha can take on special dimensions.

The great quinquennial festival (*pañcavārṣika*), practiced by Aśoka as well as other Buddhist monarchs, is the king's attempt to outdo himself at dāna. Precisely what it consisted of, however, is a matter of some scholarly debate. The editors of the *Divyāvadāna* thought it corresponded to the entertainment of all monks during the five (pañca) months of the rainy season (*varṣa*).[45] Franklin Edgerton, following Heinrich Lüders, claimed it consisted simply of a large gathering and

[44] On the kaṭhina offering in early Buddhism, see Heinz Bechert, "Some Remarks on the Kaṭhina Rite," *Journal of the Bihar Research Society* 54 (1968): 319-29. For accounts of the practice in Burma and Thailand, see Spiro, *Buddhism and Society*, pp. 226-28, 301-02, and Tambiah, *World Conqueror*, pp. 456-60.

[45] E. B. Cowell and R. A. Neil, eds. *The Divyāvadāna* (Cambridge: University Press, 1886), index, s.v. "pañcavārṣika."

entertainment of monks held every five years,[46] while Etienne Lamotte has specified that it was not necessarily held every five years, but was the occasion when kings spent whatever had accumulated in their treasuries during a five year period in honor of the sangha.[47] In any case, it is clear that the quinquennial festival was a time of offering to the sangha on a grand scale.

Our best source of knowledge on the festival itself is the Chinese pilgrim Hsüan-tsang's description of the one held by Harṣa, a North Indian emperor of the seventh-century. The ceremony took place on the great "Plain of Alms-giving," at the confluence of the Jumna and the Ganges rivers near Prayāga (Allahabad). There, Harṣa had built dozens of huts to house the vast quantities of gold, silver, and precious minerals to be given away. He also had constructed hundreds of storage sheds for the cloth to be made into monastic robes, and an immense dining hall to accommodate the ten thousand monks who had assembled for the occasion.[48]

Then, on the first day of the festival, an image of the Buddha was set up in a thatched temple, and precious goods were given away in great quantities as alms. On the second day, an image of the god Āditya (Viṣṇu), was consecrated, and again many things were distributed, but only half as many as on the first day. On the third day, an image of the god Īśvara (Śiva), was installed, and as many alms were distributed as for Āditya. Then, on the fourth day, gold pieces, cloth, food, drink, perfumes, and flowers were handed out to ten thousand Buddhist monks seated in hundreds of rows.[49]

[46] Heinrich Lüders, *Bruchstücke der Kalpanāmaṇḍitikā des Kumāralāta*, Kleinere Sanskrittexte aus den Turfanfunden, no. 2 (Leipzig, 1926), p. 44; see also Franklin Edgerton, *Buddhist Hybrid Sanskrit Dictionary* (New Haven: Yale University Press, 1953), s.v. "pañcavārṣika."

[47] Lamotte, p. 66.

[48] Watters, vol. 1, pp. 63, 119, 364. See also Radhakumud Mookerji, *Harsha* (orig. pub., 1925; rpt., Delhi: Motilal Banarsidass, 1965), pp. 75-83.

[49] René Grousset, *In the Footsteps of the Buddha*, tr. J. A. Underwood

The festival continued in this manner with further distribution of goods to the Brahmins, to the "heretics," that is, non-Buddhists, to the Jains, and finally to the masses of the poor. By the end of the festivities, as René Grousset put it, "all the wealth accumulated in the royal coffers over a period of five years was entirely spent. Nothing remained to the king but the horses, elephants, and weapons of war necessary to maintaining order in his realm."[50]

But the festival of dāna does not end there. Instead, there follows a curious ritual in which the king, Harṣa, is seized by a sort of frenzy of alms giving: "Like the Viśvantara of Buddhist Legend, a prefiguration of the Buddha Śākyamuni who had given in alms his goods and family, the emperor of Kannauj resolved to strip himself utterly. The clothes he was wearing, his necklaces, his earrings, his bracelets, the garland of his diadem, the pearls that adorned his throat and carbuncle that blazed at the crest of his hair, all this Harsha gave in alms, keeping nothing back. When the whole amount of his wealth was exhausted he asked his sister to bring him a worn and common robe and, dressing himself in this, went to worship before the Buddhas of the ten countries."[51]

There follows a rather ecstatic adoration of the Buddha, the Dharma, and the sangha, in whose favor the king has just rid himself of all his goods and, in fact, of his royalty. Eventually, however, the ritual ends and the king returns to normality: "This spate of mystical exaltation once over, there was the coming down to earth. . . . The eighteen vassal kings gathered afresh precious things and large sums from among the peoples of their realms, redeemed the rich necklace, the carbuncle and the royal garments given in alms by King Harsha, brought them back and gave them to him once more."[52]

(New York: Grossman Publishers, 1971), pp. 204-05; see also Watters, vol. 1, p. 364.

[50] Grousset, pp. 205-06.

[51] Ibid., p. 206.

[52] Ibid., p. 207, slightly altered.

This custom of divestment and then reacquisition of the royal clothes and jewels, all symbolic of the kingship itself, had become ritualized and well established in the Buddhist world even before Harṣa's time. For example, the Chinese Buddhist emperor Liang Wu-ti of the early sixth century held several great festivals of dāna in which he made tremendous offerings to the sangha, and clothed himself in a monk's robe and preached to the assembly. Before long, however, his ministers would come and pay "a billion pieces of gold" to ransom him back.[53]

It would be tempting to find in this ritual of the pañcavārṣika a Buddhist version of the rites involving humiliation of the king and renewal of the kingship that were so widespread in the ancient world and have been made so much of by James Frazer and others. More immediately, however, in a strictly Buddhist context, the symbolism involved in this ritual clearly recalls the story of the Buddha's own divestment of the accoutrements of royalty: his giving up of his princely attire and ornaments after the Great Departure from Kapilavastu. As is well known, at the time of the Buddha's birth, the fortune-tellers who examined him predicted that as a Great Man (a Mahāpuruṣa) he would have one of two careers open to him. Should he decide to stay at home, he would become a great cakravartin monarch; if, on the other hand, he should wander forth, he would become a Buddha. Thus the Great Departure represents more than just a momentous decision in the Buddha's career; it symbolizes the separation of the two Wheels of Dharma.[54]

The Great Departure also, of course, became a model for the Buddhist ordination ceremony, with its ritual forsaking

[53] Lévi and Chavannes, p. 42, esp. n. 1. See also Ch'en, p. 125. Compare the case of the Sinhalese king, Mahinda II, in Wilhelm Geiger, tr. *Cūḷavaṃsa*, 2 vols. (London: Pali Text Society, 1973), 1:123.

[54] André Bareau, "La jeunesse du Buddha dans les sūtrapiṭaka et les vinayapiṭaka anciens," *Bulletin de l'Ecole Française d'Extrême-Orient* 61 (1974): 199-274, esp. 246ff.

of royal symbols at the moment of the candidate's entrance into the monkhood. Unlike the Buddha, however (and unlike most bhikṣus), Harṣa does not remain a monk; he instead reacquires the royal garments and ornaments, is recrowned, and becomes once again a great dharmarāja-cakravartin. This suggests the custom still followed in some Theravāda lands where the king (or any layman) enters the sangha for a while and then returns to his kingship.[55]

Much is made in the description of these ceremonies of the fact that the king actually becomes a monk; but it is clear that the end result of the ritual is just as much to renew and reemphasize his kingship. The pañcavārṣika was thus not only an occasion on which the king, at least symbolically, gave everything (including himself) to the sangha; it was also a time when he reaffirmed his role and position as a cakravartin. It was, moreover, something only a cakravartin could do, since it required dominion and kingship to begin with. It was thus not possible for ordinary laypersons.

Harṣa's pañcavārṣika provides us with a context in which to understand Aśoka's. In the *Aśokāvadāna*, Aśoka invites a great assembly of monks to Pāṭaliputra,[56] and then announces his intention to hold a great quinquennial festival when he will make an offering of a hundred thousand pieces of gold to the sangha and bathe the Bodhi tree with a thousand pots of scented water. This, however, hardly represents the totality of his assets. There follows, therefore, a comic scene in which Aśoka's young son Kunāla gradually increases the size of his father's gift. When Aśoka first announces his offering, Kunāla indicates with a hand gesture to the crowd that he will double the amount. The crowd laughs and Aśoka is forced to "outbid" his son by tripling his original offer; Kunāla quadruples

[55] See, for example, Spiro, *Buddhism and Society*, pp. 234-47, and Tambiah, *Buddhism and the Spirit Cults*, pp. 97-115.

[56] There is some confusion in the text as to precisely when the assembly begins; the announcement of it is made twice. See Mukhopadhyaya, pp. 94, 100.

it. This goes on until finally, Aśoka, retaining only the state treasury, makes a total gift to the sangha of his whole kingdom, his harem, his ministers, his self, and his son Kunāla.[57] This is the ultimate potlatch, and Kunāla, finding himself part of his father's gift, cannot very well outdo him.

Then, however, having given everything away to the sangha, having made the total offering, Aśoka, just like Harṣa and Liang Wu-ti, buys it all back. His ministers dispense four hundred thousand pieces of gold from the reserved state treasury, and the king thereby redeems from the sangha his kingship, his wives, his ministers, his son, and his self.[58]

The sangha apparently has very little choice in whether or not to go along with this repurchase. In fact, it is clear that there are always some very real strings attached to the total gifts given by kings in pañcavārṣikas. Just as Harṣa kept control of the army and the "weapons or war necessary to maintaining order," so Aśoka sets aside the state treasury so as to keep the wheel of state rolling and to be able to regain his royal status. And despite the fact that they have, at least nominally, been given away to the sangha, it is the ministers (who as we have seen most fully embody the interests of the state) who "buy back" the king and his kingship.[59]

The Gift of Half a Myrobalan

This repurchase of the kingship from the sangha, however, sets up another situation: it enables the king to give it away again.[60] The great quinquennial festival is not the only occasion on which Aśoka gets carried away by a "frenzy of dāna," and makes a total gift to the sangha. Toward the end

[57] Moreover, he will bathe the Bodhi tree with milk "scented with sandalwood, saffron, and camphor and contained in five thousand pitchers of gold, silver, crystal, and cat's eye." See Mukhopadhyaya, p. 101.

[58] Ibid., pp. 103-04.

[59] Ibid., 132.

[60] Liang Wu-ti, for instance, did so at least three times. See Kenneth K. S. Ch'en, *Buddhism in China* (Princeton University Press, 1964), p. 125.

of his life, desiring fame as a great Buddhist donor, he adds up all of the offerings he has so far made in support of the Buddhist religion. He recalls his donations of one hundred thousand pieces of gold to each of the eighty-four thousand stūpas, and to each of the four major places of pilgrimage, and the four hundred thousand spent on entertainment of the monks, and the additional four hundred thousand spent to redeem his gift of himself and his kingdom to the sangha. He tallies all of this up and, with an arithmetic only possible in legends of this sort, he arrives at the figure of ninety-six koṭis[61] of gold pieces. This leaves him four koṭis short of the legendary record for dāna (one hundred koṭis) established during the lifetime of the Buddha by the householder Anāthapiṇḍada.[62]

Aśoka would like to equal that sum, but unfortunately he is old and ill and he soon becomes despondent because he will not be able to fulfill his intention. He resolves to try, however, and starts drawing on the state treasury in order to make donations to the Kukkuṭārāma Monastery. His ministers become worried immediately for this goes against the established pañcavārṣika ritual of reserving state funds, and for the first time threatens, in a real way, the kingship itself. Thus, claiming that "the power of kings lies in their treasury," they convince Aśoka's grandson, the heir-apparent Sampadin, to countermand his grandfather's orders and prohibit the treasurer from further disbursing state funds to the sangha.[63]

This essentially amounts to a coup d'état, at least on a limited scale. But Aśoka is not to be thwarted. He starts sending the gold dishes on which his meals are served to the monks at the Kukkuṭārāma. Soon, however, his ministers have his meals brought on silver dishes. He then gives these away too, and they serve him on copper plates. When he sends these to the sangha as well, his food is brought in on clay plates. Finally, after thus continuing to give away all his personal

[61] A large sum, usually said to be 10 million.
[62] Mukhopadhyaya, p. 126.
[63] Ibid., pp. 127-28.

possessions, Aśoka is left only with half of a myrobalan fruit. From having been a great king, ruler of the whole world, vying to be the greatest Buddhist donor of all time, he has suddenly become seemingly powerless and more destitute than the poorest Buddhist layman. And yet he does not hesitate to do what he can; he holds the myrobalan in his hand, contemplates it for a while, and then sends it to the Kukkuṭārāma where it is cut up, put in the monks' soup, and so distributed to the whole sangha.[64]

The myrobalan (*āmalaka*) was famous in India for its medicinal properties.[65] In the Buddhist tradition, it came to be closely associated with the cult and iconography of Bhaiṣajyaguru, the "Buddha of Medicine,"[66] but it was also, as Alex Wayman has pointed out, a symbol for the "creative power of thought, which in high levels of meditative praxis can materialize the unseen worlds in the manner of the myrobalan berry concretized upon the palm of the hand."[67] Thus, "this fruit is not just a medicine . . . but represents blessings from unseen realms like the healing energy radiating upon devotees in their worship."[68]

What is marvelous about the myrobalan is that though it is very small, it goes a long way and brings about tremendous results, not only in the context of medicine, but symbolically in the context of meditation and in the context of faith and karmic action. There is a story in one of the sacred biographies of Śaṅkara, the great Hindu philosopher and saint, which

[64] Ibid., pp. 128-30. The deed became famous; eventually a stūpa, visited by Hsüan-tsang, and called the Āmalaka stūpa, marked the spot where the gift was supposed to have been made (see Watters, vol. 2, p. 100). The story was also retold later by the poet Kṣemendra (see Vaidya, *Avadānakalpalatā*, 1:457).

[65] There were actually three sorts of myrobalan in India, of which the āmalaka is one. See Alex Wayman, "Notes on the Three Myrobalans," *Phi Theta Annual* 5 (1954): 63-77.

[66] Raoul Birnbaum, *The Healing Buddha* (Boulder, Colo.: Shambala, 1979), pp. 82-84, 102.

[67] Alex Wayman and Hideko Wayman, *The Lion's Roar of Queen Śrīmālā* (New York: Columbia University Press, 1974), p. 52, n. 94.

[68] Birnbaum, pp. 83-84.

illustrates this latter point well. Śaṅkara goes begging at the home of a poor Brahmin couple. The woman of the house laments that they have absolutely nothing to give him, but then she finds a single myrobalan fruit and makes an offering of it. Śaṅkara is impressed by this example of devotion and asks Lakṣmī, the goddess of wealth, to help the couple; soon their house is filled with myrobalans of solid gold.[69]

Similarly, in the context of the *Aśokāvadāna*, the myrobalan is symbolic of Aśoka's destitution, and thus of the impermanence and vagaries of royal sovereignty and all worldly life. As the elder Yaśas, at the Kukkuṭārāma, puts it when he accepts the gift from Aśoka's envoy:

> A great donor, the lord of men,
> the eminent Maurya Aśoka,
> has gone from being lord of Jambudvīpa
> to being lord of half a myrobalan.[70]

But at the same time, the gift of the myrobalan, though seemingly insignificant and symbolic of Aśoka's loss of power, is paradoxically what restores him to sovereignty. Of course, he does not suddenly acquire a fortune in gold like the woman in the story of Śaṅkara, but he does, after giving the myrobalan, appear to have his kingship reestablished. His ministers and his own grandson have usurped his powers, but when, just after his gift of the fruit, he asks his prime minister, Rādhagupta, "Tell me, who is now lord of the earth?" the latter responds that Aśoka is. Then, struggling to his feet, Aśoka uses this renewed authority to make his final gift: "Except for the state treasury, I now present the whole earth, surrounded by the ocean, to the community of the Buddha's disciples."[71] Having performed this final act, Aśoka dies, leaving his ministers in a quandary; the king is dead, but the

[69] David Lorenzen, "The Life of Śaṅkarācārya," in *The Biographical Process*, ed. Frank Reynolds and Donald Capps (The Hague: Mouton, 1976), p. 98.

[70] Mukhopadhaya, p. 131.

[71] Ibid., p. 132.

kingdom has been given away to the sangha. Before they can install a new king, therefore, they are forced to buy the Earth back again, at the going price—four koṭis of gold. Thus, in the end, Aśoka does achieve his goal of giving a total of one hundred koṭis, and becomes posthumously the equal of Anāthapiṇḍada, a contemporary of the Buddha, and the greatest donor of all times.

Conclusion

The story of Aśoka's gift of the half of myrobalan reflects, perhaps better than any of the other tales we have looked at in this chapter, the dual nature of Aśoka's relationship to the sangha. In his reduced straits, at the end of his life, Aśoka is seen as no different from any ordinary layperson, and his offering to the sangha becomes a model for even the most destitute of Buddhists. Who, after all, cannot afford to give a myrobalan? At the same time, it is the gift of this myrobalan that restores to Aśoka his balacakravartinship—his sovereignty over Jambudvīpa—and that enables him to give the earth away again and to achieve the perfect, complete gift to the sangha.

Much of the appeal of the figure of Aśoka in the *Aśokāvadāna* lies precisely in the fact that he is both great king and simple layman. On a personal level, this involves him, on the one hand, with charismatic Buddhist saints who represent the Buddha and confirm for him his royal status; and, on the other hand, with abbots and ordinary members of the sangha with whom he enjoys a routinized relationship. At the same time, however, as a legendary model for Buddhists everywhere, this duality of roles represents a powerful combination; for as balacakravartin and greatest donor of all time, Aśoka clearly was an ideal to inspire, while as giver of ordinary gifts and routine supporter of the community, he was an example to actually be followed.

CHAPTER FOUR

Aśoka and the Buddha

It should be clear from the discussion in the last chapter that the question of Aśoka's relationship to the Buddhist community is intimately tied up with that of Aśoka's relationship to the person of the Buddha.

Any attempt to deal with this issue immediately encounters an obvious major difficulty; apart from the episode of the gift of dirt, the Buddha is never actually said to be present in the text. The time frame of the story simply does not allow it; Aśoka is born "one hundred years after the Buddha's parinirvāṇa" and so cannot possibly meet him face to face in his lifetime. We have already seen how certain members of the sangha such as Upagupta and Piṇḍola remind Aśoka of the person of the Buddha; they re-present him in their time and help fill the spiritual and charismatic gap left by the death of the Master. When he looks at these monks, Aśoka asserts he can "see" the Buddha even though he has gone beyond.

This, however, is by no means the only way Aśoka manages to enjoy a personal relationship with the Tathāgata. As we shall see in this chapter, by his various actions as king—his construction of the eighty-four thousand stūpas, his pilgrimage with the elder Upagupta, his worship of the Bodhi tree—Aśoka repeatedly creates a situation in which the Buddha, despite his parinirvāṇa, may in some sense be said to be present.

Such an assertion might initially seem to fly in the face of certain theories about the nature of the Buddha in nirvāṇa. Aśoka, these theories would contend, cannot be said to relate personally to the Buddha because the Buddha is "out of relation"; he has gone beyond, has transcended this world, and it is useless to try to deal with him in this-worldly terms. After all, did not the Buddha himself deliberately refrain from elucidating the matter of whether, after death, the Tathāgata could be said to exist, or not exist, or both exist and not exist, or neither exist nor not exist?[1] Or, as the great philosopher Nāgārjuna was to put it (in Stephan Beyer's unforgettable translation):

After his final cessation
the Blessed One isnt is
(isnt isnt) isnt is and isnt
isnt isnt is and isnt.[2]

The paradox, of course, is that this has never stopped Buddhists from making offerings to the Buddha, from having faith in the Buddha, from bowing down to the Buddha, and engaging in all sorts of activities and sentiments vis-à-vis the Buddha that almost anywhere would qualify as worship. If the Buddha in nirvāṇa has truly gone beyond, he nonetheless often seems to be remarkably "present."

In the three-hundred-page "preface" to his *Barabuḍur* and elsewhere, Paul Mus has tried to resolve some of the paradoxes and problems engendered by the question of the Buddha in nirvāṇa. The whole issue, he claims, has too often been treated by Buddhist and non-Buddhist scholars alike from an ontological perspective. Within the Buddhist tradition itself, this has resulted in nirvāṇa being seen as "so ungraspable that one can only propose for it a formula bristling with contradictory negations."[3] Yet at the same time, in order to cut through this "excessively subtle logic," Buddhists have turned to certain magical and cultic practices, "so as to assure themselves

[1] I. B. Horner, tr., *The Middle Length Sayings (Majjhima-Nikāya)*, Pali Text Society Translation Series, nos. 29-31 (London: Luzac & Co., 1954-59), 2:101.

[2] Stephan Beyer, *The Buddhist Experience* (Encino, Calif., Dickenson Publishing Co., 1974), p. 214.

[3] Paul Mus, "La mythologie primitive et la pensée de l'Inde," *Bulletin de la Société Française de Philosophie* 37 (1937): 91.

of satisfactions and certainties of an affective order, without which there is no religion."[4]

Mus believes that we should not look for ontology when the question of Being is unresolvable; instead we should investigate the matter of what he calls "magical projection."[5] The Buddha's nirvāṇa, according to Mus, was *theoretically* considered by the Buddhists as a "new kind of absence," but *practically* dealt with by traditional Indian magical techniques that had devised ways "for overcoming the absence of objects or persons and acting on them from a distance, wherever they might be or no longer be."[6] This magic was accomplished by ritual action directed toward certain objects formerly associated with the absent person. Hence, Mus likes to point to the veneration in Buddhism not only of the Buddha's relics (bones), but of his cut hair, nails, begging bowl, footprints, and shadows left on a wall—all classic foci for the operations of contagious magic.[7]

Mus's use of the word "magic" here was perhaps unfortunate, at least for those of us who tend to think of the term in a limited Frazerian sense.[8] For him, magic was much more akin to what his teacher, Marcel Mauss, meant by the word. He, as the British anthropologist Mary Douglas has pointed out, tended to use "magic" as "a vague literary term, described but never rigorously defined [that] does not connote a particular class of rituals, but rather the whole corpus of ritual and belief of primitive peoples."[9]

[4] Ibid.

[5] Paul Mus, *Barabuḍur*, 2 vols. (Hanoi: Imprimerie d'Extrême-Orient, 1935), 1:89-90.

[6] Ibid., 1:74.

[7] Ibid., 1:76-77, 2:236, 239.

[8] For this classic formulation of the concept of magic, see James George Frazer, *The Golden Bough*, abridged ed. (London: MacMillan and Co., 1950), pp. 11-47.

[9] Mary Douglas, *Purity and Danger* (London: Routledge and Kegan Paul, 1966), p. 59. See also Marcel Mauss, *A General Theory of Magic*, trans. Robert Brain (New York: W. W. Norton and Co., 1972).

Magic, then, for Mus, is ritual action; it is cultic worship. It is an act that breeches the break between this saṃsāric world and nirvāṇa, and that enables one to experience the presence of the absent Buddha, without, however, infringing upon his ontological otherness.[10]

Mus's interest, however, lay not so much in Buddhist ritual action per se, as in the nature or structure of the immediate cultic objects. For him, these were best exemplified by the Buddhist stūpa. The stūpa was, paradigmatically, what Mus liked to call a "mesocosm," that is, a focal point of religiously relevant reality which is in tune with various other cosmological levels (microcosm, macrocosm) and which forms a "magical structural milieu" for a cultic operation which "can evoke or make real the absent Buddha in Nirvāṇa."[11]

We should not fail to note in the use of this term the emphasis placed on the cosmological dimension of Buddhist practice. Cosmology, to be sure, is an important part of all religions, but it is a crucial one in the case of Buddhism. Perhaps because of the absence in Buddhism of belief in any creator God, Buddhists have turned to cosmological knowledge for a sense of order in the world. Indeed an understanding of the world as it exists, that is, as it is said to exist, is a fundamental part of the whole process of enlightenment. The stūpa is an efficacious mesocosm because not only was it originally the funerary mound of Buddhas and great kings (and hence presently a potent symbol of the person of the Buddha), but also because it is a cosmogram—a model of the world that enables one to relate to and understand the basic structure of reality.

As a mesocosm, the stūpa is also readily comparable to other Buddhist mesocosms such as the Buddha image, the Dharma, the Bodhi tree, and importantly for our purposes, the king. In fact, the king and his kingdom, for Mus, are essentially a sort of "living stūpa," with all that this implies: "Does the Buddha exist? It is not true that he is no more, nor

[10] Mus, *Barabuḍur*, 1:100.

[11] Ibid., 1:94, 100.

is it true that he still lives. But the stūpa and the king *are* present, and it is at their level that we should ask the question of existence. Is the stūpa really a stūpa of the Buddha? Is the king really a Dharmarāja? If it is and if he is, they will, by that fact alone, grasp something of the Buddha. But we should understand by this that they will grasp it magically and not *really*."[12]

Dharmakāya and Rūpakāya

We shall see shortly how these views can be helpful in analyzing Aśoka's relationship with the Buddha as it is portrayed in the *Aśokāvadāna*. The situation, however, is made more complex by reference in our text to the theories of the two bodies of the Buddha. Scholars are generally agreed that the earliest stage in the development of speculation about the bodies (*kāya*) of the Buddha ascribed two bodies to the Buddha, a rūpakāya and a dharmakāya.[13] The rūpakāya is simply the physical form of the Buddha in which he was born at Lumbinī and died at Kuśinagarī. The dharmakāya is his doctrinal body. In this context, it should not be confused with the ineffable, transcendent, and eternal Dharmakāya it was to become later on in Mahāyānist speculation; it should, more simply and somewhat naively, be thought of as nothing more (nor less) than the body of the Buddha's doctrine, the collection of his Teachings.[14]

Both of these bodies were considered to be "visible" in some

[12] Ibid., 1:91.

[13] Paul Demiéville, "Busshin" in *Hōbōgirin: Dictionnaire encyclopédique du bouddhisme d'après les sources chinoises et japonaises*, ed. Paul Demiéville (Tokyo: Maison Franco-japonaise 1929-); Gadgin Nagao, "On the Theory of Buddha-Body (Buddha-kāya)" *Eastern Buddhist* 6 (1973): 25-53; Lewis R. Lancaster, "An Early Mahāyāna Sermon about the Body of the Buddha and the Making of Images," *Artibus Asiae* 36 (1974): 287-91.

[14] In addition to the sources in n. 13, see Louis de la Vallée Poussin, "Appendice iii: Notes sur les corps du Bouddha," in his *Vijñaptimātratāsiddhi, la siddhi de Hiuan-tsang*, Buddhica, vol. 5 (Paris: Paul Geuthner, 1929), p. 766.

sense. The rūpakāya could be seen with the ordinary eyes of flesh (*maṃsacakṣu*) by anyone fortunate enough to meet the Buddha during his lifetime. The dharmakāya could be seen only by the "eye of wisdom" (*prajñācakṣu*) of those enlightened beings who had realized the truth of the Buddha's doctrine (Dharma).[15]

After the Buddha's parinirvāṇa, however, this situation became more complex. The dharmakāya—the corpus of the Buddha's Teachings—could still be "seen" by enlightened arhats. They were the ones, in fact, who symbolically gathered this body together and preserved it at the First Buddhist Council when they rehearsed the whole of the Sūtra and Vinaya. (It is probably in this light also that we should remember that the Buddha appointed the Dharma as his successor, that, as several Pali texts put it, "anyone who sees the Dharma sees the Buddha,"[16] and that Buddhist legends are full of monks who claim, even long after the parinirvāṇa to have "seen the dharmakāya" of the Buddha.)[17]

The physical rūpakāya, on the other hand, was cremated, and what remained of it—the relics—were dispersed, taken off by various petty kings of the times. As a body, after the Buddha's parinirvāṇa, it no longer held together, and could no longer be seen, in any ordinary sense.

This, however, did not stop devotees from trying to visualize

[15] See on this, Maryla Falk, *Nama-Rūpa and Dharma-Rūpa* (Calcutta: University of Calcutta Press, 1943), pp. 114-15.

[16] See, for example, T. W. Rhys Davids, tr., *The Questions of King Milinda*, 2 vols., Sacred Books of the East, nos. 35-36 (orig. pub. 1890-94; rpt. New York: Dover, 1963), 1:110; and F. L. Woodward, tr., *Itivuttaka: As It Was Said*, Sacred Books of the Buddhists, vol. 8 (London: Oxford University Press, 1948), p. 181.

[17] In addition to the story of Upagupta and Māra, see P. L. Vaidya, ed. *Divyāvadānam*, Buddhist Sanskrit Texts, no. 20 (Darbhanga, Bihar: Mithila Institute, 1959), pp. 11-12; Edouard Huber, tr. *Aśvaghoṣa Sūtrālamkāra* (Paris: E. Leroux, 1908), p. 217; and Lévi, *Mahākarmavibhaṅga*, pp. 160, 174-75. See also the discussion of this theme in Edward Conze, tr. *The Perfection of Wisdom in Eight Thousand Lines and its Verse Summary* (Bolinas, Calif.: Four Seasons Foundation, 1973), pp. 291-92.

this physical form of the Buddha. Let us consider again the example of Upagupta who, as we have noted, requests Māra to take on the physical form of the Buddha and show it to him. Upagupta does this because, as he puts it, although he has seen the dharmakāya of the Blessed One (as an enlightened arhat), he still has not seen his rūpakāya (since he has been born a century after the parinirvāṇa).[18]

This is more than just a complex way of saying that Upagupta wants to know what the Buddha looked like. He is, rather, craving a religious experience—one that will complement the vision he already has of the dharmakāya (by virtue of his enlightenment) and that will thus give him a total understanding of the Buddha in both of his bodily forms. And this is ironically what Māra, the "Evil One" of Buddhism, the chief god of the realm of the senses, provides for him. By means of his magical powers of transformation, Māra "becomes" (at least temporarily) the rūpakāya of the Buddha. He takes on his form, complete with the thirty-two marks of the Great Man, and fashions around him the figures of Śāriputra, Maudgalyāyana, Ānanda, and thirteen-hundred-fifty other disciples.[19]

Seeing the Buddha at the center of this living maṇḍala, Upagupta then gets carried away in an ecstasy of devotion, and bows down and worships the Buddha-in-Māra. Māra protests that Upagupta should not bow down to him for this is idolatry! But Upagupta answers that it is not. He knows full well that the Buddha "has gone altogether to extinction," but just as people bow down to a clay image of a god, knowing that what they are worshipping in the image is the god and not the clay, so too he has bowed down to a Māra-fashioned image of the Buddha, knowing that what he was worshipping in the image was the Buddha and not Māra.[20]

[18] Sujitkumar Mukhopadhyaya, ed., *The Aśokāvadāna* (New Delhi: Sahitya Akademi, 1963), p. 23.

[19] Ibid., p. 25.

[20] Ibid., p. 26.

It is important to see just what is going on here. Upagupta is not saying and is not acting as though the Buddha were somewhere else than before him. For him, the image of the Buddha, fashioned by Māra, that is, his form, his rūpakāya, "is" the Buddha. What it is made of—clay, wood, metal, or, in this case, Māra—is not the Buddha; but it itself comes to re-present the Buddha in a way that is obviously religiously real. In Musian terms, Māra has become a magical mesocosm in which Upagupta can grasp something of the absent Buddha. What he grasps, however, is not the total Buddha, but only one aspect of him, his rūpakāya. And this he now has to put together with his vision of the dharmakāya which, as an enlightened arhat, he has already achieved.

Frank Reynolds has spoken of the usefulness of distinguishing, even in Theravāda Buddhism, between what he calls the "dhammakāya and the rūpakāya legacies."[21] The distinction should be recalled. Indeed, the Buddha was not the only one to have these two bodies. In Aśvaghoṣa's *Sūtrālaṃkāra*, for example, we read of an enlightened layman who refuses to obey the immoral order of a king. When the king becomes furious and threatens him, he is not perturbed, for, as he puts it, although the king may well torture and break his physical rūpakāya, he cannot touch his dharmakāya which he has acquired by virtue of his enlightenment.[22] And in the story of the blinding of Aśoka's own son Kunāla, as we shall see, the same point is made in terms of Kunāla's two eyes: his physical eye can be gouged out but his dharma eye (*dharmacakṣu*) cannot.[23]

In a sense, then, we are dealing here with two whole dimensions of Buddhist religious practice; the one, meditative and scholastic, is oriented toward an understanding of the

[21] Frank E. Reynolds, "The Several Bodies of the Buddha: Reflections on a Neglected Aspect of Theravāda Tradition," *History of Religions* 16 (1977): 377.

[22] Huber, *Sūtrālaṃkāra*, p. 217.

[23] Mukhopadhyaya, p. 115.

doctrine of the Buddha and might be called the "dharmalogical" dimension. The other, visionary and emotive, is oriented toward the physical form of the Buddha and might be called the "rupalogical" dimension.[24]

With all of this in mind, we can now return to a more careful analysis of Aśoka's relationship to the deceased figure of the Buddha. We shall focus on three distinct episodes in the *Aśokāvadāna*: (1) Aśoka's gathering and redistribution of the relics of the Buddha into eighty-four thousand stūpas; (2) his establishment of and pilgrimage to important sites connected with the life of the Buddha; and (3) his special worship of the Bodhi tree at Bodhgaya, the place of the Buddha's enlightenment.

The Building of the 84,000 Stūpas

No legendary act of Aśoka was so famous as that of his construction of the eighty-four thousand stūpas or dharmarājikās over the relics of the Buddha.[25] For centuries pilgrims visiting the holy sites of India habitually ascribed almost every stūpa they came across to the reign of Aśoka, and Buddhist rulers as far away as Japan looked back on Aśoka as the stūpa builder par excellence, some even seeking to emulate his legendary construction of eighty-four thousand of them.[26]

[24] For further discussion of this theme, see John Strong, "The Transforming Gift: An Analysis of Devotional Acts of Offering in Buddhist Avadāna Literature," *History of Religions* 18 (1979): 222-27. See also Paul Mus, "Barabuḍur, sixième partie: genèse de la bouddhologie Mahāyāniste," *Bulletin de l'Ecole Française d'Extrême-Orient* 34 (1934): 193.

[25] In the *Aśokāvadāna*, the eighty-four thousand stūpas are most commonly called dharmarājikās, i.e., "[monuments] pertaining to the King of Dharma." On the ambiguity implicit in this appellation, see below. In the *Mahāvaṃsa*, the story refers to the construction of eighty-four thousand vihāras (monasteries).

[26] See, for example, Thomas Watters, *On Yuan Chwang's Travels in India*, 2 vols. (orig. pub., 1905; rpt. Delhi: Munshi Ram Manohar Lal, 1961), index, s.v. "Aśoka topes." See also the discussions in Kenneth K. S. Ch'en, *Buddhism in China* (Princeton: University Press, 1964), pp. 200-201 and Arthur Wright, "The Formation of Sui Ideology, 581-604," in *Chinese Thought and Insti-*

Moreover, there can be little doubt of the important place this deed occupies in our text. The motif of "Aśoka, builder of the eighty-four thousand stūpas" is a constantly recurring theme that helps define his character and determine important events in his life. The Buddha's prediction at the time of the gift of dirt, for example, states explicitly that Aśoka will build the eighty-four thousand stūpas, and the recall of this prophecy by the monk Samudra is, in part, what contributes to his conversion.[27] The actual building of the stūpas marks Aśoka's nominal change in status from "Aśoka-the-Fierce" to "Dharmāśoka," and is also used to determine when other events in the story take place; thus Aśoka's son Kunāla is born "on the very same day on which King Aśoka built the eighty-four thousand dharmarājikās,"[28] and the Vītaśoka episode occurs "shortly after the completion of the eighty-four thousand dharmarājikās."[29]

For purposes of analysis, it is useful to divide the story of the eighty-four thousand stūpas into two distinct episodes: (1) the collection of the relics of the Buddha from the ancient droṇa stūpas where they were enshrined immediately after the Buddha's death, and (2) the redistribution of those relics throughout Aśoka's kingdom followed by the simultaneous completion of the eighty-four thousand stūpas to house them.

The story of the gathering of the relics from the ancient droṇa stūpas is intimately bound up with Buddhist traditions concerning the fate of the Buddha's physical remains after his death and cremation.[30] According to the "Mahāparinibbana

---

tutions, ed. John K. Fairbank (Chicago: University Press, 1957), pp. 98-102. For a Southeast Asian example of a festival commemorating the construction of the eighty-four thousand stūpas, see Pierre-Bernard Lafont, "Le That de Muong-Sing," *Bulletin de la Société des Etudes Indochinoises*, n.s. 32 (1957): 43.

[27] Mukhopadhyaya, p. 51.

[28] Ibid., p. 105.

[29] Ibid., p. 56.

[30] See Jean Przyluski, "Le partage des reliques du Buddha," *Mélanges Chinois et bouddhiques* 4 (1936): 341-67; T. W. Rhys Davids, "Aśoka and the Buddha Relics," *Journal of the Royal Asiatic Society*, 1907, pp. 397-410.

Sutta," the relics—initially taken over by the Mallas in whose territory the Buddha was cremated—were soon divided into eight shares, one for each of eight kings of that time. Each of these monarchs then built a stūpa over his portion of the relics and worshipped it. These were called the droṇa stūpas because they enshrined one *droṇa* (literally a bucket, a measure of capacity) of relics, and also because the division of the relics had been made by a Brahmin named Droṇa.[31] The sutta adds that there were also two other ancient stūpas, a ninth one built by this Brahmin Droṇa over the measuring bucket (droṇa) that he had used to parcel out the relics, and a tenth one built by the Moriyas of Pipphalivana over the embers of the cremation fire. They—interestingly enough for our purposes since they are the presumed ancestors of Aśoka and the whole Mauryan line[32]—had arrived too late to receive an actual share of the relics and had to settle for the ashes from the fire.[33]

Now according to some texts, the town of Rāmagrāma where one of the eight droṇa stūpas had been built, was not long thereafter flooded by the waters of the Ganges, and the relics there were swept away and sank down to the underwater palace of the *nāga* (snake) king. The nāgas, however, continued to worship them with all due honors. As an admittedly late addition to the "Mahāparinibbana Sutta" put it:

> Eight measures of relics there were of him of the far-seeing eye,
> of the best of the best of men. In India [Jambudvīpa] seven are worshipped,
> and one measure in Rāmagrāma, by the kings of the serpent [nāga] race.[34]

[31] T. W. Rhys Davids, tr., *Dialogues of the Buddha*, 3 vols., Sacred Books of the Buddhists, nos. 2-4 (London: Pali Text Society, 1899-1921), 2:187-89.

[32] K. A. Nilakanta Sastri, *Age of the Nandas and Mauryas* (Delhi: Motilal Banarsidass, 1967), p. 143.

[33] Davids, *Dialogues*, 2:189-90. See also E. J. Thomas, *The Life of Buddha* (London: Routledge and Kegan Paul, 1927), p. 156.

[34] Davids, *Dialogues*, 2:191.

There are, of course, other traditions concerning the Buddha's relics,[35] but it is this story featuring the Rāmagrāma stūpa being worshipped by the nāgas that figures most prominently in the *Aśokāvadāna*. King Aśoka sets out to collect the relics; he goes first to the droṇa stūpa built by Ajātaśatru, and then to the next six, removing the relics from each of them. Then, we are told, he goes to Rāmagrāma; the nāgas take him down to their palace but will not let him have their relics. They want to continue honoring their droṇa stūpa themselves and Aśoka, realizing that he could never match the nāgas in their offerings, agrees to let them keep their relics, and departs empty-handed.[36] Much the same story is told by the Chinese pilgrims Fa-hsien and Hsüan-tsang,[37] and was popularly depicted in bas-reliefs on the stūpas at Sāñchī and Amarāvatī.[38]

The legend of Aśoka's failure to retrieve the relics from the nāgas was to spawn a later Sinhalese tradition that those relics had been reserved for enshrinement in the Great Stūpa on the island of Sri Lanka. According to the tale in the *Mahāvaṃsa*, when Aśoka went to the nāga palace to get the Rāmagrāma relics, he was informed that he could not have them because the Buddha himself had set them aside for King Duṭṭhagāmaṇi of Sri Lanka (101-77 B.C.).[39] The story then goes on to relate

[35] See, for example, N. A. Jayawickrama, ed. and tr., *The Chronicle of the Thūpa and the Thūpavaṃsa*, Sacred Books of the Buddhists, 28 (London: Luzac and Co., 1971), pp. 53-54, for the story of Ajātaśatru returning to collect all the relics into a single stūpa whose location is then (almost) completely forgotten. There are, in addition, many legends focussing on the fortune of the Buddha's tooth relics rather than on the fate of his ashes, but these represent a separate tradition.

[36] Mukhopadhyaya, p. 52.

[37] Watters, vol. 2, pp. 20-25; James Legge, ed. and tr., *A Record of Buddhistic Kingdoms* (orig. pub., 1886; rpt., New York: Paragon Book Co., 1965), pp. 68-69.

[38] Etienne Lamotte, *Histoire du bouddhisme indien* (Louvain: Institut Orientaliste, 1958), p. 264.

[39] Wilhelm Geiger, tr., *The Mahāvaṃsa, or the Great Chronicle of Ceylon* (London: Pali Text Society, 1912), p. 211; see also Jayawickrama, *Thūpavaṃsa*, p. 125.

how the elder Soṇuttara, on Duṭṭhagāmaṇi's behalf, descends to the nāga palace where he accuses the snake lords of not honoring the Buddha properly, more or less steals the relics from them, and returns with them to Sri Lanka where they are enshrined with great ceremony.[40]

The divergence between this version of the story and the *Aśokāvadāna*'s reflects, of course, the different orientation of the two texts touched upon in Chapter One. In the *Aśokāvadāna*, the stress is at least nominally on the value of devotion to the relics, whether it be the devotion of Aśoka or of the nāgas. In the *Mahāvaṃsa*, on the other hand, the emphasis is on the glory of Sri Lanka and on its possession of some genuine Buddha relics. Simply put, Duṭṭhagāmaṇi is shown to have succeeded where Aśoka had failed. Nevertheless the failure of Aśoka to collect all the relics of the Buddha in the *Aśokāvadāna* highlights once again the less-than-perfect aspect of Aśoka's rule. Even in this great deed of gathering the relics, Aśoka encounters certain obstacles that, ideally, he should have been able to overcome, but, in reality, was not.

Having said this, however, we must hasten to note that there are other Sanskrit traditions that directly contradict this view. In the *Samyuktāgama*, for example, exactly the same story is told as in the *Aśokāvadāna* except that Aśoka does get the relics from the nāgas.[41] Moreover, there exists another entirely different tradition about Aśoka's collection of the relics, preserved among other places in the last section of the *A-yü wang chuan*, a chapter of unrelated Aśoka stories unfortunately no longer extant in Sanskrit.[42]

In this tale, Aśoka is also successful in obtaining the relics from a nāga king. King Ajātaśatru, we are told, had deposited all the Buddha relics in the Ganges where they were guarded

[40] Geiger, tr., *Mahāvaṃsa*, p. 214.

[41] Lamotte, pp. 264-65. See also Watters, vol. 2, p. 21.

[42] See Jean Przyluski, *La légende de l'empereur Açoka* (Paris: Paul Geuthner, 1923), pp. 425-26, and Appendix, no. 10 below. Similar accounts are given by Tāranatha and in the *Thūpavaṃsa*, pp. 53-54.

by a huge revolving water wheel with sharp swords that spun around and effectively prevented anyone from passing. Aśoka, however, manages, by clever means, to stop the wheel from turning, but then he encounters a nāga king who further bars his way.[43] Not knowing how to proceed, Aśoka turns to a bhikṣu for advice. The monk tells him that he will be successful in getting the relics only if his merit is greater than that of the nāga. Their relative merit is then calculated as follows: two statues of identical size are made—one of Aśoka and one of the nāga—and are then weighed. The implication is that he whose statue is the heaviest will be the one who has the most merit. At first, the nāga's statue weighs twice as much as that of Aśoka. Aśoka then hastens to acquire more merit, and gradually his statue gets heavier and heavier until finally it outweighs that of his adversary and he is able to pass and take away the relics.[44]

We are left, then, with two basic traditions about Aśoka's collection of the relics: one emphasizing his success at overcoming obstacles blocking his way, and the other hinting at his failure to obtain all the relics of the Blessed One. The ambiguity should not surprise us in view of what we already know of our text's double attitude toward the king. Once again, Aśoka is being presented here as the paradigm of a

[43] In the *A-yü wang chuan*, Aśoka throws prunes into the water which block the mechanism of the wheel and keep it from turning. In the *Thūpavaṃsa*, where the relics are said to be guarded by wooden figures with revolving hands carrying swords, Viśvakarman, the divine artificer, intervenes on Aśoka's behalf and disarms the figures. In Tāranātha, in which the revolving wheel throws fire, Aśoka diverts the course of the water to keep it from spinning.

[44] Przyluski, *Légende*, p. 426. The account in the *Thūpavaṃsa* (p. 54) makes the connection between this story and the eighty-four thousand stūpas quite explicit. Aśoka is said to find in the relic chamber a gold plaque that reads: "In the future, a prince named Piyadāsa will raise the parasol of state and become a righteous monarch called Aśoka. He will take these relics and have them widely dispersed." Aśoka then takes them and deposits them in eighty-four thousand caityas in eighty-four thousand monasteries throughout Jambudvīpa.

perfect and powerful monarch, while at the same time, in subtle ways, questions are being raised about him in that role.

The story of the gathering of the relics, however, is only a prelude to the more important account of the redistribution of those relics in the eighty-four thousand stūpas. In the *Aśokāvadāna*, after collecting the relics, Aśoka has eighty-four thousand urns prepared, places the relics in them, and, with the help of the *yakṣas*, he sends off one share of relics to every city of one hundred thousand people throughout the earth as far as the surrounding ocean.

There then follows a humorous but significant interlude in which the people of Takṣaśilā, because they number thirty-six hundred thousand, request thirty-six shares of relics. Aśoka turns them down by threatening to execute thirty-five hundred thousand of them! In fact, he realizes that were he to accede to their demand, he would not be able to distribute the relics far and wide. We are thus left with the image that the relics—the body of the Buddha—must be spread evenly throughout the whole of Jambudvīpa. There can be no lopsidedness or deformity in this symbolic reconstruction of the Blessed One.

For much the same reason, it is important that all of the reliquaries be enshrined at precisely the same moment. The dedication of a stūpa, much like the consecration of a Buddhist image, or, for that matter, of any other Buddhist mesocosm, marks the moment when the mesocosm "comes alive," when the Buddha is thought to be present in it.[45] For this reason, the dedication of the eighty-four thousand stūpas must take place simultaneously since it is collectively that they represent the Buddha. To this end, Aśoka goes to see the elder Yaśas and asks him to signal the moment of the completion of all eighty-four thousand stūpas throughout the kingdom. He agrees to do so by eclipsing the sun with his hand. When he does,

[45] See, on this, Richard Gombrich, "The Consecration of a Buddhist Image," *Journal of Asian Studies* 26 (1966): 23-26.

the stūpas are ready, the relics are enshrined, the mesocosm has been established.[46]

It is possible to give two interpretations of this episode of the stūpas, one running along "rupalogical" and the other along "dharmalogical" lines.

The intimate relationship between the relics and the Buddha's rūpakāya is clear in the Buddhist tradition. After all, the relics are the remains of the physical body of the Buddha. As Mus puts it, "they are the Buddha on a magical plane. Offerings are made to them of flowers, of ornaments, of food, of clothes which are tailored to the Buddha's size. Once again, we find here the fundamental notion that the measure of a man *is* a man. . . . The daily cult of the relics reproduces the daily routine of the Buddha. It is clear that such symbolism projects onto the relics the personal image of the Buddha."[47]

The same notion is reinforced in Buddhism by stories recounting how the relics miraculously "come alive" and take on the bodily form (rūpakāya) of the Buddha himself, with all of his physical traits. In the *Mahāvaṃsa*, for example, when Duṭṭhagāmaṇi is about to enshrine the relics in the Great Stūpa, the casket rises up into the air. It then opens of itself and the relics come up out of it and "taking the form of the Buddha, gleaming with the greater and lesser signs, they performed, even as the Buddha himself . . . that miracle of the double appearances that was brought to pass by the Blessed One during his lifetime."[48]

[46] Mukhopadhyaya, p. 54. According to Hsüan-tsang, it is Upagupta who eclipses the sun (see Watters, 2:91). In the *Mahāvaṃsa* (tr., p. 41), there is no eclipse; instead eighty-four thousand letters arrive from eighty-four thousand cities on the same day announcing the completion of the eighty-four thousand vihāras.

[47] Mus, *Barabuḍur*, 1:77.

[48] Geiger, tr., *Mahāvaṃsa*, p. 217. Similar events are sometimes said to take place at the time of the "nirvāṇa of the relics," at the end of the aeon just prior to the arrival of the future Buddha Maitreya. See Sylvain Lévi and Edouard Chavannes, "Les seize arhat protecteurs de la loi," *Journal asiatique* 8 (1916): 13, and Marinus Willem De Visser, "The Arhats in China and Japan," *Ost-asiatische Zeitschrift* 10 (1922-23): 64.

In the *Aśokāvadāna*, we do not find such a spectacular coming alive of the relics, but it is quite clear that in Aśoka's organized distribution (and subsequent worship) of the relics an attempt is being made to recapture, to make present, the Buddha's rūpakāya. The number eighty-four thousand is naturally significant in this regard. It is generally symbolic of totality, but it corresponds more specifically here to the traditional number of atoms in a body.[49] Thus, in building eighty-four thousand stūpas over eighty-four thousand minute relics, Aśoka is trying to reconstruct the Buddha's physical body on the face of his own realm, Jambudvīpa.

This reconstruction, however, also takes place in the dharmalogical dimension. As Mus puts it, the stūpas are the Dharma in stone.[50] The number eighty-four thousand not only represents the number of atoms in the Buddha's body; it is also equal to the number of sections in the Buddha's Teachings.[51] In fact, the *Mahāvaṃsa* records that when Aśoka learns that there are eighty-four thousand sections of the Dharma he decides to undertake his construction project and honor each one of those sections by building a vihāra.[52] Thus, by building the eighty-four thousand stūpas (or vihāras), Aśoka is also symbolically reconstructing the body of the Buddha's Teachings—his dharmakāya.

This is more, however, than just a matter of a symbolic reconstruction; for Aśoka, it is also a genuine religious experience. The completion of the stūpas marks his own achievement of a dharmalogical understanding. As we have already mentioned, in the *Aśokāvadāna*, the stūpas are not generally referred to as "stūpas" but as "dharmarājikās," that is, as monuments pertaining to the King of Dharma (dharmarāja). This, of course, reinforces their connection with the Buddha,

[49] See Legge, p. 69, n. 1.
[50] Mus, *Barabuḍur*, 1:245.
[51] Lamotte, p. 162.
[52] Geiger, tr., *Mahāvaṃsa*, p. 32. The *Mahāvaṃsa* tells of the construction of the vihāras (monasteries) instead of stūpas.

since "King of Dharma" is an epithet of the Blessed One;[53] but at the same time, it asserts their intimate relation with the person of Aśoka who is also, of course, a King of Dharma (dharmarāja). The building of the stūpas, then, does not just symbolize the reconstruction of the Buddha's body, it also represents Aśoka's own establishment as Dharma king, that is, his dharmalogical understanding of his kingship. It is for this reason that, in all versions of the story, it is the construction of the stūpas (and not some other event such as his conversion by Samudra) that is said to mark Aśoka's change in status from being "Aśoka-the-Fierce" to being "Dharmāśoka." This event is for him the definitive dharmalogical experience.[54]

In the *Mahāvaṃsa*, the visionary dimensions of this experience are stressed even more. As soon as the eighty-four thousand vihāras are completed, there occurs a miracle known as "the unveiling of the world." Standing in his capital, Aśoka is suddenly able to see, all at once, all eighty-four thousand vihāras and the whole of Jambudvīpa adorned for their festival.[55] This, as Paul Mus has made clear, is tantamount to a vision of the dharmakāya,[56] and as such it is just as much an enlightenment experience as Upagupta's arhatship which also provided a vision of the dharmakāya. But, as we have seen, it is also a vision of the rūpakāya, and in this we can find something new. Where Upagupta had to pursue two separate roads—a dharmalogical one to arhatship and a rupalogical one with Māra—to obtain his total vision of the Buddha, Aśoka only has to pursue one. He can find both dimensions right there in the mesocosm of the stūpas.

It now becomes clearer why the construction of the eighty-

[53] On the use of the epithet Dharmarāja to designate the Buddha, see Franklin Edgerton, *Buddhist Hybrid Sanskrit Dictionary* (New Haven: Yale University Press, 1953), s.v. "dharmarāja."

[54] See, for example, Mukhopadhyaya, p. 55; Geiger, tr., *Mahāvaṃsa*, p. 52.

[55] Geiger, tr., *Mahāvaṃsa*, p. 52.

[56] Mus, *Barabuḍur*, 1:245.

four thousand stūpas occupies such an important position not only in the legend of Aśoka but in the history of Buddhism. In this act, Aśoka has brought together two dimensions of the Buddha that had been separated since the parinirvāṇa: his rūpakāya and his dharmakāya. In the process, he has somewhat changed our understanding of these two bodies of the Buddha in that he has explicitly "cosmologized" them by identifying them with the territory of his kingdom, with Jambudvīpa. No longer are the Buddha's physical remains randomly dispersed here and there; they are now cosmologically organized and spread throughout the kingdom. And no longer does the dharmakāya represent quite so naively just the corpus of the Buddha's Teachings; it is now more cosmological and has been systematically implanted in and identified with the kingdom. It is thus in his kingdom, in Jambudvīpa, that Aśoka manages by means of the eighty-four thousand stūpas to establish a potent mesocosm, that is both rupalogical and dharmalogical, and that will also allow at the same time for a relationship with the total person of the Buddha, even though he has gone beyond.

Aśoka's Pilgrimage

We shall return to this important theme later on in this chapter. At this point, however, it may be useful to examine another episode that can help further illustrate the relationship between Aśoka and the departed Buddha in nirvāṇa.

Shortly after his meeting with the elder Upagupta, Aśoka resolves to go on a pilgrimage in order to honor all the places where the Blessed One lived, and to mark them with signs, as a favor to future pilgrims. He asks Upagupta to act as his guide and together they set out.

There follows an account of their journey as they visit various sites associated with the Buddha, starting with his birthplace in Lumbinī and finishing with the place of his parinirvāṇa at Kuśinagarī. Their pilgrimage thus reconstructs the entire life of the Buddha in the sense that, as they move physically from one site to another, they retrace and remember the events of his career.

The close connection between Buddhist pilgrimage and the sacred biography of the Buddha is, of course, well known. Alfred Foucher, in fact, wrote his classic *Life of the Buddha* following the same pattern. In the *Aśokāvadāna,* however, Aśoka's pilgrimage goes beyond a simple retracing of the Buddha's career; it is, like the building of the eighty-four thousand stūpas, the establishment of a mesocosm where Aśoka himself can experience the presence of the Buddha. In this, however, as we shall see, the emphasis is almost exclusively on the rūpakāya, the physical form in which the Buddha lived the life that is being experienced.

At each of the major sites of the pilgrimage, Aśoka builds a *caitya*, a commemorative monument, for himself and posterity to worship. André Bareau has sought to distinguish between caityas and stūpas, claiming that while the latter always contain bodily relics, the former are associated with places of pilgrimage, ancient sanctuaries, and especially groves of trees. A caitya, he says, is a monument intended to recall (*anu-smṛ*) in the minds of the faithful an important event in the life of the Buddha, and thereby give rise to meritorious thoughts.[57]

The vividness of this recollection (or perhaps visualization) is made explicit in our text by several episodes in which Upagupta summons a local deity connected with a particular pilgrimage site to come and describe for Aśoka the physical form of the Buddha. Thus, for example, at Lumbinī, Upagupta summons the tree spirit who dwelt and still dwells in the tree under which the Buddha was born. Aśoka says to her:

> You witnessed his birth and saw
> his body adorned with the marks!

[57] André Bareau, "Le parinirvāṇa du Buddha et la naissance de la religion bouddhique." *Bulletin de l'Ecole Française d'Extrême-Orient* 61 (1974): 290.

You gazed upon his large lotus-like eyes!
You heard in this wood
the first delighful words
of the leader of mankind. . . .

Tell me, goddess, what was it like—the magnificent moment
of the Blessed One's birth?
And the deity answers:

I did indeed witness the birth of the best of men,
the Teacher who dazzled like gold.
I saw him take the seven steps,
and also heard his words . . .
Throughout Indra's three-fold world,
there shone a supernatural light,
dazzling like gold and delighting the eye.
The earth and its mountains
ringed by the ocean,
shook like a ship being tossed at sea.[58]

A very similar episode occurs a little later on, on the road to Bodhgaya where Upagupta summons the nāga king, Kālika. Aśoka says to him:

You saw my peerless Master,
his complexion like blazing gold,
and his face like the autumn moon.
Recount for me some of the Buddha's qualities,
tell me what it was like—
the splendor of the Sugata![59]

And Kālika obliges him by recalling the appearance of the Buddha when he saw him, right there, walking along the road to Bodhgaya.

These eyewitness reports send Aśoka into an ecstasy of

[58] Mukhopadhyaya, pp. 82-83, slightly rearranged.

[59] Ibid., pp. 86-87. On the identification of Mahākāla and Kālika see Edgerton, *Buddhist Hybrid Dictionary*, s. v. kāla.

bhakti, and in this they recall the similar testimonials of Piṇḍola who, as we have seen, also recounts for Aśoka the several times when he saw the Buddha face to face. It is noteworthy that in all of these reports, the emphasis is as much on the person of the Buddha—his charismatic qualities—as on the specific event that occurred in the life of the Buddha at a particular place and time. Aśoka already knows what happened at each of the sites of the pilgrimage; what he wants is to relive these events, to experience the Buddha himself in all his glory.

This is made even more graphic in another episode concerning Aśoka and Kālika in the *Mahāvaṃsa*. One day, we are told, Aśoka meets the nāga king Mahākāla (Kālika),

> and when he had brought him and made him sit upon the throne under the white canopy, when he had done homage to him with gifts of various flowers, and had bidden the sixteen thousand women of the palace to surround him, the king spoke thus: "Let us behold the bodily form of the omniscient Great Sage, of Him who hath the boundless knowledge, who hath set rolling the wheel of the true doctrine. The nāga king created a beauteous figure of the Buddha, endowed with the thirty-two greater signs and brilliant with the eighty lesser signs of a Buddha, surrounded by the fathom long rays of glory and adorned with the crown of flames. At the sight thereof the king was filled with joy and amazement.[60]

The similarity between this account and that of Māra taking on the form of the Buddha for the elder Upagupta need hardly be pointed out. In both cases, there is a vision of the physical form, the rūpakāya, of the Buddha, although he is in parinirvāṇa. And this, of course, is precisely the intent of Aśoka's pilgrimage. Like the building of the eighty-four thousand stūpas, his pilgrimage reconstructs a structural milieu—a mes-

[60] Geiger, tr., *Mahāvaṃsa*, pp. 33-34.

ocosm—where the presence of the Buddha can be experienced even now.

It is interesting to note in the account we have just cited, however, that before the nāga is experienced as the Buddha, he also becomes the king: Aśoka sits him on the throne, pays homage to him, and surrounds him with the women of his harem. It is thus not only the nāga who "becomes" the Buddha, but the nāga as king who does so. We have already seen how it is in this kingdom that Aśoka establishes the mesocosm of the eighty-four thousand stūpas; here the importance of this emphasis on royalty is reinforced by the identification of the nāga with the figure of the king.

The same notion, perhaps, is implicit in another aspect of Aśoka's pilgrimage. It is rather striking that, in the *Aśokāvadāna*, the number of sites visited by Aśoka and Upagupta totals exactly thirty-two, the same as the number of distinguishing marks on the body of a Great Man (Mahāpuruṣa). It is always difficult to know how much significance to attribute to such details. Although the pilgrimage sites are not actually numbered in the text, each is introduced by the formula "asmin pradeśe," which I have variously translated as "over here," "in this place," "in this direction."[61] In a few

[61] The pilgrimage sites listed are as follows: (1) The Lumbinī wood, (2) the place where the Buddha's father was shown his son and fell at his feet upon seeing the thirty-two marks on his body, (3) the temple of the Śākya clan where the young Buddha was presented to the gods, (4) the place where he was shown to the fortunetellers, (5) the place where Asita predicted he would be a Buddha, (6) the place where he was nourished by Mahāprajapatī, (7) the place where he learned the art of writing, (8) where he mastered the martial arts, (9) where he trained in the martial arts, (10) the place where he pursued pleasure with his sixty-thousand wives, (11) the place where he saw the old man, sick man, and dead man, (12) the Jambu tree in the shade of which he meditated, (13) the gate through which he left Kapilavastu on the Great Departure, (14) the place where he sent back the groom and his horse, (15) the place where he exchanged his clothes for the robe of a hunter, (16) the hermitage of the potter, (17) the place where Bimbisāra offered him half of his kingdom, (18) the place where he met Arāda and Udraka, (19) the place where he practiced fierce austerities for six years, (20) the place where he was offered the milk-rice, (21) the place where the nāga king met

cases, moreover, there appears to have been an unnecessary doubling of sites; this might reflect an attempt at some point, to have come up precisely with the total of thirty-two. Thus, "the place where the bodhisattva mastered the various martial arts" (site no. 8) is distinguished from the training hall where he practiced the martial arts (site no. 9), or again, the place where, as a child, he was shown to the fortune tellers (site no. 4) is distinguished from the place where he was shown to the fortuneteller Asita (site no. 5).

A thirty-two fold scheme (thirty-three if one counts the center) was, in Indian cosmology, a very popular way to arrange units symmetrically around a center. Thus, for example, Indra's heaven had, in addition to himself, thirty-two gods arranged around Mount Meru. Moreover, certain earthly kingdoms were organized administratively on the basis of this same maṇḍala-like pattern. One might especially mention in this regard the early Mon kingdom in Lower Burma, that was divided into thirty-two districts, each the seat of a subordinate prince, with the whole united by the cult of a bodily relic of the Buddha that had miraculously been multiplied by thirty-two soon after its arrival from India.[62]

It is not surprising, therefore, that in the thirty-two places of pilgrimage, we have not only an attempt to recall the various events in the life of the Buddha, but, once again, a systematic establishment of his whole person—his life as a Ma-

---

him on the road to Bodhgaya, (22) the tree of Enlightenment, (23) the place where he received the four stone begging bowls from the gods, (24) the place where he received alms from the two merchants Trapuṣa and Bhallika, (25) the place where he was praised by the ājīvika, (26) the deer park in Sārnāth, (27) the place where a thousand ascetics were converted, (28) the place where King Bimbisāra perceived the truths, (29) the place where the Buddha taught the Dharma to Indra, (30) the place of the great miracle, (31) the place where he came down from Trāyastriṃśa Heaven and (32) the place of the parinirvāṇa at Kuśinagarī.

[62] H. L. Shorto, "The Thirty-two Myos in the Medieval Mon Kingdom," *Bulletin of the School of Oriental and African Studies* 26 (1963): 572-91. See also Stanley J. Tambiah, *World Conqueror and World Renouncer* (Cambridge: University Press, 1976), pp. 108-09.

hāpuruṣa—on the face of the kingdom. Thus the thirty-two sites set up for posterity by Aśoka can, like the eighty-four thousand stūpas, be thought of separately and as a unit; they form a single mesocosmic "chronogram" that allows one to relive gradually, and then all at once, the whole life and person of the Buddha.[63]

At the same time, however, they also recall the figure of the cakravartin. As is well known, the category of Mahāpuruṣa is itself ambiguous; it implies either Buddhahood or great kingship (cakravartinhood). Thus Aśoka's pilgrimage, in symbolically reconstructing the body of a Mahāpuruṣa, would be establishing on the face of India not only the body of the Buddha but also the body of a cakravartin, both of whom possess the thirty-two marks of the Great Man. Aśoka, of course, does not have the thirty-two marks of the Mahāpuruṣa himself (we have seen, in fact, that he is physically ugly). Nevertheless, there may be here an attempt at glorifying his kingship by identifying it with that of a cakravartin, and through the Mahāpuruṣa connection, with that of the Buddha himself. We would therefore have a situation quite similar to that of the building of the eighty-four thousand dharmarājikās which, as we have seen, also recalls the overlap between Aśoka and the Buddha in terms of the ambiguity contained in their common epithet, "dharmarāja."

Aśoka and the Bodhi Tree

Much the same point is made in a humorous episode that is a sort of addendum to the account of Aśoka's pilgrimage. After the king has finished honoring all the places of pilgrimage, he returns to the site of the Buddha's enlightenment at

[63] On this intersection, in the mesocosm, of time and space and its relationship to circumambulation and the maṇḍala, see Paul Mus, "Un cinéma solide," *Arts asiatiques* 10 (1964): 21-34, and also idem., "Thousand-Armed Kannon: A Mystery or a Problem?" *Indogaku bukkyōgaku kenkyū/ Journal of Indian and Buddhist Studies* 12 (1964): 6.

Bodhgaya. Because "his faith was particularly aroused by the Bodhi tree," he wants to make further offerings there and starts "sending to Bodhi" all of his most precious jewels.[64]

The use of the unqualified name "Bodhi" here is significant and is the basis of the story that follows. It apparently refers to a number of things. First of all, of course, it indicates the Bodhi tree itself. Secondly, it refers to what took place at that spot: the Buddha's Bodhi, his enlightenment. Thirdly, however, in the mind of Aśoka's queen Tiṣyarakṣitā, it is the name of a woman, a new mistress of the king called "Bodhi." Confused and jealous, Tiṣyarakṣitā wants to know why the king is sending all of the best jewels to this Bodhi, and she hires a sorceress to put a spell on her so as to effect the destruction of her rival. The sorceress, who knows Bodhi's true identity, is a little confused as to why the queen should be jealous of a tree, but she does not ask any questions, and simply sets about her business. Making use of her black magic, she ties a thread around the trunk of the tree, mutters some mantras, and "Bodhi" soon begins to wither.[65]

Aśoka's reaction is noteworthy. He falls on the ground in a faint, and then, when he recovers his senses, he reveals the double cause of his emotion. On the one hand, as a pilgrimage site, the Bodhi tree was a potent mesocosm where Aśoka could perceive the Buddha. As he puts it, in his lament: "When I looked at the king of trees, I knew that even now I was looking at the Self-Existent Master."[66] The loss of the tree, therefore, represents the loss of (access to) the Buddha. On the other hand, Aśoka has also come to identify himself and his reign with the Bodhi tree. In the *Mahāvaṃsa*, we are told explicitly, in fact, that Aśoka bestowed his own kingship upon the Bodhi tree.[67] Here the identification is even more emotional: "If the

[64] Mukhopadhyaya, p. 93.
[65] Ibid.
[66] Ibid.
[67] Geiger, tr., *Mahāvaṃsa*, p. 125.

tree of the Lord comes to die," Aśoka declares, "I too shall surely expire."[68]

Fortunately for Aśoka, this does not happen. Tiṣyarakṣitā comes to realize her error and asks the sorceress to undo the spell. This she does in time and the Bodhi tree (and Aśoka) recover. But the point has been made: the Bodhi tree is identified not only with the Buddha in nirvāṇa but with Aśoka as well.

The Aśoka Tree

The close identification of the person of the Buddha with various types of trees in early Buddhism is, of course, well known. According to legend, even during his lifetime, the Buddha asked his disciple Ānanda to break off a branch from the Bodhi tree and plant it in Śravastī, for "he who worships it will receive the same reward as if he worshiped me."[69] Moreover, as we have seen, many of the most important events in the life of the Buddha were portrayed as taking place in a wooded grove or beneath a tree. Thus, before the advent of the Buddha image, the Blessed One was often represented by one tree or another (as well as other symbols) that marked his presence in a particular place. In this way, the Bodhi tree came to represent him at Bodhgaya at the moment of his enlightenment and the twin sal trees indicated his parinirvāṇa at Kuśinagarī.

In a related tradition, each of the Buddhas of the past was also represented in the form of a different tree. Thus, while iconographically the bodhi tree stood for Gautama, the ban-

[68] Mukhopadhyaya, p. 93. The moment has been captured on one of the bas-reliefs at Sāñchī; see John Marshall, *A Guide to Sāñchī*, 3rd ed. (Calcutta: Government of India Press, 1955), p. 54.

[69] See Monier Monier-Williams, *Buddhism in its Connexion with Brahmanism and Hinduism* (orig. pub. 1889; rpt., Varanasi: The Chowkhamba Sanskrit Series Office, 1964), p. 517.

yan indicated the presence of Kāśyapa Buddha, the udumbara of Kanakamuni, and so on.[70]

Scholars have not hesitated to trace this particular figuration of the Buddha back to ancient indigenous practices of tree worship.[71] Although the sacred character of certain trees in India and their relationship to fertility and to various gods and goddesses is a subject that cannot be gone into here, we must note that in the *Aśokāvadāna*, the Bodhi tree is not the only sacred tree mentioned. By virtue of his name, Aśoka also comes to be identified with the aśoka tree (*Saraca indica*). The text itself makes this clear in several instances. Just prior to his conversion, when Aśoka goes out to the royal pleasure garden with his harem, he comes across an aśoka tree whose blossoms are at their peak. Thinking "this tree is my namesake," he becomes sexually aroused; but, as we have mentioned, because he has rough skin the young women in his harem do not enjoy caressing him. And, out of spite, they express their contempt for him by chopping all the flowering branches off the aśoka tree while the real Aśoka is asleep. When he wakes up and gazes upon his dismembered namesake, he is so mad that he has five hundred of his wives burned at the stake.[72] In another instance, at the very end of his life, when Aśoka is left with only the half of myrobalan fruit, he again compares himself to an aśoka tree, in a stanza that perhaps refers to this episode:

> Just like an aśoka tree
> when its flowers are cut off
> and its leaves have shrivelled and fallen
> this king is drying up.[73]

[70] Ibid., p. 515.

[71] See, for example, Odette Viennot, *Le culte de l'arbre dans l'Inde ancienne*. (Paris: Musée Guimet, 1954), pp. 99-239.

[72] Mukhopadhyaya, p. 43.

[73] Ibid., p. 129.

In both these instances, then, Aśoka, during some of the darker moments of his kingship, compares himself to a dying, withering, deflowered aśoka tree. When it dies, he will die, just as he will when the Bodhi tree dies. This is in stark contrast to certain depictions of Aśoka in happier times. For example, when the poet Kṣemendra wants to portray the greatness of King Aśoka and the prosperity of his reign, he describes how all the aśoka trees of the countryside, of their own accord, offer up their blossoms to the king.[74]

In order better to understand these passages, we must delve a bit further into their popular context. The aśoka tree in India was renowned for its beauty, but was also the subject of a curious myth: it was not supposed to bloom until it was touched or gently kicked by a beautiful girl or young woman.[75] The tradition, as Heinrich Zimmer has pointed out, was well known to early Buddhist artists who did not hesitate to sculpt at Bhārhut and elsewhere, the voluptuous figures of sylvan nymphs who "with one arm entwining the trunk of a tree and the other bending a branch down, give the trunk, near the root, a gentle kick."[76]

The story of Aśoka and his harem women readily fits into this scenario; he identifies himself with the aśoka tree, and then wants the women to caress him. They refuse and he "fails to blossom": all the flowers are cut off his tree. (In this context of sexuality, fertility, and tree goddesses, it becomes more understandable now how the Bodhi tree could so readily be confused with a woman, Aśoka's mistress.)

There is another piece of Buddhist iconography that readily fits into this artistic and mythological milieu. The Buddha's

[74] P. L. Vaidya, ed., *Avadāna-Kalpalatā*, 2 vols., Buddhist Sanskrit Texts, nos. 22-23 (Darbhanga, Bihar: Mithila Institute, 1959), 2:346.

[75] See references in Margaret Stutley and James Stutley, eds., *Harper's Dictionary of Hinduism* (New York: Harper and Row, 1973), s.v. "aśoka."

[76] Heinrich Zimmer, *Myths and Symbols in Indian Art and Civilization* (New York: Harper and Row, 1946), p. 69, fig. 19.

mother, Queen Māyā, is depicted as giving birth to him at Lumbinī, while holding onto the branch of a blossoming tree. Now it is curious that while generally in the Buddhist tradition, the tree at Lumbinī is said to have been a sal-tree,[77] in the *Aśokāvadāna* it is specified as an aśoka tree.[78] Moreover, as we have seen, it "comes alive" in the sense that the tree goddess herself appears and tells Aśoka of the Buddha's birth and its glories. There is a curious set of interconnections here between the aśoka tree, King Aśoka, the tree goddess, the Buddha's mother, and the Buddha himself. It would be wrong, of course, to claim that they are all one and the same; but it is part of the richness of our text and its tradition and the many-faceted appearance of Aśoka in his relationship to the Buddha that these homologies suggest themselves.

Conclusion

A whole history of Buddhism could probably be written on how Buddhists throughout the centuries have tried to deal with the problems posed by the Buddha's parinirvāṇa. Some (for example the Theravādin monastics and certain early followers of the Prajñāpāramitā) took an approach that was almost exclusively dharmalogical. They frankly recognized the Buddha's physical absence in nirvāṇa but chose to emphasize his presence in his Teachings, his Doctrine, to the point of asserting that one could only relate to the Buddha if one perceived the Dharma. Others, more docetically inclined (Mahāyānists), stressed the eternal transcendent reality of the Buddha and thus the unreality of his life as well as of his death. Still others, while accepting the fact of the parinirvāṇa, looked forward to the coming of another Buddha, either in the distant or the imminent future (Maitreyists). Yet another group projected the Buddha not in time but in space into one or several paradises (Pure Lands) where they hoped to rejoin him after

[77] Thomas, *Life of the Buddha*, p. 33.

[78] Mukhopadhyaya, p. 82.

death; while others interiorized the Buddha within their bodies or minds, and sought to find him therein (Tantra and Zen).

The *Aśokāvadāna*, too, presents its own particular solution to this problem of the Buddha's parinirvāṇa. As we have seen in this chapter, Aśoka, as king, discovers or establishes certain cosmological settings, what Mus would call mesocosms, in order to relate to the Buddha in this world. The eighty-four thousand stūpas, the thirty-two places of pilgrimage, the Bodhi tree, even to some extent the aśoka tree—each provides in its own way a focus, a structure where Aśoka can ritually and experientially relate to the Buddha despite his parinirvāṇa.

The same, of course, would be true for any Buddhist devotee encountering a stūpa, or a place of pilgrimage. What is different in the case of Aśoka is that he goes beyond mere worship of already existing ritual centers; he is a builder of mesocosms. He does not just go to the places of pilgrimage, he establishes them, "as a favor to posterity." He does not simply worship the relics of the Buddha, he goes and gets them, and reorganizes them into the grand scheme of the eighty-four thousand stūpas.

As we have seen, this reorganization, this building of new mesocosms, may follow along rupalogical and/or dharmalogical lines; but it is important to note that it is consistently done with reference to a cosmology related both to the Buddha and to the figure of the king. The eighty-four thousand dharmarājikās refer to both the Buddha and Aśoka as dharmarājas; the sites of pilgrimage feature both the Buddha and the king as Mahāpuruṣas; and, as we have just seen, Aśoka finds not only the Buddha but himself in the trees at Bodhgaya and Lumbinī. In promoting the Buddhist religion, in establishing the Buddha throughout Jambudvīpa, Aśoka is clearly also promoting his own kingship and establishing himself.

Some later Buddhist kings were to push these affinities even further, to the point of claiming that they themselves, as kings, actually were the Buddha. In China, for example, it was maintained as early as the fourth century that T'ai-tsu, the first emperor of the Northern Wei, was "in his very person the Tathāgata"; thus anyone bowing down to him was not doing obeisance to the emperor but was worshipping the Buddha.[79] Somewhat similar developments took place in Southeast Asia where Buddhist kings were commonly viewed as deities, bodhisattvas, or Buddhas. Stanley Tambiah has outlined for Cambodia and Thailand how the Buddhist notion of dharmarāja combined with the Brahmanical notion of *devarāja* ("king as god") to result in the new notion of Buddharāja ("king as Buddha") best exemplified, perhaps, by the figure of the Khmer King Jayavarman VII (twelfth century).[80] In fact, throughout the region, there was more generally, as Georges Coedès put it, "a tradition which appears to have been widespread in Buddhist monarchies according to which the king identified himself with one of the great figures of the Buddhist pantheon, and even went so far as to play the role of a "living Buddha."[81]

These are all, however, much later developments reflecting the influence of both the Mahāyāna and the Hindu traditions in full bloom. In the context of the *Aśokāvadāna*, there is no claim that Aśoka actually is the Buddha. Indeed, we have seen enough of our text's tendency to denigrate and render ridiculous the figure of Aśoka and the institution of kingship so as to make such a proposition impossible.

What we have instead is a more subtle relationship. If the people of the legendary Aśoka's time did not expect to meet the Buddha in their king, they did look for him in the mes-

[79] See Zenryū Tsukamoto, "Wei Shou on Buddhism and Taoism," trans. Leon Hurvitz in *Yün-kang, the Buddhist Cave Temples of the 5th Century A.D.*, ed. Mizuno Teiichi and Nagahiro Toshio (Kyoto, 1956), vol. 16, suppl., p. 53. See also Ch'en, p. 146, and Erik Zürcher, *The Buddhist Conquest of China* (Leiden: E. J. Brill, 1959), pp. 309-10.

[80] Tambiah, *World Conqueror*, pp. 98-101. Even more common is the identification in an eschatological context of the king with the figure of the future Buddha Maitreya.

[81] Georges Coedès, "Les inscriptions malaises de Çrīvijaya," *Bulletin de l'Ecole Française d'Extrême-Orient* 30 (1930): 57-58.

ocosms that their king established in the kingdom. Aśoka's greatness lies not in himself but in what he does, in what he makes possible. As Paul Mus puts it: "We should not speak of "living Buddhas" in the context of the early Buddhist royal cults. The king is not the Buddha. . . . The Buddha does not incarnate himself in the king; that would be a monstrous suggestion. The king is simply a magical instrument who puts his kingdom in touch with the vanished Master."[82]

Here then we encounter another important dimension of Aśoka's kingship: in his building of the eighty-four thousand stūpas, in his marking of the thirty-two places of pilgrimage, in all of these mesocosmic activities, Aśoka is motivated by more than his own personal religious self-interest. As we shall see in our next chapter, he is, at the same time impelled by compassion. He is concerned with making the Buddha present in this world not simply for himself but for others—for the subjects of his kingdom—as well.

[82] Mus, *Barabuḍur*, 1:91.

CHAPTER FIVE

Aśoka: Master of Good Means and Merit Maker

In an interesting story preserved in the last chapter of the *A-yü wang chuan*, but not in the Sanskrit text of the *Aśokāvadāna*, we read of Aśoka's visit to a soothsayer attached to his royal court. The diviner tells him that he bears on his body certain inauspicious marks that can only be erased if he performs great deeds of merit. Aśoka therefore sets about building the eighty-four thousand stūpas. When he finishes, he returns to the diviner, but the inauspicious marks are still there. At a loss as to what to do next, Aśoka consults Yaśas, the abbot of the Kukkuṭārāma. The elder explains to him that so far, in his building of the eighty-four thousand stūpas, he has only been acquiring "light" merit for himself; if he truly wishes to get rid of his evil marks, he needs to acquire "heavy" merit by exhorting others to acquire merit also.[1]

Students of the Aśokan edicts have long noted what might be called Aśoka's "initiative" in doctrinal matters. Not only does he declare in his inscriptions his own views on Dharma, he advocates them for others, and takes certain specific measures for promoting Dharma, for teaching it to others.

The *Aśokāvadāna* too records not only Aśoka's great deeds for himself; it also presents the king as a teacher, a promoter of Buddhist doctrine. Moreover, his teaching is not without its own originality. Several times Aśoka is called a "master of good means" (*upāya*), and he does not hesitate to take the initiative, in his own way, in aiding others to come to a true appreciation of the Buddhist faith. In so doing, he quite naturally focuses on a number of traditional themes dear to his

[1] Jean Przyluski, *La légende de l'empereur Açoka* (Paris: Paul Geuthner, 1923), p. 423. See below Appendix, No. 9.

own heart such as the value of merit making and the worthiness of the Buddhist sangha. But at the same time, as we shall see, he is presented as adopting a deeper doctrinal stance, and proposing a doctrine of the "essence" (*sāra*) of all beings.

It is this whole side of Aśoka's legend—his actions in converting others and the arguments he uses to do so—that we shall focus on in this chapter. Again, we shall proceed by looking first at a number of relevant episodes from the text, and then examine the content of Aśoka's teaching for both its originality and continuity with Buddhist doctrine in general.

Aśoka and his Brother Vītaśoka

Shortly after his conversion by the monk Samudra, Aśoka takes it upon himself to encourage others to turn toward the Buddhist religion. His first convert is his younger brother, Prince Vītaśoka, who is said to favor the non-Buddhist heretics. Vītaśoka especially admires the ascetic practices of certain Brahmanical *ṛṣis*, and even maligns the Buddhist monks as being soft, attached to the passions, and inclined to enjoy life.[2]

Aśoka decides to teach his brother the truth of the matter. By an elaborate stratagem, he tricks him into putting on the royal crown and sitting on the throne, and then accuses him of trying to usurp the kingship.[3] He condemns Vītaśoka to die but at the last moment agrees to a seven-day reprieve during which he will let him be king and enjoy the pleasures of that state. Aśoka then surrounds Vītaśoka with dancing girls, delicacies, and all the delights of royalty, but places

[2] Sujitkumar Mukhopadhyaya, ed., *The Aśokāvadāna* (New Delhi: Sahitya Akademi, 1963), p. 56.

[3] In a Chinese version of the story, Aśoka has his harem seduce his brother and then accuses him of illicit conduct. See Edouard Chavannes, *Cinq cents contes et apologues extraits du Tripiṭaka chinois*, 4 vols. (Paris: Imprimerie Nationale, 1934), 3:299.

fearsome executioners at his door to remind him every day of exactly how much time he has left to live. Vītaśoka is completely unable to enjoy the pleasures of his new position. Thus when, at the end of the week, Aśoka asks him how he liked the kingship, he replies:

> I did not see the dance, O king,
> nor did I hear the sound of the music.
> I did not smell the perfumes today
> nor did I recognize any tastes.
> I did not feel the touch of the women
> their bodies bedecked with gold. . . .
> The choicest bed gave me no pleasure
> for I could see the executioners,
> dressed in blue, standing at my door.
> I could hear the ghastly sound of their bells,
> and I became dreadfully afraid
> of death, O chief of kings.[4]

The whole scenario, of course, is only a trick—an elaborate ruse to get Vītaśoka to change his ways. Aśoka never intends to have his brother executed, but only to emphasize the lesson that, just as he could not enjoy any physical pleasure because of the fear of death, so too the Buddhist monks, who constantly meditate on death—not just in one but in hundreds of lives—do not delight in any of the pleasures of the senses. Vītaśoka needs no further convincing; he gives up his support for the heretics, takes refuge in the Triple Gem (the Buddha, the Dharma, and the sangha), and becomes in every way a devout layman.[5]

[4] Mukhopadhyaya, p. 59.

[5] The story is also found, it might be pointed out, in the *Mahāvaṃsa*'s account of Aśoka's brother Tissa, which repeats in a summary fashion the gist of our tale:

> One day Tissa when hunting saw gazelles sporting joyously in the wild. And at this sight he thought: "Even the gazelles sport thus joyously, who feed on grass in the wild. Wherefore are not the bhikkhus joyous and gay, who have their food and dwelling in comfort?

Soon, however, Vītaśoka wants to go a step further than this; he wishes to become a monk. At this point, interestingly, Aśoka balks. It is one thing for members of the royal household to support the saṅgha, quite another for them to join it; and he seeks to dissuade Vītaśoka from his resolve by pointing out how difficult and trying the life of a monk is. He lists for Vītaśoka's benefit the five sufferings characterizing this world that, he claims, the monks constantly recall: "In hell, the suffering brought on by a blazing fire that causes great pain to the body; among the animals, the suffering coming from the fear of eating one another; among the pretas the suffering of hunger and thirst; among humans the suffering of the practice of striving; among the gods, the suffering that marks their fall from the divine state."[6]

This list is noteworthy for several reasons. First of all, it states clearly the specific kinds of suffering characterizing the five *gatis* (literally "courses") or realms of rebirth in the Buddhist scheme of *saṃsāra.*[7] Secondly, it reveals that the uniqueness of the enlightened Buddhist monk lies not in the intensity of his own suffering (as for example in the case of an ascetic) but in the breadth of his cosmological vision, of his awareness of suffering in the world. Like the Buddha during the night of his enlightenment, he can see into and meditate upon the sufferings of beings reborn in all the realms of existence. The

---

> Returned home he told the king his thought. To teach him the king handed over to him the government of the kingdom for one week, saying: "Enjoy, prince, for one week, my royal state; then will I put thee to death." . . . And when the week was gone by he asked: "Wherefore art thou thus wasted away?" And when Tissa answered: "By reason of the fear of death," the king spoke again to him and said: "Thinking that thou must die when the week was gone by thou wast no longer joyous and gay; how then can (the monks) be joyous and gay, who think ever upon death?"

(See Wilhelm Geiger, tr., *The Mahāvaṃsa or the Great Chronicle of Ceylon* [London: Pali Text Society, 1912], pp. 39-40.)

[6] Mukhopadhyaya, p. 60.

[7] The *Aśokāvadāna* knows the scheme of the five realms of rebirth rather than the later one of the six. On this whole question see Paul Mus, *La lumière sur les six voies*, Travaux et mémoires de l'Institut d'Ethnologie, no. 35 (Paris: Institut d'Ethnologie, 1939), pp. 18-32.

important thing, then (and Aśoka states this explicitly) is not so much the individual's ascetic or indulgent lifestyle but the depth—or perhaps rather the breadth—of his insight into the transience and suffering of this world.

All of this, of course, is perfectly good standard Buddhist doctrine. The originality of Aśoka's teaching lies in his skill in means (*upāya*) at making others aware of this transiency and suffering.

In the analysis of the Buddha's smile in Chapter Two, we noted how the dharmalogical activities of the different beings in the Buddhist cosmos had various scopes or fields. The activity of the Buddha, at the top of the hierarchy, encompassed the largest field, in fact, the whole cosmos. The activities of the hell-beings, at the bottom of the system, had almost no field at all. As a balacakravartin, Aśoka stands in the middle of the scheme, immediately above the denizens of the hells, preta realms, animal and human worlds, but below the lofty reaches of the Buddhas, pratyekabuddhas, and arhats. In other words, his field of activity encompasses all the classic realms of rebirth,[8] but no more than that.

This is significant because it defines for us in a rather precise way the scope of Aśoka's teachings. This is not to say that he literally starts preaching to the animals, pretas, or hell-beings; rather, through his kingship, he now creates situations that translate into this-worldly human terms the sufferings characterizing the various realms of rebirth, and he does so in such a way that those sufferings can be understood and overcome.

We have already seen how, before his conversion, Aśoka builds a terrible prison that becomes known as "Aśoka's hell." The text, in fact, is even more specific than this: the inspiration for the building of the prison and for the sufferings being inflicted on people there, comes to Aśoka's executioner, Caṇḍagirika, when he overhears a monk reading the graphic description of the Buddhist hells found in the "Bālapaṇḍita Sū-

[8] Except that of the devas; but, as we shall see, kingship and divinity may be equatable in Aśoka's scheme.

tra."[9] The prison thus is a sort of concretization of the sūtra. It gives form (*rūpa*) to the Buddhist Teaching (Dharma), and as such it can serve definite religious ends. Thus, it is in this setting of a hell-on-earth built by Aśoka, that Samudra first attains enlightenment and then brings about Aśoka's own conversion.

Similarly, in the story of Vītaśoka, we have a setting up of a heaven-on-earth in Aśoka's throne room, with an emphasis on the sufferings that characterize the divine state. According to Buddhist tradition, life in heaven, no matter how long it may seem to go on, is nevertheless impermanent. Suffering in the heavens comes only in the last few days of a god's tenure there, when he realizes that he will soon fall from his divine state, and no longer enjoy the pleasures and delights of divinity. It does not involve any intense physical suffering but is rather an acute realization of impermanence (death) that prevents the deity from rejoicing in his privileged status.

It is quite apparent that the elaborate setup where Vītaśoka is unable to enjoy the pleasures of the kingship because of the constant reminder of his death replicates this same scenario. Vītaśoka on the throne is like a god in heaven during the last few days before his fall.

The homologies between king and deity, palace and heaven, in ancient India are well known.[10] In the case of Aśoka, one need only mention here a specific instance of a comparison made between Aśoka's palace and Indra's heaven. In a story no longer extant in Sanskrit but preserved in the Chinese Tripiṭaka, a monk enters Aśoka's palace and acts strangely, examining everything there very closely. Aśoka, rather suspicious of this character, asks him what he is doing. He replies that he is comparing Aśoka's throne room to the palace of

[9] Mukhopadhyaya, p. 45. See I. B. Horner, tr., *The Middle Length Sayings (Majjhima-Nikāya)*, 3 vols., Pali Text Society Translation Series, nos. 29-31 (London: Luzac and Co., 1954-59), 3:209-23.

[10] See, for example, Jan Gonda, *Ancient Indian Kingship from the Religious Point of View* (Leiden: E. J. Brill, 1966).

the gods in the Trāyastriṃśa Heaven, and has found the two to be exactly alike.[11]

In this divine setting, then, Vītaśoka suffers just as surely as if Aśoka had thrown him into the infernal prison. And like Samudra, Vītaśoka also benefits from the situation: he takes refuge in the Triple Gem and becomes a Buddhist layman.

However, as mentioned, Vītaśoka then wants to go further than this and become a monk; and Aśoka seeks to change his mind by pointing out how difficult and trying the life of a monk is.

"Forego this resolution," he says, "the ascetic life results in a worsening of one's appearance: your garments will be rags from the dust-heap and your cloak something which was thrown out by a servant; your food will consist of alms collected from strangers; your bed and your seat will be a layer of grass and a pile of leaves at the foot of a tree. When you are sick, food will not be easy to obtain, and urine will be your medicine; and you are very delicate and unable to endure the suffering of heat and cold, hunger and thirst! I beg you to change your mind."[12]

It is perhaps understandable that Aśoka does not want his brother to become ordained, even though he has just made him convert to Buddhism, but there is still a curious contradiction here that needs to be explained. In seeking to dissuade his brother from joining the sangha, Aśoka stresses the hardships of the religious life—the dust-heap robes, the poor quality of the food, the discomforts of hunger and thirst—all of those things that, in Aśoka's day, characterized not monastic life in general but the ancient ideal life style for those monks who were particularly ascetically inclined.[13] Earlier, however, when he was convincing his brother of the worthiness of the Buddhist monks as opposed to the heretic ascetics, his argu-

[11] Chavannes, 1:370.

[12] Mukhopadhyaya, p. 62.

[13] On the practice of these dhūtāṅga, see Etienne Lamotte, *Histoire du bouddhisme indien* (Louvain: Institut Orientaliste, 1958), p. 60.

ment was that in spite of appearances, the bhikṣus did not really enjoy physical pleasures, because they were constantly meditating on death and impermanence. The implication was that, at least physically, the Buddhist monastic life did not generally involve ascetic suffering.

In fact, it is well known that in India, certain monks did join the Buddhist sangha because they sought therein a relatively easy and comfortable life.[14] Aśoka does not initially dispute the possibility that they might, at least outwardly, have indeed found such a comfortable life, but then he contradicts himself by emphasizing the strenuous hardships involved in the life of a monk.

There would seem to be only one way to resolve this paradox. Aśoka, it would appear, is here merely continuing to employ his skill in good means in teaching his brother. He wants to test Vītaśoka's resolve further, and therefore stresses the difficulties of the monastic life. More interestingly for our purposes, however, his test associates the life of the ascetic monk with yet another of the Buddhist realms of rebirth. Having replicated the sufferings of the Buddhist hells in his prison, and the sufferings of the gods in his throne room, Aśoka stresses the sufferings of the realm of the pretas, the hungry ghosts. He sets up for his brother a sort of hermitage under a tree in the palace grounds, and has him visit the royal apartments on his alms rounds. Then, curiously, when the women of the harem fill his begging bowl with delectable and sumptuous foods, Aśoka immediately intervenes and orders them to give him mashed rotten beans instead.

The specifics of this further test are noteworthy. In the Buddhist tradition, the pretas, with their huge bellies and needle-like gullets are famous for their intense hunger and thirst. Moreover, the food and drink that they do consume, no matter how delicious it is, turns to ordure, feces, pus, and blood as

[14] See, for example, the case of Piṇḍola (Mukhopadhyaha, p. 64). See also John Strong, "Legend of the Lion-Roarer: A Study of the Buddhist Arhat Piṇḍola Bhāradvāja," *Numen* 26 (1979): 61-68.

soon as they partake of it.[15] In a somewhat similar fashion, Vītaśoka's food changes from being a sumptuous royal meal to being "mashed rotten beans."

We cannot here go into the whole question of the homologies between the figure of the Buddhist monk—the bhikṣu—and that of the preta or ghost in the Indian tradition. Both, of course, are recipients of "*piṇḍa*," a word that in the Brahmanical tradition represents the rice-ball offerings given to the departed ancestors and, in the Buddhist tradition, the alms food put in a monk's begging bowl. Food offerings to Buddhist monks thus can allay the suffering of departed ancestors in the preta realm.[16] More generally, both the bhikṣu (especially if ascetically inclined) and the preta live apart from society and frequent cremation grounds.

The most convincing parallel, however, comes from another version of the Vītaśoka story preserved in a Chinese commentary on the *Ekottara-āgama*, no longer extant in Sanskrit but translated probably sometime in the second century.[17] In it, after eating the disgusting nauseating food prepared for him, Vītaśoka is sent by the king to the city of Takṣaśilā where he ends up in a cemetery, in the midst of a company of pretas. There, in conversation with the ghosts, he comes to a realization of the suffering and impermanence of this world and attains arhatship.[18] Just as Samudra's enlightenment came in the setting of prison/hell, and Vītaśoka's conversion in the midst of a palace/heaven, so here Vītaśoka's final enlighten-

[15] See, for example, the stories in Henry S. Gehman, tr., *Peta vatthu: Stories of the Departed*, Sacred Books of the Buddhists, no. 12 (London: Luzac and Co., 1942).

[16] We have here the ideological roots of the Avalambana festival. See John Strong, "Buddhism and Filial Piety: The Indian Antecedents to a "Chinese Problem," *Traditions in Contact and Change*, ed. Peter Slater, Maurice Boutin, Harold Coward, and Donald Wiebe (Waterloo, Ontario: Wilfrid Laurier, University Press, 1983).

[17] Taishō Tripiṭaka 1507. See the translation of relevant passages in Przyluski, *Légende*, pp. 221-22.

[18] Ibid.

ment takes place in the context of an ascetic/preta life. The same is true in the *Aśokāvadāna* where Vītaśoka consumes the rotten beans and Aśoka, seeing his resolve, agrees to let him wander forth. He does so and soon attains arhatship as a result of his ascetic life.

Aśoka and his Minister Yaśas

This pattern of deliberate reminders of the realms of rebirth continues in the very next episode of the *Aśokāvadāna*, that of the encounter of Aśoka and his minister Yaśas.[19] Although Yaśas is a Buddhist devotee, as a minister, he is also concerned about matters of royal protocol. Specifically he is worried about Aśoka's practice of bowing down to all Buddhist monks because some of them are low caste individuals, and he does not think it proper for a king to prostrate himself in front of them.[20]

Aśoka resolves to teach Yaśas a lesson. He orders each one of his ministers to bring him the head of a particular kind of animal (cow, sheep, deer, bird, etc.) and then to go and sell it in the marketplace. Yaśas's task is to do likewise, but with the head of a human being. He has no difficulty procuring the head of man (from a corpse), but then he finds it impossible to sell it. No one in the market will buy it, no one will even take it free of charge. Frustrated and insulted by the merchants, Yaśas comes to a realization of the worthlessness not just of this but of all human heads, and understands that it is therefore quite all right for Aśoka to bow down his worthless head at the foot of Buddhist monks.[21]

The simile is a bit awkward but the lesson is quite clear and Aśoka does not hesitate in stressing the point for Yaśas:

[19] Not to be confused with Yaśas, the abbot of Kukkuṭārāma.

[20] Mukhopadhyaya, p. 71.

[21] Ibid., p. 72; compare the same story in Edouard Huber, tr., *Aśvaghoṣa Sūtrālaṃkāra* pp. 90-96.

You, sir, are obsessed with matters of form and superiority, and because of this attachment you seek to dissuade me from bowing down at the feet of the monks.

But if I acquire some merit
by bowing down a head so disgusting
that no one on earth would take it,
even free of charge,
what harm is there in that?
You, sir, look at the caste [jāti]
and not at the inherent qualities of the monks.
Haughty, deluded and obsessed with caste,
you harm yourself and others.
When you invite someone,
or when it is time for a wedding,
then you should investigate the matter of caste,
but not at the time of Dharma.
For Dharma is a question of qualities
and qualities do not reflect caste.[22]

This passage is noteworthy for a number of reasons. First of all, it makes a simple statement from a Buddhist perspective about caste, viewing it as irrelevant in matters of Dharma but applicable on occasions such as weddings and invitations. There is nothing very extraordinary about this view, at least in the Buddhist context, but the manner in which caste is denigrated is interesting; Aśoka turns, for his didactic example, to the animal world. When all the different animal heads are assembled and sold for food, the marketplace in this story becomes a replica, in human terms, of the animal gaṭi. As such it is marked, as we have seen, by the "suffering coming from the fear of eating one another." In the larger perspective established by this look at the animal realm, distinctions between human beings (including even kings) be-

[22] Mukhopadhyaya, pp. 72-73. P. L. Vaidya, ed., *Divyāvadānam*, Buddhist Sankrit Texts, no. 20 (Darbhanga, Bihar: Mithila Institute, 1959), pp. 185-86.

come meaningless. At the same time, there is here the further implication that the human caste system with its classification of people into different "species" and its fear—if not of eating each other, at least of eating with each other—is also similar to this animal kingdom. Yaśas with his obsession with caste is suffering the suffering of animals. When he goes to the marketplace, he suffers further, but in such a way that he comes to realize and overcome his limitation.

Cosmological Vision

In each of the examples we have considered, Aśoka's skill in means lies in his ability to replicate in human terms the various Buddhist realms of rebirth and thus give to others an awareness of suffering in a larger cosmological field. A god in heaven is like a king on a throne and experiences the same suffering: fear of losing his status. A denizen of hell is like a prisoner in a gaol and like him experiences physical suffering. A preta on a cremation ground is like an ascetic monk, undergoing hunger and thirst. An animal in the wild is like an animal in the marketplace or a man caught up in the caste system: afraid and threatened by others.

In thus setting up the sufferings of the gaṭis, Aśoka is in effect painting in real terms a saṃsāra-maṇḍala, a Wheel of Life (*bhavacakra*) depicting the different realms of rebirth.[23] His purpose in doing so is not to satisfy others' curiosity about the cosmos but to stimulate them to dharmalogical action and understanding. In this, he is also following the example of the painters of the Wheel of Life who, according to the *Divyāvadāna*, always inscribed on the wall, right next to their depic-

[23] On the Wheel of Life in Indian Buddhism, see Louis de La Vallée Poussin, *Bouddhisme: études et matériaux* (Brussels, 1898), pp. 98-100; and L. Austine Waddell, "The Buddhist Pictorial Wheel of Life," *Journal of the Royal Asiatic Society of Bengal* 61 (1892): 33-55. For an English translation of the relevant passage from the *Divyāvadāna*, see Bhikkhu Khantipalo, *The Wheel of Birth and Death*, Wheel Publications, nos. 147-49 (Kandy: Buddhist Publication Society, 1970).

tion of the sufferings in the various realms of rebirth, the following exhortatory verse:

> Start now! Leave home! Apply yourselves to the
> Buddha's Teaching.
> Overthrow the army of Death the way an elephant
> smashes a reed hut!
> For whoever goes forth intent on the Doctrine and
> Discipline
> will put an end to suffering and abandon this cycle of
> rebirth.[24]

This stanza is also cited in the *Aśokāvadāna* in the stereotyped description of the Buddha's smile that, as we have seen, is itself revelatory of the different realms of rebirth.

Aśoka's ability to paint such a cosmological picture of suffering and to use it to prod others into dharmalogical action is rooted not only in his power and position as king, but in his own personal religious experience as well. We have already seen in Chapter Two that Aśoka's dharmalogical career begins in his past life with his gift of dirt to the Buddha. On that occasion, he not only makes his vow to become a great monarch, but he is also accorded, through the intermediary of the Buddha's smile, a vision of a larger, structured universe. Most directly the rays of light that leave the Buddha's mouth reveal (as they relieve) the sufferings in the heavens and the hells. This cosmic picture is then filled in by reference in the Buddha's explanation of the smile to all the other gatis.

[24] Vaidya, *Divyāvadānam*, p. 186. The same verse may be found in the *Aśokāvadāna* (Mukhopadhyaya, pp. 32-33); in the stereotyped description of the Buddha's smile in the *Avadānaśataka* (see P. L. Vaidya, *Avadānaśatakam*, Buddhist Sanskrit Texts, no. 19 [Darbhanga, Bihar: Mithila Institute, 1958], p. 298); in the Sanskrit *Dharmapada* (see Emile Sénart, "Le manuscrit kharosthi du Dhammapada; les fragments Dutreuil de Rhins," *Journal asiatique* 12 [1898]: 193-308, esp. p. 208); and, in Pali, in the *Samyutta Nikāya* (see C.A.F. Rhys Davids, tr., *The Book of the Kindred Sayings*, 5 vols., Pali Text Society Translation Series, Nos. 7, 10, 13, 14, 16 [London: Pali Text Society, 1917-30], 1:195).

The same theme of a cosmological vision is then repeated in Aśoka's construction of the eighty-four thousand stūpas where, as we have seen, there occurs the miracle of the "unveiling of the world" that enables Aśoka to see at once all eighty-four thousand stūpas and the whole of Jambudvīpa. This represents not only an establishment of Aśoka's and the Buddha's rule throughout the known world, but Aśoka's realization of the world's basic structure, something which is then reflected in his acquisition of the new epithet "Dharmāśoka."[25]

The connection between this type of awareness of the total picture of the cosmos and the process of enlightenment is something that has not been emphasized enough in Buddhist studies. In a sense, some sort of cosmic vision—whether of Jambudvīpa or of all the realms of rebirth—is a necessary part of a full realization of the significance of the First Noble Truth of suffering. For to be properly understood, the truth of suffering—*duḥkha*—must be seen to characterize all existence everywhere, not simply this life or this human state.

The Buddha himself in the second watch of the night of his enlightenment at Bodhgaya had such a vision. With his divine eye, he looked down at the entire world and saw all the beings in it transmigrating from one realm of rebirth to another.[26] Only then did he go on to a more strictly dharmalogical enlightenment in the third watch with his realization of the Four Noble Truths and of the doctrine of Dependent Origination. Similarly, we have seen in the story of Vītaśoka that one of the factors that distinguishes enlightened monks from heretics (as well as from Buddhist laypersons) is the breadth of their cosmological perception. As Aśoka put it, they see the suf-

[25] Geiger, tr., *Mahāvaṃsa*, p. 42. See also on this theme the discussion above and Paul Mus, *Barabuḍur*, 2 vols. (Hanoi: Imprimerie d'Extrême-Orient, 1935), 1:245.

[26] For a classic description of this vision of the second watch of the night, see E. H. Johnston, ed. and tr., *The Buddhacarita or Acts of the Buddha* (orig. pub., 1936; rpt. Delhi: Motilal Banarsidass, 1976), pp. 158, 204. Mus (*La lumière*, p. 206) connects this vision to the bhavacakra.

fering not just in this life but in all lives, in all possible realms of rebirth.[27]

At an earlier stage, however, the situation of suffering has to be set up and structured before it can be "seen." Only in this way can relatively unenlightened persons extract from it something positive, something dharmalogical. Sheer chaotic suffering is totally consuming and affords a person no hope at all, but if it is ordered, if it is put into a greater cosmological context, this will enable those suffering in it to see their own suffering in the setting of a structured whole. In this way a liberating insight can be engendered in the very midst of suffering.

This is, of course, precisely what Aśoka does for Samudra, Vītaśoka, and Yaśas; thanks to him and thanks to his good means in communicating his greater cosmological perspective, they all achieve some initial perception of the greater world and its cosmological structure and so are spurred on to attaining enlightenment.

The Doctrine of Essence

There is implicit in all of this a more developed metaphysic—one revolving around the notion of realizing one's dharmalogical core or essence (sāra), an idea that is mentioned several times in the *Aśokāvadāna*. The notion is not totally foreign to Buddhist canonical literature. Indeed in the *Majjhima Nikāya*, there are two suttas devoted to equating the attainment of enlightenment with the finding of the core or pith (sāra) of a log of wood.[28] In a somewhat different vein, Aśoka himself, in his twelfth rock edict, claims that one of the prin-

[27] Mukhopadhyaya, p. 60.

[28] See the "Mahāsāropama Sutta" and the "Cūḷasāropama Sutta" in Horner, *Middle Length Sayings*, 1:238-53. See also Joaquin Pérez-Rémon, "The Simile of the Pith (Sāra) in the Nikāyas and its Bearing on the Anattavāda," *Boletín de la Asociación Española de Orientalistas* 15 (1979): 71-93.

ciples of his Dharma is the "furthering of essence" (*sāravaḍḍhī*) or "progress in the essential." This is what is shared by all the various religious sects and unites them in a common goal.[29]

In the *Aśokāvadāna*, however, the notion of essence takes on somewhat different connotations. For its fullest elucidation, we must return to Aśoka's sermon to his minister Yaśas:

> Have you not heard that saying
> of the compassionate leader of the Śākyas
> that the wise are able to grasp the essence (sāra)
> of this world's essenceless constructs (yantras)?
> . . . .
> When my body lies in the ground,
> discarded like the pulp of sugarcane,
> it will be of no use for merit making;
> it won't be able to perform strenuous activities:
> getting up, bowing down, and making añjalis.
> Therefore, right now, I should endeavor to save
> my meritorious essence from perishing in the grave.
> Those who do not extract the essence
> from this body that must inevitably perish
> are like those who fail to save a chest of jewels
> from a burning house or a ship sinking at sea.
> Unable to distinguish essence from non-essence,
> they never see the essence at all
> and are totally distraught
> when they enter the jaws of Death.
> Once one has enjoyed curds,
> ghee, fresh butter, and buttermilk,
> the best part of the milk—its essence—is gone.
> If the jar is then accidentally broken,
> it is hardly something to get upset about.

[29] Jules Bloch, ed. and tr., *Les inscriptions d'Aśoka* (Paris: Les Belles Lettres, 1950), pp. 121-24.

So too there should be no sorrow at death
if one has already extracted from one's body,
its essence—good conduct.

. . . .

The wise in this world make merit
by getting up, bowing down, and performing
other acts of obeisance,
relying on this most vile body,
hoping for the essence.[30]

There are several themes running through this passage that should be examined carefully.

First of all, there is the notion found throughout Buddhism that one should take advantage of this rare opportunity—rebirth as a human being—and make the best use of it before death. Aśoka's similes make this clear. The essence in the body is like the juice in sugarcane, like a chest of jewels in a burning house, like ghee or curds in a milk-pitcher about to be broken. One should grasp it in time, before it perishes.[31]

Secondly, the text itself, in this and other references to essence, seems to encourage a return to our distinction between the dharmalogical and rupalogical dimensions of Buddhist religious activity. Sāra, it is clear, is a dharmalogical element that is distinct from, yet located in physical forms (*rūpa*), either the human body or the world as a whole. As such it is to be understood or grasped by the wise. The same point is made in the story of the blinding of Aśoka's son Kunāla. As has been mentioned, through the evil workings of his step-

[30] Mukhopadhyaya, pp. 73-74.

[31] The reference to the burning house reminds one, of course, of the famous parable in the *Lotus Sūtra* that equates saṃsāra to a burning house (see Hendrik Kern, tr., *Saddharma-Puṇḍarīka or the Lotus of the True Law*, Sacred Books of the East, no. 21 [Oxford: Clarendon Press, 1884], pp. 72 ff.). The other similes intriguingly recall those used by the Sarvāstivādin teacher Dharmatrāta to explain how an element, although it changes as it moves through the three times, nonetheless remains the same. See Surendranath Dasgupta, *A History of Indian Philosophy*, 5 vols. (Delhi: Motilal Banarsidass, 1975), 1:115.

mother Tiṣyarakṣitā, as well as because of his own bad karma, Kunāla, who is known for his righteousness and for the beauty of his eyes, is to suffer by having his eyes plucked out. Kunāla, however, remains unperturbed by this prospect since he "has already grasped the essence of [his] eye," and it therefore makes little difference to him "whether his eyes are ripped out or not." Thus the occasion that might have been a tragic one is transformed into something joyful because it confirms Kunāla's enlightenment. He realizes the truth of suffering and impermanence and although his "eyes of flesh" (which see forms—rūpa) are torn out, his "eye of wisdom" (which sees Dharma) is opened.[32]

Thirdly, the human body itself is valuable only because it somehow contains this essence, this dharmalogical pith or core of value that is to be separated from it and saved from the

[32] Mukhopadhyaya, pp. 114-115. The Kunāla story itself was very popular throughout the Northern Buddhist world. Different versions of it may be found in the *A-yü wang chuan*, the *A-yü wang ching* (see Przyluski, *Légende*, pp. 281-95), Kṣemendra's *Avadānakalpalatā* (Vaidya ed., pp. 346-67), Tāranātha (*History of Buddhism in India*, trans. Lama Chimpa and Alaka Chattopadhyaya [Simla: Indian Institute of Advanced Study, 1970], pp. 76-77), and the *Aśokāvadānamālā* (see G. M. Bongard-Levin and O. F. Volkova, *The Kunāla Legend and an Unpublished Aśokāvadānamālā Manuscript* [Calcutta: Indian Studies Past and Present, 1965], pp. 13-39). His story has also been carried over into the Jain tradition (see Hermann Jacobi, ed., *Sthavirāvalīcharita or Parisishṭaparvan by Hemachandra*, Bibliotheca Indica, n.s. 537 [Calcutta: Asiatic Society, 1885], pp. 259-70), and has interesting parallels in the tale of Hippolytus as well as the Byzantine legend of Crispus, Constantine the Great, and Fausta (see Emile Sénart, "Un roi de l'Inde au IIIe siècle avant notre ère," *Revue des deux mondes* 92 [1889]: 108). The site of his blinding in Takṣaśilā was marked by a stūpa and became an important place of pilgrimage where, according to Hsüan-tsang, the blind came to pray for the restoration of their sight (see Thomas Watters, *On Yuan Chwang's Travels in India*, 2 vols. [orig. pub., 1905; rpt., Delhi: Munshi Ram Manohar Lal, 1961], 1:246), and his legend continued to inspire blind bards as far away as Japan (see Susan Matisoff, *The Legend of Semimaru: Blind Musician of Japan* [New York: Columbia University Press, 1978]). Finally, a persistent tradition associates Kunāla with the establishment of Buddhism in Khotan (see Lamotte, pp. 281-83 and R. E. Emmerick, *Tibetan Texts Concerning Khotan*, London Oriental Series, vol. 19 [London: Oxford University Press, 1967], p. 15).

sufferings of death. The language of our text here is somewhat reminiscent of Brahmanical or Jain discussions of the *ātman* (self) or *jīva*, or perhaps even more of the Sāṃkhya school's dualism of *puruṣa* and *prakṛti*.

The notion that there is an essence, a sāra contained within the body and separable from it, is, of course, one that certain Buddhists, notably the Sanskrit and Pali Abhidharmists (and scholars following them), have consistently fought. For them such an essence would resemble too much a self or soul, and so threaten to contradict the *anātman* (no-self) doctrine.

But even within Buddhist circles, especially in popularly oriented groups who were concerned more with personal devotion and karmic continuity from one life to the next than with abhidharmic analysis, the anātman doctrine was always causing difficulties. This was the case, for example, in the book of the *Jātaka* that needed to focus on the Buddha's personal identity and continuity as he moved from one life to another and so foster a sense of importance for individual identity. It could hardly maintain in very strict terms the no-self doctrine, and yet at the same time, as a Buddhist work, it could hardly explicitly contradict it either. Its solution, as John Jones has recently pointed out, was simply to remain more or less silent on the whole issue.[33]

In other cases, however, theoretical elaborations were proposed to circumvent the problem. Thus the Pudgalavādins (Personalists) argued for the existence of a *pudgala* (person) who fulfilled several important religious functions. The person was the doer of deeds, pure and impure, the recipient of the fruit of those deeds, and the "enjoyer" who wanders in saṃsāra and is reborn in life after life.[34] As Edward Conze views it: "The Personalists . . . taught that the Person is a reality in the ultimate sense, which provides a common factor or link

[33] John Garrett Jones, *Tales and Teachings of the Buddha* (London: George Allen & Unwin, 1979), p. 24.

[34] Edward Conze, *Buddhist Thought in India* (Ann Arbor: University of Michigan, Press, 1962), p. 128

for the successive processes occurring in a self-identical individual, over many lives, up to Buddhahood."[35]

The Personalists, of course, were often accused of heterodoxy, despite their careful insistence that their theory did not contradict the no-self doctrine of the Buddha.[36] It would be wrong, however, to think of them simply as a minor deviant group. At the time of Hsüan-tsang, the Pudgalavādins numbered as many as one-fourth of all Buddhist monks in India,[37] and there can be no doubt that they were trying to respond to real religious and philosophical demands for some sort of unity of the personal continuum.

They were, however, by no means the only Buddhists engaged in doing this. Other schools besides the Personalists felt the practical and theoretical demand for a notion of some type of "person," and although they always refrained from using the word ātman, they did introduce a number of different conceptions which might well be called "pseudo-selves."[38]

Conze gives a number of examples of these pseudo-selves, including the late Theravādin theory of a "life-continuum," the Mahāsaṅghika notion of a "basic consciousness," the Saṃkrantika teaching that the five *skandhas* (the constituent factors of the individual) themselves transmigrate, the Mahīśāsaka distinction of three kinds of skandhas (those which endure a single instant, those which last a lifetime, and those which remain until the end of saṃsāra), and the Sautrāntika theory of a "seed of goodness" that "leads to Nirvana, exists from time immemorial, never changes its nature, and abides with us in all our lives."[39]

"All these theoretical constructions," Conze concludes, "are attempts to combine the doctrine of 'not-self' with the almost instinctive belief in a 'self', empirical or true."[40]

[35] Edward Conze, *A Short History of Buddhism* (London: George Allen & Unwin, 1980), p. 36.

[36] Conze, *Buddhist Thought in India*, p. 128.

[37] Ibid., p. 123.

[38] Ibid., p. 131.

[39] Ibid., pp. 132-33.

[40] Ibid., p. 133.

In Aśoka's sermon about essence (sāra) it might at first seem that we have another such attempt, albeit in a much less theoretical and philosophical context. The notion of sāra clearly provides a basis for personal religious action and realization, while at the same time our text is careful not to deny the orthodox doctrine of anātman. There is one important difference, however, between sāra and these other theories. While they, for the most part, are attempts to respond to philosophical and psychological pressures for some sort of personal continuum from one life to another, sāra seeks to emphasize personal realization *in this lifetime*. Indeed, Aśoka's sermon to Yaśas makes it clear that one's essence does not transmigrate, that in fact it needs to be grasped here and now before it perishes at death. Rather than trying to provide an individual with a sense of personal continuity the notion of essence seeks to give him a sense of personal urgency in realizing Dharma.

Individual essence is thus not the self in disguise; it is rather the Dharma in the individual. In this sense, it is much more akin to the later Mahāyānist notions of the embryo of the Tathāgata (Tathāgatagarbha) inherent in all creatures, or the Dharma-element (Dharmadhātu) that is the "ultimate reality to be understood in enlightenment,"[41] the "omnipresent germ of Buddhahood which indwells all beings."[42]

These and other similar theories were all used "to emphasize the immanence of the Unconditioned. Just as within all material dharmas there is an element of space, so within all [beings] there is a Nirvana-nature. This is called 'the element of Dharma.' "[43] Or, as the *Ratnagotravibhāga* (one of the basic texts propounding the early Tathāgatagarbha theory) remarks:

[41] A. K. Warder, *Indian Buddhism* (Delhi: Motilal Banarsidass, 1970), p. 405.

[42] Conze, *Buddhist Thought in India*, p. 229.

[43] Ibid.

All beings are potentially Tathāgatas

....

If the Element of the Buddha did not exist (in everyone)
There could be no disgust with suffering
Nor could there be a wish for Nirvana
Nor striving for it, nor a resolve to win it.[44]

Philosophically speaking, of course, the doctrine of essence is much less sophisticated, much less developed than these other theories.[45] Aśoka, in his sermon to Yaśas, is not concerned with doctrine per se but with stressing the immediate possibilities of soteriological action. The notion of essence, then, should be seen in the context of Aśoka's larger enterprise: his use of good means to lead others to the Buddhist way.

At the same time, essence (like the Tathāgatagarbha and the Dharmadhātu) does not just dwell in the individual person, but in the entire world of appearances as well. It is thus also to be found in the midst of saṃsāra that, paradoxically, is itself characterized by essencelessness, that is, by non-self. Only those who can distinguish essence from non-essence can ever see this essence. Sāra, as our text has it, is "the essence of this world's essenceless constructs."[46]

Essence and Merit Making

The word "constructs" in our text is significant. It is a translation of the Sanskrit "yantra" which generally refers to any constructed, artificial instrument or device, and also de-

[44] Quoted in Edward Conze, ed., *Buddhist Texts through the Ages* (New York: Harper and Row, 1964), p. 181.

[45] For a detailed study of these doctrines, see David Seyforth Ruegg, *La théorie du Tathāgatagarbha et du gotra*, Publications de l'Ecole Française d'Extrême-Orient, vol. 70 (Paris: Ecole Française d' Extrême-Orient, 1969); and Jikido Takasaki, *A Study on the Ratnagotravibhāga* (Rome: Istituto Italiano per il Medio ed Estremo Oriente, 1966).

[46] Mukhopadhyaya, p. 73.

notes a "magical diagram" somewhat akin to a maṇḍala. Like a maṇḍala, it is essenceless in its outer aspect, but is constructed in such a way that it can contain within it an essence that can be found by the wise. In fact the word "maṇḍala" means an "enclosing of essence." As one etymology defines it: " '*Maṇḍa*' means essence (or 'pith', **sāra*, **hṛdaya*); '-la' means seizing that—thus 'seizing the essence' (*maṇḍala*)."[47]

All of this raises an important point: the body, or for that matter saṃsāra as a whole, is not a yantra or maṇḍala by nature; it has to be made into one. What the wise come to understand is the essence not of chaotic suffering but of a structured world whose form is in itself essenceless but encloses the potentiality for meaning.

We have so far been focussing on Aśoka's use of good means in making evident to various individuals the structure of saṃsāra so as to enable them to attain a liberating perspective, and we have traced this in terms of what might be called the cosmological dimension. At a more generalized level, it would appear from Aśoka's sermon to Yaśas that much the same thing can be accomplished by the individual himself by means of ordinary merit making activities. It is the wise, Aśoka declares, who manage to grasp their essence; but who are "the wise" in this context? They are not primarily the erudite scholars or the great meditators (although Aśoka would, of course, not doubt that they too understand Dharma). The "wise" are, rather, those who engage in formal, physical merit making activities:

> The wise in this world make merit
> by getting up, bowing down, and performing
> other acts of obeisance,
> relying on this most vile body,
> hoping for the essence.[48]

[47] Ferdinand D. Lessing and Alex Wayman, *Introduction to the Buddhist Tantrica Systems*, 2nd ed. (Delhi: Motilal Banarsidass, 1978), p. 270, n. 1.

[48] Mukhopadhyaya, p. 74.

This is a rather striking view. Essence is not primarily to be sought through the traditional practices of meditation or through the reflective pursuit of knowledge but through devotion and the ordinary practice of merit making. This does not mean that the body itself or this physical world is glorified. The wise merit makers know that the body is "most vile"; in itself, it is valueless, but its activities are absolutely necessary for religious realization. As our text put it: "Aśoka knew that although the body was even more worthless than ground-up eggshells mixed with sand, the rewards of prostration and other bodily acts of worship were greater than dominion for many aeons over the whole world."[49]

Of course, merit making and devotional activities, especially in Theravāda Buddhism, have often been seen as basically divorced from the quest for enlightenment. They result, we are told, only in karmic rewards and a happy rebirth. In his sermon to Yaśas, however, Aśoka makes it clear that these same activities can also lead to a real religious realization, an understanding in this lifetime of one's dharmalogical essence. This can happen, I would suggest, because acts of merit and devotion have the effect of restructuring the world in such a way that a dharmalogical realization can take place. This realization, of course, is not identical to attaining full enlightenment, but it is in the same dharmalogical dimension; it is a conversion or reconversion experience—an initial awakening to Dharma and a guarantee that one is on the right dharmalogical path. Thus, though doctrinally the individual's essence may resemble the Tathāgatagarbha or the Dharmadhātu, soteriologically, "grasping one's essence" is more akin to the Mahāyāna notion of the production of the thought of enlightenment (*bodhicitta*). This event, which marks the start of a bodhisattva's career, has as some of its necessary antecedents "faith, worship, prayer, . . . and other practices of piety and

[49] Ibid.

devotion."[50] Alternatively, in Hīnayāna terms, "grasping one's essence" might be said to correspond to the notion of "entering the stream" (*śrotāpanna*), the first of the four stages of religious development leading to arhatship, with the understanding, however, that essence is specifically connected to merit making and devotion.

For a fuller comprehension of this connection, it is useful to return, once again, to some of the tales of the *Avadānaśataka* that we touched on briefly in our discussion of Aśoka's gift of dirt. This anthology, as we have seen, is a collection of one hundred stories devoted primarily to illustrating the workings of merit. In it, a typical act of merit consists of several elements. First, it involves a simple physical offering or expression of devotion (the gift of a flower, prostration, etc.) that eventually, in a future lifetime, leads to some equally physical result (a particular kind of body, birth in a particular family, etc.). Secondly, as we have seen, it also involves the making of a praṇidhāna, a mental or verbal declaration of one's dharmalogical intent, and this, in a future lifetime, results in the attainment of enlightenment. This pattern, as we have shown, is the same as that of Aśoka's gift of dirt and may readily be analyzed in terms of the two dimensions of Buddhist religious activity we have been discussing, the rupalogical and the dharmalogical one.[51]

For the moment, however, let us focus on another aspect of the act of merit: the ways in which it, more immediately, has the effect of restructuring the world of the merit maker. It is a striking feature of the acts of merit performed in the *Avadānaśataka* that they are often accompanied by a magical transformation of the whole milieu in which they are taking place. Thus, for example, a simple, single lotus blossom piously

[50] Har Dayal, *The Bodhisattva Doctrine in Buddhist Sanskrit Literature* (orig. pub., 1932; rpt., Delhi: Motilal Banarsidass, 1975), p. 50.

[51] See the discussion above in Chapter Two, and also John Strong, "The Transforming Gift: An Analysis of Devotional Acts of Offering in Buddhist Avadāna Literature," *History of Religions* 18 (1979): 231-32.

offered to the Buddha, is suddenly pictured as becoming a huge flowery wheel that rises up into the air and crowns the figure of the Blessed One;[52] or a handful of blossoms given by a gardener is transformed immediately into a flowery pavilion that magically remains suspended in mid-air;[53] or a toothstick presented to the Buddha magically grows into a giant banyan tree in whose shade the merit maker then listens to the Dharma.[54] Even more spectacular, as we have seen, are the cases in which the act of merit occasions the Buddha's smile and its subsequent illumination not just of the immediate surroundings but of the whole cosmos from the highest heaven to the lowest hell.

These and other similar miracles are more than just signs of the power of faith; they also transform the whole setting of the act of merit, and thereby reorder the merit-maker's perception of his immediate surroundings and ultimately of the world as a whole. And with this new, larger perspective on things, he takes his first dharmalogical step and makes his praṇidhāna. This is then confirmed by the Buddha, who typically proceeds to make a prediction that the individual in question will indeed attain full enlightenment in such and such a future lifetime. From that point, the devotee is not only on the path, he is guaranteed to reach the goal, for strictly speaking the Buddha does not predict the future, he *sees* it.

An act of merit, then, when correctly carried out, is far more than a banal karmic deed. It can be a significant soteriological action that has immediate experiential effects and can lead, as Aśoka put it, to a realization of one's dharmalogical essence. Indeed, Aśoka himself claims, in the *Aśokā-*

[52] Vaidya, *Avadāna-śatakam*, pp. 18-19; cf. Léon Feer, tr., *Avadāna-çataka: cent légendes (bouddhiques)*, Annales du Musée Guimet, vol. 18 (Paris: E. Leroux, 1891), p. 42.

[53] Vaidya, *Avadāna-śatakam*, p. 1; cf. Feer, p. 25. On this flowery symbolism, see also John Strong, "Gandhakuṭī: The Perfumed Chamber of the Buddha," *History of Religions* 16 (1977): 394-95.

[54] Vaidya, *Avadāna-śatakam*, p. 73; cf. Feer, p. 109.

vadāna, to have attained just such an awareness. As he declares at one point to the elder Upagupta:

I have profited from the human condition I attained,
by making hundreds of offerings.
With the vacillating powers of royal sovereignty,
I have grasped the supreme essence.
I have ornamented this world with hundreds of caityas
resplendent as cumulus clouds.
In fulfilling today the Teaching of the peerless Master
have I not done the difficult to do?[55]

Conclusion

In this chapter, we have seen Aśoka operating in a number of different ways as a teacher and master of good means. In the absence of the Buddha, he functions as a cosmological kingpin who can provide Buddhist devotees with a greater realization of the structure of the world. He makes graphic for them in this-worldly human terms the nature of suffering in the various realms of rebirth. In a rather similar vein, he builds the eighty-four thousand stūpas and establishes the thirty-two sites of pilgrimage; these too are ways of ordering the world, although they use an alternative cosmological scheme, one which is based on the Buddha's body or on his biography rather than on the representation of the gatis.

In all of these examples, Aśoka is, so to speak, making maṇḍalas in this world of suffering so that saṃsāra can be seen for what it is. Thus his function, as Paul Mus has pointed out, is not to launch a direct attack against the realities of suffering, but rather to organize those realities, to structure saṃsāra in such a way that it is seen as the very stuff that is to be understood.[56]

At the same time, in his sermon to Yaśas and by his own

[55] Mukhopadhyaya, p. 92.
[56] Mus, *Barabuḍur*, 1:243.

example, Aśoka enjoins others to make their own maṇḍalas in the midst of saṃsāra, to structure their own world of suffering through the simple activities of merit making and devotion. In this way they too can come to a genuine dharmalogical realization.

Conspectus

The study of any religious text is as much an exploration of a world of meaning as it is a dissection of the meaning of words. We have in the first part of this book, tried to examine certain aspects of the world of meaning[1] of the *Aśokāvadāna.*

In Chapter One, we have seen how this world differs from that of the Sinhalese chronicles, and how it is rooted in the concerns of the Buddhist community of Mathurā and the Northwest. In Chapter Two, we have examined how its view of kingship modifies the full-blown mythic ideal of the cakravartin to present in Aśoka the picture of a balacakravartin, a monarch who "gets his hands dirty," who is suited to this day and age, but who nevertheless retains some of the mythic qualities of the king. In Chapter Three, we have looked at the relationship between this king and the Buddhist community of monks, and found him acting toward it in two ways: as a great munificent monarch so magnificent as to be closely associated with the figure of the Buddha, but also as an ordinary Buddhist layman routinely engaging in the support of the sangha. In Chapter Four, we then turned to examine the relationship between Aśoka and the Buddha, and discovered the way he establishes certain mesocosms (to use the term adopted from Mus) in which he could enjoy a religiously real relationship despite the fact of the parinirvāṇa. These mesocosms included most predominantly the eighty-four thousand stūpas and the thirty-two places of pilgrimage, but also such things as the Bodhi Tree and the aśoka tree. Finally, in Chapter Five, we have looked at the ways Aśoka sought to share with others his own Buddhist perspective by making relevant for them, in human terms, the sufferings of the different realms of re-

[1] I borrow this term from Joseph M. Kitagawa who has used it in the context of Japanese religions. See Joseph M. Kitagawa, "Some Reflections on the Japanese World of Meaning," *Journal of the Oriental Society of Australia* 11 (1976): 1-16.

birth, and by proposing merit making as a means of finding in this lifetime one's own dharmalogical essence.

If there is a common thematic thread running through all of these chapters, it is the following: the *Aśokāvadāna* constantly seeks solutions enabling it to maintain the ideals of the Buddhist tradition—the Buddha, the Dharma, the sangha, the cakravartin, the goal of enlightenment—while making these relevant to the ordinary Buddhist in his everyday religious activities.

Every religion, of course, must deal in some way with the basic problem of translating the absolute ideals it sets up into this-worldly realizable terms. But Buddhism in India potentially faced several difficulties in this regard. As we have seen, the Buddha, after his parinirvāṇa, was, at least in certain circles, considered to be truly transcendent, "out of this world." No further revelation could come from him, no contact could be made with him; how then could he remain a personage to be worshipped and revered here and now? (The answer of some Buddhists was that he could not, but this answer did not satisfy all parties.) Or again, the full-fledged cakravartin was given such truly mythic qualities that his reign could be seen (at least by some) as one reserved strictly for the Golden Age at the beginning of time. How then could he serve as a model for rule in this world? Or, the attainment of salvation (enlightenment) could be seen as so complex and full time an endeavor as to remain the exclusive preserve of monks and meditators. As some Buddhists put it: "No realization outside the monastery!"[2] How then could ordinary laypersons lead meaningful religious lives?

The *Aśokāvadāna*, in its own way, attempts to deal with all of these questions. With its mesocosms it seeks to recapture the presence of the Buddha in this world while not trespassing on the ontological otherness of his parinirvāṇa. With its portrayal of Aśoka's kingship, it manages to bring down to earth

[2] See Paul Mus, *Barabuḍur* 2 vols. (Hanoi: Imprimerie d'Extrême-Orient, 1935), 1:29.

and use effectively the cakravartin ideal. With its doctrine of essence, it seeks to connect, dharmalogically, practices such as merit making and soteriology, and thus to insure a meaningful religious lifestyle for the laity.

There were, of course, other Buddhist attempts to deal with these questions. It is tempting, for example, to find in the *Aśokāvadāna*'s solutions parallels to certain features of early Mahāyāna Buddhism. Indeed, we have had occasion to remark on a number of these throughout our study, and several scholars have not hesitated to attribute the rise of the Mahāyāna itself to just such developments as we have been looking at: the worship of stūpas, the importance of the laity, the use of good means, and the emphasis on cosmology and on the person of the Buddha.[3] It may even be possible to look upon the figure of Aśoka as pointing in the direction of the bodhisattva ideal.[4] Like the bodhisattva, Aśoka is a master of upāya; like the bodhisattva, he has a curious combination of personal striving for his own enlightenment and compassion for others; and like the bodhisattva, he has a somewhat ambiguous attitude toward saṃsāra; it is a most vile world full of suffering, but it is the only arena where enlightenment can take place. Thus Aśoka, like the bodhisattva, realizes that, in order to help sentient beings, he must address them within the saṃsāric context.

Such comparisons, however, should not make us forget that the *Aśokāvadāna* is technically a Hīnayānist text. Whether or not it is a Sarvāstivādin work, it clearly belongs to the Sanskritic Hīnayānist milieu of Northwest India, and we have, throughout these chapters, sought to ground our findings by

[3] See, for example, Akira Hirakawa, "The Rise of Mahāyāna Buddhism and its Relationship to the Worship of Stūpas," *Memoirs of the Research Department of the Toyo Bunko* 22 (1963): 57-106.

[4] For a fine discussion of the relationship of royal symbolism to the figure of the bodhisattva, see Paul Mus, "Le Buddha paré. Son origine indienne. Çākyamuni dans le mahāyānisme moyen," *Bulletin de l'Ecole Française d'Extrême-Orient* 28 (1928): 153-278.

reference to other avadānas and Sanskrit works from that milieu.

But perhaps it is wrong to worry about such categorizations. At the popular level, among the lay-oriented Buddhists whose interests the *Aśokāvadāna* addressed, these sectarian affiliations were of little concern. More important were the attraction of new converts, the reinforcement of the faith of established followers, and the encouragement of both devotion and donation. And all of this was best accomplished by the telling of popular, appealing stories about the religious exploits of others. Whatever else can be said about it, it is in this guise—as a good legend about a great king—that the *Aśokāvadāna* belongs to the whole of Buddhism.

PART TWO. THE LEGEND OF AŚOKA: A TRANSLATION OF THE *AŚOKĀVADĀNA*

Introduction to the Translation

The following translation of the Sanskrit text of the *Aśokāvadāna* is, as far as I know, the first one to be available in the English language. It is based on Sujitkumar Mukhopadhyaya's annotated edition of the text, *The Aśokāvadāna* (New Delhi: Sahitya Akademi, 1963). The most generally cited edition of the *Aśokāvadāna* used to be that found in E. B. Cowell and R. A. Neil, eds., *The Divyāvadāna* (Cambridge: University Press, 1886), where it occupies chapters 26-29 (pp. 348-434). This, in turn, was reedited in *devanāgarī* script in P. L. Vaidya, ed., *Divyāvadānam*, Buddhist Sanskrit Texts, no. 20 (Darbhanga [Bihar], 1959), pp. 216-82.

Mukhopadhyaya's edition differs from these older ones in the following ways: (1) It is based on a larger number of original manuscripts and so it corrects some of Cowell and Neil's errors, and lists virtually all known variants of the text. (2) It takes into account the Chinese versions of the text, especially the *A-yü wang chuan*. (3) Following the lead of the Chinese texts, it inverts the order of two of the four chapters of the Cowell and Neil edition. Thus, where Cowell and Neil (and Vaidya) place the legend of Kunāla (Kunālāvadāna) preceding that of Vītaśoka (Vītaśokāvadāna), Mukhopadhyaya reverses that order.

I have followed Mukhopadhyaya in this, but omitted his chapter headings, replacing them with titles of my own, and interspersing the text with additional subtitles for easier reading.

In one or two instances, I have preferred the reading of the Vaidya edition over that of Mukhopadhyaya, and have indicated these occasions in footnotes. Also, in a very few cases, for the sake of clarity, I have added a sentence or two on the basis of the Chinese text, or slightly rearranged the order of the Sanskrit. This too is indicated in notes.

Everywhere, I have translated prose as prose and verse as

verse, but have not tried to retain or imitate the meter of the latter. A number of words have been left untranslated. Some of these, such as cakravartin, balacakravartin, dharmarāja, dharmarājikā, have already been introduced in our discussion; others, such as añjali (a salutation consisting of cupping one's hands and bringing them to one's forehead), or yojana (a measure of distance, variously estimated to be somewhere between one and one half and nine miles), proved too clumsy to translate succinctly. In any case, all untranslated terms may be found in the glossary.

The numbers in the margin of the translation refer to the page numbers of the Mukhopadhyaya edition. These have been included for the convenience of those wishing to check the original text. Bracketed passages are my own interpolations for the sake of clarity. I have tried to keep these, as well as explanatory textual notes, at a minimum.

The Sanskrit text as we have it was probably composed sometime in the second century A.D. It was first translated into Chinese by Fa-ch'in circa 300. Although this translation has been given various titles, it is best known today as the *A-yü wang chuan* (Taisho Tripiṭaka No. 2042). It contains, in addition to those chapters corresponding to our Sanskrit text, several chapters no longer extant in the original: the legends of the different masters of the law, a chapter on the end of the Dharma, and a miscellaneous collection of additional stories about Aśoka. The latter have been summarized in the Appendix. The whole of the *A-yü wang chuan* has been rendered into French by Jean Przyluski in his *Légende de l'empereur Açoka*, pp. 225-427.

A somewhat different version of the text was translated in 512 by the monk Sanghabhara (Seng-ch'ieh-p'o-lo) as the *A-yü wang ching* (Taishō Tripiṭaka No. 2043). Its precise relationship to the *A-yü wang chuan* and to our Sanskrit text is a matter of some debate, and interested readers are referred to pp. xi-xiv of Przyluski's work.

There is no full Tibetan translation of the *Aśokāvadāna*,

although the chapter on Kunāla was rendered into that language in the eleventh century by Padmākaravarman and Rinchen bZangpo (see Mukhopadhyaya, p. lix).

In 1844, Eugène Burnouf translated much of the Sanskrit text of the *Aśokāvadāna* into French and included it in his *Introduction à l'histoire du buddhisme indien* (Paris: Adrien Maisonneuve, 1844; 2nd ed., 1876), pp. 319-85. (These pages were in turn rendered into English [without reference to the Sanskrit text] by Winifred Stevens as *Legends of Indian Buddhism* [London: John Murray, 1911].) There are a number of mistakes in Burnouf's work, but considering the state of buddhology in his time and the fact that he based his translation on the raw manuscripts of the text he had just received from Nepal, it was a remarkable achievement.

The text, as we have it in the Mukhopadhyaya edition, does not actually begin with the story of Aśoka. It starts rather with the legend of the elder Upagupta (pp. 1-28) which serves as a sort of prelude to the account of Aśoka's life, and which, as we have seen, is not unrelated to our understanding of the work as a whole.

The Legend of Aśoka

Prologue

1 [The Buddha] made sacrifices
with the flesh of his own body,[1]
and out of compassion practiced austerities
for the well-being of the world.
Good people, listen devotedly now
to what is being said,
so that his exertions may bear fruit.

"Thus have I heard. Once, when the Blessed One was dwelling in Śrāvastī . . ."[2] Thus a sūtra is to be spoken.

In the presence of our teachers for whom the mud-piles of passion, hatred, delusion, intoxication, arrogance, duplicity, and rascality have all been washed away by the flowing rain showers of the words of the Blessed Tathāgata, issued forth from his open cloud-like mouth; for whom the obscurantist teachings of the heretical treatises have been dispelled by the light of wisdom born from understanding the scholarly works on grammar, logic, and other subjects; who are themselves addicted to drinking the water of the most excellent true Dharma that cuts off the thirst for saṃsāra—in their presence, let us recall together a dharmic tale that brightens the minds of gods and men. It begins with the story of the elder Upagupta, the foremost of all the preachers, whose teaching was unmatched even by Śakra, Brahmā, Īśāna, Yama, Varuṇa, Kuvera, Vā-

[1] This undoubtedly is a reference to the Buddha's past lives, recounted in the *Jātaka*, in which he gave up his life and/or limbs for the sake of others.

[2] This formulaic line—the traditional opening sentence of Buddhist sūtras—seems to have been introduced here to give the impression that the *Aśokāvadāna* is indeed a sūtra. This, in fact, is boldly (and rather unusually) stated to be the case in the next sentence. Although the *Aśokāvadāna* was classified as a sūtra in certain Sanskrit Buddhist circles, it, of course, cannot be thought of as literally being the word of the Buddha. This appears to be recognized in the next paragraph which attributes what follows to the teachers (gurus).

sava, Soma, Aditi, and the other gods, a hero sweeping away the pride of Kandarpa [Kāma], a magnanimous being with very great supernatural powers. Listen, then, to the teachers with attentive ears.

Upagupta's Past Life

2 It is said that when the Blessed One, around the time of his parinirvāṇa, had converted the nāga Apalāla, the potter, the outcaste woman, and Gopālī, he reached the city of Mathurā. There he spoke to the Venerable Ānanda: "Ānanda, right here in Mathurā, one hundred years after my parinirvāṇa, there will be a perfumer named Gupta. He will have a son named Upagupta, a Buddha without the marks, who, in those days, will carry on the work of a Buddha. Through his teaching, many monks will rid themselves of all their defilements and experience arhatship—[so many that] they will fill up a cave eighteen cubits long and twelve cubits wide with their tally-sticks (śalākā) four inches in length. Furthermore, Ānanda, this same monk Upagupta will be the foremost of all my disciples who are preachers.

"Ānanda, do you see over there that dark line on the horizon?"

"Yes, your reverence."

"That, Ānanda, is the mountain called Urumuṇḍa. There, one hundred years after the parinirvāṇa of the Tathāgata, a monk called Śāṇakavāsin will build a monastery and initiate Upagupta into the monastic life. Moreover, Ānanda, in Mathurā, there will be two guild masters, the brothers Naṭa and
3 Bhaṭa. They will build a monastery on Mount Urumuṇḍa; it will be known as the Naṭabhaṭika, and will be the best of all my forest hermitages where the beds and seats are conducive to meditation."

Then the Venerable Ānanda said to the Blessed One: "Your reverence, it is marvellous that the Venerable Upagupta will do such things for the benefit of many people!"

The Blessed One replied: "This is not the only time, Ānanda; in a previous life too, in a body that is now no more, Upagupta worked right here for the benefit of many people. At that time [various beings lived on each of] the three slopes of Mount Urumuṇḍa: five hundred pratyekabuddhas dwelt together in one place, five hundred ṛṣis (brahmanical ascetics) in another, and five hundred monkeys in a third. One day, the leader of the five hundred monkeys left his band and went to the mountainside where the five hundred pratyekabuddhas were living. As soon as he saw those pratyekabuddhas, his faith was engendered. He made an offering of withered leaves, roots, and fruits to them, and, when they sat down cross-legged in meditation, he prostrated himself in front of the eldest members of the group, and then went to where the novices were and sat down cross-legged himself.

"Before long, the pratyekabuddhas attained parinirvāṇa. The monkey [again] presented withered leaves, roots, and fruits to them, but, of course, they did not accept them. He pulled at the folds of their robes, and grabbed their feet, [but they did not move]. Finally, he thought to himself 'Surely they have passed away,' and, full of sorrow, he lamented and went to the other side of the mountain where the five hundred ṛṣis were dwelling.

4 "Now some of these ṛṣis had couches of thorns, and others had beds of ashes; some were standing holding their hands aloft, and others were practicing the penance of the five fires.[3] The monkey began to disrupt their various ascetic performances; he pulled out the thorns of the couches of thorns, he scattered the ashes of the beds of ashes, he caused those whose hands were raised to lower them, and he put out the fires of those sitting between five fires. Then, when he had thus disrupted their ascetic performance, he assumed a cross-legged posture in front of them.

"In time, the ṛṣis reported all of this to their teacher; he

[3] An ascetic practice consisting of sitting between four fires built in the four cardinal directions, with the fifth fire, the sun, blazing above.

told them also to assume a cross-legged position. Accordingly, those five hundred ascetics sat down cross-legged, and, without a preceptor or an instructor, they understood the dharmas that are the thirty-seven aids to enlightenment, and experienced pratyekabodhi.[4] They then reflected: 'This most excellent thing that we have attained is all due to this monkey.' So they provided the monkey with ample roots and fruits, and, when his time came, they cremated his body with fragrant wood.

"Now what do you think, Ānanda? The one who was the leader of this band of five hundred monkeys, he is this very Upagupta. Even then, in a body that is now no more, he worked for the benefit of many people, right here on Mount Urumuṇḍa. So too, in a life to come, one hundred years after my parinirvāṇa, he will work for the benefit of many people in this same spot." And just so, we will illustrate it.

The Śāṇakavāsin Episode

5 When the elder Śāṇakavāsin had built his monastery on Mount Urumuṇḍa, he focussed his mind on [the question of] whether or not Gupta, the perfume merchant, had yet been born; and he saw that he had.[5] He then focussed his mind on [the question of] whether or not his son Upagupta—a Buddha without the marks who, it was foretold, would carry out the work of a Buddha one hundred years after the parinirvāṇa—had been born; and he saw that he had *not*.

Now eventually, through skillful means, Gupta the perfumer came to be favorably disposed toward the Teaching of the Blessed One. One day, after this had happened, the elder

[4] The thirty-seven *bodhipakṣadharma* are qualities characterizing or contributing to enlightenment and are often referred to in Buddhist sources. One of the characteristics of pratyekabuddhas is that they attain enlightenment on their own, without the direct assistance of an instructor or master.

[5] It is understood that he "focusses his mind" (samanvāharati) with the aid of his meditative powers.

Śāṇakavāsin went to his house along with many monks; then, on another day, he went there with only one other monk; and, on a third day, he went there all alone.

When Gupta saw that the elder Śāṇakavāsin was all by himself, he asked:

"How is it that the Noble One has no attendant?"

"Why," replied the elder, "should we, who are subject to old age, have any attendants? If someone, moved by faith, should be initiated into the monastic life, then he would truly be an attendant and a follower of ours."

6 "Noble One," said the perfume merchant, "I have always been greedy for the householder's life and taken delight in the field of the senses; it is not possible for me to be initiated into the monastic life. However, when I have a son, I will give him to your lordship as an attendant."

"So be it, my child," said the elder, "but you should remember this firm promise."

Now eventually a son was born to Gupta the perfumer, and he was given the name "Aśvagupta." When he had grown, the elder Śāṇakavāsin went to Gupta and said: "My child, you promised that when you had a son, you would offer him to us as an attendant. Now this son has been born to you; give your consent, and I will initiate him into the monastic life."

"Noble One," said the perfumer, "this is my only son. Please exempt him. I will have another, a second son, and will give him to your lordship as an attendant."

Then the elder Śāṇakavāsin focussed his mind [on the question] "Is this boy Upagupta?" And seeing that it was not, he declared: "So be it."

After some time, a second son was born to Gupta the perfumer, and he was given the name "Dhanagupta." And again, when he had grown, the elder Śāṇakavāsin said to Gupta: "My child, you promised that when you had a son, you would offer him to us as an attendant. Now this son has been born to you; give your consent, and I will initiate him into the monastic life."

"Noble One," said the perfumer, "please exempt him. My eldest son will go gathering goods abroad; this second one will have to assure the protection at home. However, I will have a third son, and he will be given to your lordship."

7 Then the elder Śāṇakavāsin focussed his mind [on the question] "Is this boy Upagupta?" And seeing that it was not, he said: "So be it."

Finally, Gupta the perfumer had a third son. He was pleasing, handsome, amiable, surpassing men in appearance, and almost resembling a divinity. And when his full birth ceremonies had been carried out, he was given the name "Upagupta." When he too had grown, the elder Śāṇakavāsin went to the perfumer and said: "My child, you promised that when you had a third son, you would offer him to us as an attendant. This third son of yours has now been born; give your consent, and I will initiate him into the monastic life."

"Noble One," said Gupta the perfumer, "it is agreed. When, [as they say], 'there will be neither profit nor loss,' then I will grant him leave."

Some time after this agreement had been made, it happened that Māra filled the whole city of Mathurā with a [foul] odor. All the citizens of the town consequently bought perfumes from Upagupta, and he sold a great many. The elder Śāṇakavāsin then went to Upagupta who was selling perfumes in the perfume bazaar where he conducted business honestly.[6] The elder addressed him: "My child, how are the mental states of your mind—defiled or undefiled?"

8 "Noble One," replied Upagupta, "I don't even know which kind of mental states are defiled and which kind are undefiled."

Śāṇakavāsin said: "My child, if you are able to comprehend fully a single thought, you will overcome this obstacle." Then

[6] Literally, "he did business according to Dharma (dharmeṇa)."

he gave him some black and some white strips of cloth, and instructed him as follows: "If a defiled thought arises, put aside a black strip, but if an undefiled thought arises, put aside a white one. Meditate upon impurity and foster the recollection of the Buddha."

Now, until undefiled mental states began coming to him [regularly], he put aside two pieces of black cloth for every one of white. After a while, however, he was putting aside half black and half white strips. Then, he was putting aside two pieces of white cloth for every one of black; and, eventually, all of his thoughts became pure and he put aside white strips of cloth only. He did business according to Dharma.

The Story of Vāsavadattā

Now in Mathurā, there was a courtesan named Vāsavadattā. One day, her servant girl happened to go to Upagupta to purchase some perfumes. And [when she had returned], Vāsavadattā said to her: "Dear girl, you must have robbed that merchant; you bring back so many perfumes!"[7]

"Mistress," replied the girl, "Upagupta, the perfumer's son—
9 an altogether handsome man of perfect cleverness and charm—
does business honestly!" When Vāsavadattā heard this, she developed an amorous longing for Upagupta, and she sent her servant girl to him announcing that she would come to him, for she wished to pursue pleasure with him. But when the servant girl communicated this to Upagupta, he only replied that it was not yet time for her to see him.

Now Vāsavadattā['s price] was five hundred pieces of gold. It occurred to her that Upagupta was unable to pay this amount,

[7] Perfumers in ancient India were apparently known for their disreputable practices. P. K. Gode cites a sarcastic passage from the *Pañcatantra* as evidence: "Of all trades, the trade of perfumer is the best; other trades like those of dealers in gold, etc., are of no avail. In the case of the trade in cosmetics and perfumes, what one purchases for one (rupee) can be sold for one hundred (rupees)." See "Indian Science of Cosmetics and Perfumery," *The International Perfumer* 3 (1951): 1.

so she sent her servant back again saying that she did not intend to receive even a penny from her lord; she only wanted to pursue pleasure with him. But when the servant girl communicated this to Upagupta, he again replied that it was not yet time for her to see him.

Some time later, the son of a certain guildmaster was staying with Vāsavadattā, when a caravaneer, who had captured five hundred horses and brought them for sale from the North country, arrived in Mathurā. "Which courtesan," he wanted to know, "is the best of all?" He was told that it was Vāsavadattā. So, taking five hundred pieces of gold and many presents, he set out for her house. [Hearing that he was coming], and moved by greed, Vāsavadattā [quickly] had the guildmaster's son beaten up and thrown out onto the dungheap; she then pursued her pleasure with the caravaneer.

10 The guildmaster's relatives, however, [found out about this]. They rescued the son from the dungheap, and reported the matter to the king. And the king ordered his men to go [and arrest] Vāsavadattā, to cut off her hands, feet, nose, and ears, and leave her on the cremation ground. They did so.

Now when Upagupta heard that Vāsavadattā had been abandoned on the cremation ground with her hands, feet, nose, and ears cut off, this thought occurred to him: "Previously she wished to see me for sensual reasons, but now her hands, feet, nose, and ears have been cut off; this is the time to see her." And he said:

When her body was covered with excellent clothes
and bedecked with variegated ornaments,
then it was better for those who have turned away
from rebirth, and are set on liberation,
not to see her.
But now that she has lost her pride,
her passion and her joy,
and has been wounded with sharp swords—
this is the time to see her form
in its true intrinsic nature.

Then, accompanied by a single servant carrying a parasol, he went to the cremation ground, tranquil, and observing the practices of a religious mendicant.

Now Vāsavadattā's servant girl, out of appreciation for her mistress's past virtues, had remained close to her, and was chasing away the crows and other carrion birds. [When she saw Upagupta coming] she said to Vāsavadattā:

11 "My lady, that Upagupta to whom you sent me again and again has arrived; surely, he must have come impelled by passion and desire."

When Vāsavadattā heard this, she said:

How will he have any passion or desire
when he sees me on the ground,
red with blood, my lustre gone,
afflicted by suffering?

And she told her servant to gather the hands, feet, nose, and ears that had been cut from her body, and to cover them with a piece of cloth. Upagupta then arrived and stood in front of Vāsavadattā. Seeing him standing there, Vāsavadattā said: "My lord, when my body was uninjured and well-disposed for sensual pleasure, I sent a servant girl to you again and again, but you only said: 'Sister, it is not yet time for you to see me.' Now my hands and feet and ears and nose have been cut off, and I sit in the mire of my own blood. Why have you come now?"

And she added:

When this body of mine was fit to be seen,
soft like the womb of a lotus,
and bedecked with costly garments and jewels,
then I, the unfortunate one, did not meet you.
Why have you come here to see me now
that my body is unfit to be looked at,
plastered with mud and blood, causing fear,
having lost its wonder, joy, pleasure, and play?

Upagupta replied:

Sister, I have not come to you impelled by desire,
but have come to see the intrinsic nature
of desires and impurities.
When you were covered with clothes, ornaments,
and all the other variegated externals
conducive to passion,
those who looked at you
could not see you as you truly are,
even when they made the effort.
12 But now, free from outer trappings,
your form may be seen in its intrinsic nature.
Unlearned and wicked are those who take pleasure
in this gross living carcass.
Who would, how could, anyone feel attracted
to a body that is held together with skin,
encircled by blood, covered with hide,
plastered with lumps of flesh, and surrounded
on all sides by a thousand muscles and veins?

Furthermore, sister:

Seeing forms that are beautiful on the outside,
a fool is attracted to them.
Knowing them to be corrupt on the inside,
a steady man remains indifferent.
A corpse that is clearly vile is impure;
what is pure is the suppression of desire
by one who has desires but knows what is good.

Truly now:

A foul odor is covered up by various perfumes
which themselves are piles of impurity.
A change may be brought about externally
by ornaments and garments and other things,
and impurities such as sweat, moisture, and dirt

can be washed away with water.
In this way, this foul impure skeleton
is cherished by those whose essence is desire.
But those who abandon the desires
that engender weariness, sorrow, and suffering,
and that are always despised by the good,
and who go out to a tranquil wood,
with their minds free from the causes of desire,
and who cross to the other shore
of the great ocean of becoming,
taking refuge in the boat that is the path—
they are the ones who hear and carry out
the word of the Fully Enlightened One
who is mild in speech.

13 Upon hearing this, Vāsavadattā became terrified of saṃsāra. Her heart was humbled by the recollection of the virtues of the Buddha, and she said:

All of this is just as the wise one says.
Since I have met you, may it please you
that I should hear the word of the Buddha.

Upagupta, therefore, preached to her a step-by-step discourse,[8] and then exposed to her the Truths. And coming to an understanding of the inherent nature of Vāsavadattā's body, he himself became disgusted with the realm of desire, and, from this clear understanding of the Truth that came with his own preaching of the Dharma, he attained the fruit of a non-returner; and Vāsavadattā attained the fruit of entering the stream.[9]

[8] The step-by-step discourse (pūrvakālakaraṇīyā kathā) consisted of preliminary stories dealing with such topics as dāna (donation), *śīla* (morality), and *svarga* (heaven), that Buddhist preachers used to catch their audience's interest and prepare them for the teaching of the Dharma proper. It thus corresponds to the first three sections of the "graduated discourse" (*anupūrvikathā*), well known in canonical sources. See Etienne Lamotte, *Histoire du bouddhisme indien* (Louvain: Institut Orientaliste, 1958), p. 84.

[9] A non-returner (*anāgāmin*) will never be reborn again as a man but will

When Vāsavadattā perceived the Truths, she said in gratitude to Upagupta:

Thanks to you, the truly fearful path
to the lower states of rebirth,
that is yoked to many sorrows,
has been shut for me.
The very meritorious realm of heaven is open
and I have reached the path to nirvāṇa.

14 "And now I [wish to] take refuge in the Blessed Tathāgata, the completely enlightened saint, and in the Dharma, and in the community of monks." And she said:

I go for refuge to the Jina whose eye is as dazzlingly bright
as a fresh lotus blossom newly opened,
and who is attended by immortals and sages;
and I go for refuge to the dispassionate sangha.

Now, when Upagupta had finished instructing Vāsavadattā with dharmic discourses, he departed. Soon thereafter, Vāsavadattā died and was reborn among the gods, and in Mathurā, the deities proclaimed: "Having heard the Dharma preached by Upagupta, Vāsavadattā perceived the Noble Truths. Now that she is dead, she has arrived in heaven." And when the residents of Mathurā heard this, they, as a group, paid homage to the body of Vāsavadattā.

Upagupta's Ordination

Then the elder Śāṇakavāsin went to Gupta the perfumer and said: "Give your consent, and I will initiate Upagupta into the monastic life."

"Noble One," replied Gupta, "this was the agreement: 'When

attain arhatship in this life. One who has "entered the stream" (*śrotāpanna*) has seen the Truth of the Buddhist path and will attain arhatship after several more rebirths.

there will be neither profit nor loss, then I will give my permission.' "

The elder Śāṇakavāsin, therefore, by means of his magical powers, set it up so that there was neither profit nor loss. Gupta counted, and weighed, and measured, but he could find neither profit nor loss. The elder Śāṇakavāsin then told him: "Truly, the Blessed Buddha made a prediction concerning your son; he said that one hundred years after his parinirvāṇa, he would carry out the work of a Buddha; allow me to initiate him into the monastic life!" And, at last, Gupta the perfumer granted his permission.

The elder Śāṇakavāsin then took Upagupta to the Naṭabhaṭika forest hermitage, carried out the formal ordination ceremony, and made him a monk. And Upagupta, ridding himself of all the defilements, experienced arhatship.

Then the elder Śāṇakavāsin said: "Upagupta, my child, the Blessed One made a prediction about you. He said that one hundred years after his parinirvāṇa there would be a monk named Upagupta, a Buddha without the marks, who would carry out the work of a Buddha, and who would be the foremost of his disciples who are preachers. Therefore, my child, work for the well-being of the Teaching."

Upagupta replied: "So be it."

Upagupta and Māra

Soon thereafter, he was asked to preach at a Dharma meeting; and the word spread throughout Mathurā that, on that day, a Buddha without the marks named Upagupta would expose the Dharma. And hearing this, several hundred thousand persons set out.

The elder Upagupta then entered into meditation and examined the matter of how the assembly of the Tathāgata had customarily been seated. He perceived that that assembly sat down in the shape of a half-moon. Next, he contemplated the way the Tathāgata had preached the Dharma, and he perceived that the Buddha made an exposition of the Truth after giving a step-by-step discourse. Therefore, he too preached a step-by-step discourse, and then began to expose the Truth.

Just then, however, Māra caused a shower of strings of
pearls to rain down on the assembly; and the minds of those
who were about to be converted became agitated [by greed],
16 and not one of them came to see the Truth. The elder Upagupta
carefully considered the matter of who was causing this disturbance, and he perceived that it was Māra.

Then, on the second day, a very large number of men arrived in Mathurā, thinking "Upagupta preaches the Dharma and strings of pearls come down in a shower!" And again, on that day, just when Upagupta had finished the step-by-step discourse and was beginning to expose the Truth, Māra caused a shower of gold to rain down on the assembly; the minds of those who were about to be converted were agitated, and not one of them came to see the Truth. Once more, the elder Upagupta carefully considered the matter of who was causing this disturbance, and he perceived it was Māra being even more wicked.

Then, on the third day, an even larger number of men came out, thinking "Upagupta preaches the Dharma and showers of pearls or gold fall down!" And again, on that day, he had finished the step-by-step discourse and had just started to expose the Truths, when, not very far off, Māra began a theatrical performance; heavenly instruments were played and divine apsāras started to dance, and the once dispassionate crowd of men, seeing the divine forms and hearing the heavenly sounds, was drawn away by Māra.

Māra was so pleased that he had attracted Upagupta's as-
17 sembly to himself, that he hung a garland around the elder's
neck. Upagupta then focussed his mind [on the question] "Who
is this?" And he perceived that it was Māra. Then he reflected:
"This Māra causes a lot of disturbance to the Teaching of the
Blessed One; why was he not converted by the Buddha?" And

he realized: "He is to be converted by me; it was with reference to his conversion, and as a favor to all beings, that the Blessed One predicted that I should become a Buddha without the marks!"

Upagupta, therefore, focussed his mind [on the question] of whether or not the time for Māra's conversion had arrived, and he perceived that it had come. He took, therefore, three carcasses—a dead snake, a dead dog, and a dead human being—and, by means of his magical powers, he transformed them into a garland of flowers and went up to Māra. When Māra saw him [and the flowers], he was delighted and thought that he had won over even Upagupta. He resumed, therefore, his own bodily form, so that Upagupta could garland him personally. Then the elder crowned him with the snake carcass, and hung the dead dog around his neck, and the human corpse over his ears, and taking hold of them, he said:

Just as you, sir, have bedecked me with a garland,
which is inappropriate for a man who is a monk,
so I have bound around you these carcasses,
which are unfit for a man of desires.
18 Show whatever powers you have,
but today you have encountered a son of the Buddha.
Even when the water of the ocean surges up,
its swollen waves blown by the wind,
it still loses its force
in the caverns of Mount Malaya.

Now Māra started to try to take off one of the carcasses; but, as he had entered into it personally, he was not able to remove it, just as an ant cannot lift up a great mountain. Indignant, he rose up into the air and said:

If I myself am not able to remove
this dog's carcass from around my neck,
the other gods, whose power is greater
than mine, will release me!

The elder said:

Go seek refuge in Brahmā or Indra,
enter the blazing fire or the sea,
but this carcass fixed around your neck
will neither get dried out or wet,
nor will it ever break.

Māra went to Mahendra, to Rudra, to Upendra, to the Lord
of Riches; to Yama, Varuṇa, Kubera, and Vasāva, and to the
19 other gods as well, but he did not achieve his purpose. Finally,
he went to Brahmā. The latter said: "Pass me by, my child,
for

Who can break the bounds
that the disciple of the Daśabala himself
has set with his magical powers?
They are like the limit of the ocean;
it would be easier to bind and uproot
the Himālayas with ropes of lotus stalk
than for men to remove the dead dog
that is fastened around your neck.
Granted, my power is great,
but even so I am no match
for the son of the Tathāgata.
There is, without a doubt, some brilliance
in the light of the planets,
but it is not like that which is
in the fiery disk of the sun.

Māra said: "What then do you recommend? Whom shall I turn to now?"

Brahmā replied:

Go quickly and take refuge in Upagupta.
It was after encountering him that you fell
from the heights of your magical power,
fame, and happiness.

As they say, "One who has fallen on the ground
must support himself on the ground
in order to stand up again."

When Māra realized how much power the disciple of the Tathāgata had, he reflected:

The power of the Buddha must be immeasurable,
if Brahmā so reveres the Teaching
of one of his disciples!
The Holy One could have inflicted
any punishment he wanted to on me,
but he did not do so, out of forbearance.
Instead, he spared me!

But why say more?

Today, I have discovered how greatly compassionate
is the Sage who is exceedingly kind.
His mind is free from all oppressions
and his lustre is like that of a mountain of gold.
Blind with delusion, I harassed him
again and again with all sorts of schemes.
Nevertheless, not once did that Mighty One
so much as utter an unkind word to me.

Then Māra, the lord of the Realm of Desire, realized that, for him, Upagupta was the only way out [of his predicament]. Thus, he gave up all [his attempts to free himself], sought out the elder, fell at his feet, and said: "Reverend sir, you well know the hundreds of wicked things I did to the Blessed One at the Tree of Enlightenment and elsewhere:

When Gautama came to me
at a mansion in a Brahmin village,
I made him go without any food at all;
even so he did nothing unkind to me.
And when I took on the form of a carter,
and when I became a bull,

and when I raised myself up like a snake,
I tormented the Lord;
but he never harmed me.
21 You, on the other hand, O great one,
must have abandoned your innate compassion,
for today you ridicule me
in the worlds of gods, asuras, and men."

The elder said:

Evil One, how can you,
without even considering the matter,
refer to a disciple [śrāvaka] in terms
of the great virtues of the Tathāgata?
How can you equate Mount Meru
with a mustard seed, the sun
with a firefly, the ocean
with a handful of water?
The Buddha's compassion for living beings
is exceptional, my friend; a disciple
does not have great compassion.

Furthermore:

I now clearly perceive the reason for which
the Blessed One spared you in spite of your faults.

Māra said:

Tell me, tell me what was the intent
of the Glorious One who patiently kept
his vows to cut off attachment,
whom I, in my delusion, constantly tormented,
yet who always looked upon me
with thoughts of loving kindness?

22 The elder replied: "Listen, my friend, you are guilty of many offenses against the Blessed One. There is only one way to

wash away your demerits: faith in the Tathāgata, who alone can cut them out.

This is why the farseeing Sage
never said anything unkind to you,
but addressed you only with pleasant words.
By this reasoning, that man of highest wisdom
engendered devotion in your heart.
Truly, even a little devotion toward him
gives the fruit of nirvāṇa to the wise.
In short, all the wicked things that you did to the Sage,
when your mind was blind with delusion,
have now been washed away by the abundant waters
of faith that have entered your heart."

Now Māra, his hairs quivering like the buds of a kadamba tree, prostrated himself fully [in front of Upagupta] and said:

It is true, I pestered him in many ways,
and before he was successful [in attaining enlightenment,
I tempted him] with desires
for success here on earth.
But that most excellent of ṛṣis
overlooked all this, the way a kind father
does the offence of a son.

23 Then, with a mind filled with faith in the Blessed One, Māra recollected for a long time the virtues of the Buddha. He fell at Upagupta's feet and said:

Today you did me the very greatest favor,
when you introduced me to the venerability
of the Buddha.
But, out of loving kindness, do now release me
from this ornament of a great sage's anger
that is still hanging around my neck!

Upagupta replied: "I will release you on one condition."
"What condition?" asked Māra.

"First," said the elder, "from this day forth, you will no longer harass the monks."

Māra said: "I will not do so. What else do you command?"

"That," replied the elder, "was my command with regard to the Teaching, now I shall tell you about another duty of yours."

"Be gracious, elder," Māra replied nervously, "what is your command?"

"You yourself know," answered Upagupta, "that I was initiated into the monastic life one hundred years after the Blessed One entered parinirvāṇa, therefore:

I have already seen the Dharma-body
but I have not seen the physical body
of the Lord of the Triple World,
who resembles a mountain of gold.
Thus, in return for this "very greatest favor,"
[I want you] to make manifest here
the physical form of the Buddha.
Truly, nothing would be more pleasing to me
than this, for I am eager [to see]
the body of the Daśabala."

"Very well," said Māra, "but listen also to my conditions:

When you, all at once, look upon me
wearing the costume of a Buddha,
do not prostrate yourself out of respect
for the qualities of the Omniscient One.
24 If you show even a little reverence toward me,
your mind tender from the recollection of the Buddha,
I will be consumed by fire, O mighty one.
Do I have the power to endure
the prostration of one whose passions are gone?
I am like the sprouts of the eranda tree
that cannot bear the weight of an elephant's trunk."

"So be it," said the elder, "I will not bow down before you."

"Then wait a bit," said Māra, "while I enter the forest.

Previously determined to deceive Śūra,[10]
I created, out of the power of the incomparable Buddha,
a Buddha body that had
the lustre of fired gold.
I will now create that same body,
that brings joy to the eyes of men,
and, with its spread-out nimbus,
forms a shining net of rays like the sun."

Upagupta agreed to this and removed the carcasses [from Māra's neck]; he then stood by, anxiously waiting for the sight of the form of the Tathāgata. Then Māra, after he had gone far into the forest and [magically] taken on the form of the Buddha, emerged again from that wood like an actor wearing a bright costume.

Indeed, it is said:

Making manifest the Tathāgata's body,
which abounds with the highest marks
and brings tranquility to the eyes of men,
he ornamented that forest,
as though unveiling the fresh colors
of a valuable painting.

Now when he had fashioned the form of the Blessed One, adorned with a pure fathom-wide nimbus, [Māra also magically created the forms of] the elder Śāriputra on the Buddha's right, and the elder Mahāmaudgalyāyana on his left, and the Venerable Ānanda behind him, his hands busy with the Buddha's bowl. And he also created the forms of the other great disciples, starting with the elders Mahākāśyapa, Aniruddha, and Subhūti; and he made manifest the figures of thirteen

[10] A reference to the story of Māra's tricking the layman Śūra. See Edouard Huber, tr. *Aśvaghoṣa Sūtrālaṃkāra* (Paris: E. Leroux, 1908), pp. 230-36.

hundred fifty monks gathered in a half-moon around the Buddha. Then Māra approached the elder Upagupta, and Upagupta rejoiced, thinking "this is what the form of the Buddha looks like!" With a joyful heart, he quickly rose from his seat, and exclaimed:

Woe! Woe to that pitiless impermanence
that cuts off forms with qualities such as these!
For the Great Sage's body which is like this
has been touched by impermanence
and has suffered destruction.

Then, with his mind so intent on the contemplation of the Buddha that he came to think he was seeing the Blessed One, Upagupta drew near to that appearance; he made an añjali similar to the bud of a lotus, and exclaimed: "Ah! The splendid form of the Blessed One! What more can be said?

For his face surpasses the red lotus
[in beauty], his eyes the blue lotus,
his splendor a forest of flowers,
the pleasantness of his mind
the moon in its full brilliance.
He is deeper than the great ocean,
more stable than Mount Meru,
and fierier than the sun.
His gait excels the lion's,
his gentle gaze the bull's,
and his color gold."

Then Upagupta's heart was filled with joy to an even greater measure, and he exclaimed:

Oh! Sweet is the fruit of acts
that are pure in their intention.
By karma was this body made,
not by power or by accident.

26 By giving, patience, meditation,
wisdom, and restraint,
this arhat has purified that which was produced
by [the acts of] body, speech, and mind,
during innumerable koṭis
of thousands of aeons.
In this way he produced this pure form
that is pleasing to the eyes of men.
Even an enemy would be greatly delighted by it,
how much more so someone like me!

Then Upagupta, because of his affection for the Wholly Enlightened One, forgot his agreement [with Māra], and thinking that this image *was* the Buddha, he fell at Māra's feet with his whole body, like a tree cut off at the root. This worried Māra who said: "Please, reverend sir, please! Do not transgress our agreement!"

"What agreement?" said the elder.

"Did your reverence not promise," asked Māra, "that he would not bow down before me?"

At that, the elder Upagupta got up off the ground, and said with a stammering voice: "You, Evil One!

Of course, I know that the Best of Speakers
has gone altogether to extinction,
like a fire swamped by water.
Even so, when I see his figure,
which is pleasing to the eye,
I bow down before that Sage.
But I do not revere you!

"How is it," asked Māra, "that I am not revered when you thus bow down before me?"

"I shall tell you," said the elder, "how it is that I did not revere you at all, and committed no violation of our agreement.

27 Just as men bow down
to clay images of the gods,
knowing that what they worship
is the god and not the clay,
so I, seeing you here,
wearing the form of the Lord of the World,
bowed down to you,
conscious of the Sugata,
but not conscious of Māra."

Then Māra made the form of the Buddha disappear, did obeisance to the elder Upagupta, and departed. And on the fourth day, he personally began to ring a bell in Mathurā, proclaiming: "Whoever among you desires the bliss of heaven and release, let him listen to the Dharma preached by the elder Upagupta! And let those of you who never saw the Tathāgata look upon the elder Upagupta!"

And he added:

All those who wish to abandon poverty,
that is the root of calamity,
[and to attain] prosperity,
and ample splendor here below,
and those whose desire is for heaven and release,
listen with faith to the Dharma
preached by this one.
And those who have not seen
the greatly compassionate Teacher,
the self-established foremost of men,
look upon the elder Upagupta as the Teacher,
a shining lamp in the three realms of existence.

Then the word spread throughout Mathurā that Māra had been converted by the elder Upagupta; and when the citizens of the town heard this, almost all of them went as a group to Upagupta. Then, when many hundreds of thousands of Brahmins had assembled, the elder, fearless as a lion, mounted the lion's throne.

As it is said:

28 It is impossible, they say,
for an ignorant man to ascend the lion's throne;
for he who merely sits on that seat
becomes timid like a deer.
But he who roars out like a lion
in order to destroy the arrogance
of differing philosophers,
he is a lion among speakers,
and is fit to mount the lion's throne.

Then the elder Upagupta preached a step-by-step discourse and exposed the Truths. And upon hearing [his Teaching], many hundreds of thousands of living beings planted roots of merit conducive to liberation. Some attained the fruit of non-returner, and others the fruit of once-returning, and still others the fruit of stream entering. Finally, eighteen thousand persons were initiated into the monastic order, and all of them, disciplining themselves, soon attained arhatship.

Now there was, on Mount Urumuṇḍa, a cave eighteen cubits long and twelve cubits wide; and Upagupta said to those who had accomplished what they had to: "Let all those who rid themselves of the defilements and experience arhatship through my Teaching throw into the cave a tally-stick four inches in length." And on that same day, eighteen thousand arhats threw their tally-sticks [into the cave], and Upagupta's fame spread as far as the ocean. The Blessed One predicted that in Mathurā a man named Upagupta would be the foremost of preachers, and indeed that is just what happened.

When the magnanimous elder Upagupta who was fit to be a second teacher had tamed [Māra], the Lord of the Realm of Desire, gods, humans, serpents, *asuras, garuḍas, yakṣas, gandharvas*, and *vidyādharas*[11] all fell at his feet; and the rain waters of the true Dharma fell on hundreds of thousands of beings who had previously sown seeds of merit in most excellent Buddha fields, and the sprouts of liberation grew in them, there on Mount Urumuṇḍa.

The Gift of Dirt

Let us [now] recollect the gift of dirt made in a previous life by King Aśoka whose footstool is illumined by the glittering crest jewels of his vassals all dutifully bowing down before him.

29 It is said that one morning, when the Blessed One was dwelling at Kalandakanivāpa in the Veṇuvana near Rājagṛha, he put on his robes, took his bowl, and, surrounded by a group of monks and honored by the monastic community, he entered Rājagṛha for alms.

As it is said:

With his entourage of monks the Blessed One went forth,
his superlative body: a mountain of gold.
He moved with ease like the lord of elephants,
his gentle countenance: a full moon.

As soon as he arrived at the city gate, he set his foot down on the threshold stone (*indrakīla*) with a resolute mind. Now whenever Blessed Buddhas set their feet down on the threshold stone of a city gate with a resolute mind, it is usual for various marvels to occur. The blind recover their sight, the deaf become able to hear, the lame can walk again. Those who are bound by fetters and shackles find their bonds have loosened. Those who have been attached to enmity in birth after birth suddenly become full of love. Calves that have broken their tethers are reunited with their mothers. Elephants trumpet,

[11] On these various kinds of semi-mythical beings, see Franklin Edgerton, *Buddhist Hybrid Sanskrit Dictionary* (New Haven: Yale University Press, 1953), and the glossary below.

horses neigh, bulls bellow, parrots, myna birds, cuckoos, pheasants, and peacocks warble delightfully. Ornaments stored in boxes tinkle with sweet sounds, and drums, without being struck, make a pleasant noise. Those places on earth that are high are made low, and those that are low are made high, and stones, gravel and potsherds disappear. At the same time, the earth is made to tremble in six uncommon ways: the East
30 goes up, the West goes down, the edge goes down, the center goes up, there is quaking and shaking, and there is rumbling and trembling. These are but a few of the marvelous phenomena that are observed when the Blessed One enters a city.

As it is said:

A vessel is struck by the force of the wind;
so too the earth with its mountain ranges,
set in the ocean,
and adorned with cities and settlements,
is affected by the foot of the Sage.
Low ground is elevated
and high ground made low
by the power of the Buddha
the earth becomes faultless,
devoid of stones, gravel, and thorns.
The blind, the dumb, and the dimwits
instantly regain their senses,
and musical instruments without being touched
play in harmony to the delight of the town.[12]

Now the men and women [of Rājagṛha] were converted by these miracles that occurred when the Buddha entered [their city], and the whole town let out a cheer as loud as the roar of the stormy sea with its crashing wind-tossed waves; for no marvel can be found in this world to equal that of the arrival of the Buddha. The entire city was filled with the radiance of

[12] The order of the original has been slightly rearranged here.

the Lord, his golden rays more resplendent than a thousand suns.

It was said that:

The sun was eclipsed by his brilliant rays
which reached even into the forested areas
31 and filled the whole world,
bringing delightful tales of highest Dharma
to the realms of the gods, asuras, and men
whose various situations they addressed.[13]

Soon the Blessed One came to the main road where two little boys were playing at building houses in the dirt. One of them was the son of a very prominent family and was named Jaya, while the other was the son of a somewhat less prominent family and was named Vijaya. Both of them saw the Buddha whose appearance is very pleasing, his body adorned with the thirty-two marks of the Great Man. And young Jaya, thinking to himself "I will give him some ground meal," threw a handful of dirt into the Buddha's begging bowl. Vijaya approved of this by making an añjali.

As it is said:

He saw the greatly compassionate Self-Existent Lord
whose body radiated a halo a fathom wide;
his faith affirmed, and with a resolute face,
he offered some dirt
to the One who brings an end to birth and old age.

After presenting this offering to the Blessed One, Jaya then proceeded to make the following resolute wish (praṇidhāna): "By this root of good merit, I would become king and, after placing the earth under a single umbrella of sovereignty, I would pay homage to the Blessed Buddha."

[13] The image is one of the rays themselves preaching sermons appropriate to the conditions of the beings in various realms. See Jean Przyluski, *La légende de l'empereur Açoka* (Paris: Paul Geuthner, 1923), p. 226, and see below the account of the rays from the Buddha's smile.

The compassionate Sage immediately perceived the boy's
character, and recognizing the sincerity of his resolve, he saw
that the desired fruit would be attained because of his field
of merit. He therefore accepted the proferred dirt, and the
32 seed of merit that was to ripen into Aśoka's kingship was
planted.

The Buddha's Smile

The Blessed One then displayed his smile. Now whenever Blessed Buddhas smile, it is usual for rays of blue, yellow, red, white, scarlet, crystal, and silver-colored light to issue forth from their mouths, some shooting upwards and others going downwards. The rays that travel downwards enter into the various hells—the Sañjīva, the Kālasūtra, the Sanghāta, the Raurava, the Mahāraurava, the Tapana, the Pratāpana, and finally the Avīci. Becoming warm they penetrate the cold hells, and becoming cool, they enter the hot ones. In this manner, the various tortures being inflicted in the hells are allayed, and the beings dwelling in them come to wonder: "What is happening? Have we left this place? Our sufferings have been alleviated—can it be that we have been reborn elsewhere?" Then, in order to engender their faith, the Blessed One creates for these various hell-beings a magical image of himself that causes them to think: "We have not left, nor have we been reborn elsewhere. But this person we have never seen before—it must be by his power that our tortures have been reduced." And contemplating the magical apparition of the Buddha they become serene and full of faith, and casting off the karma yet to be suffered in the hells, they are reborn among the gods or men, where they become vessels of truth.

The rays that travel upwards go to the realms of the various gods—Caturmahārājika, Trayastriṃśat, Yāma, Tuṣita, Nirmāṇarati, Paranirmitavaśavartin, Brahmakāyika, Brahmapurohita, Mahābrahma, Parīttābha, Apramāṇābha, Ābhāsvara, Parīttaśubha, Apramāṇaśubha, Śubhakṛtsna, Anabhraka,

Puṇyaprasava, Bṛhatphala, Abṛha, Atapa, Sudṛśa, Sudarśana, and finally Akaniṣṭha. Everywhere they proclaim the facts of impermanence, suffering, emptiness, and non-self, and declare to the gods these two verses:

Start now! Leave home! Apply yourself to the Buddha's Teaching!
Overthrow the army of Death the way an elephant
33 smashes a reed hut!
For whoever goes forth intent on the Doctrine and Discipline
Will put an end to suffering and abandon this cycle of rebirth.

After roaming throughout the Great Trichiliocosm,[14] all of the rays then reenter the Buddha's body. If a Buddha wants to reveal a past action they vanish into him from behind; if he wants to predict a future action they disappear into him from the front. If he wants to predict a rebirth in hell they vanish into the sole of his foot; if he wants to predict a rebirth as an animal they vanish into his heel; if he wants to predict a rebirth as a hungry ghost they vanish into his big toe; if he wants to predict a rebirth as a human being they vanish into his knees; if he wants to predict the kingship of a balacakravartin they vanish into his left palm; if he wants to predict the kingship of a cakravartin they vanish into his right palm; if he wants to predict a rebirth as a god they vanish into his navel; if he wants to predict the enlightenment of a disciple they vanish into his mouth; if he wants to predict the enlightenment of a pratyekabuddha they vanish into his ūrṇā; if he wants to predict the unsurpassed complete enlightenment of a Buddha they vanish into his uṣṇīṣa.

In the case at hand, the rays circumambulated the Blessed One three times and vanished into his left palm. The Venerable

[14] Trisāhasramahāsāhasra lokadhātu: the largest unit of Buddhist cosmology, "a world system consisting of a triple thousand great thousand worlds." See Edgerton, *Dictionary*, s.v.

Ānanda, making an añjali, then said to the Buddha: "Blessed One, it is not without cause nor without reason [that Tathāgatas display the smile; why therefore has the Blessed One done so?"][15]

And he added this stanza:

Buddhas have no more arrogance;
they are free from affliction and passion.
Their causes are the highest in the world.
Victors who have vanquished the enemy,
it is not without reason
that they display the smile
whiter than the conch or the lotus.
O Valiant One, O Śramaṇa, O most eminent Jina,
you have already divined
the questions that plague your listeners.
Dispel their doubts, O Best of Sages,
with firm, brilliant, most excellent words.
O foremost of men, whose speech is like thunder,
whose appearance is like that of the best of bulls
reveal what will be the fruit
34 of the gift of dirt!

The Blessed One said: "You are right, Ānanda, completely enlightened Tathāgata Arhats do not display their smile gratuitously; rather they do so for both a cause and a reason. Ānanda, do you see that boy who threw a handful of dirt into the Tathāgata's bowl?"

"Yes, Bhadanta."

"Because of that meritorious deed, Ānanda, one hundred years after the Tathāgata has attained parinirvāṇa, that boy will become a king named Aśoka in the city of Pāṭaliputra. He will be a righteous dharmarāja, a cakravartin who rules over one of the four continents, and he will distribute my bodily relics far and wide and build the eighty-four thousand

[15] Added on the basis of the Chinese text, see Przyluski, *La légende*, p. 227.

dharmarājikās. This he will undertake for the well being of many people."

And he added:

After I die there will be an emperor;
his name will be Aśoka and his fame widespread.
He will adorn Jambudvīpa with my reliquaries
and cause them to be honored by gods and men.
His meritorious gift was just this:
he threw a handful of dirt into the Tathāgata's bowl.

Then the Blessed One gave all the dirt to the Venerable Ānanda and said: "Mix this with some cowdung and spread it on the walkway (*caṅkrama*) where the Tathāgata walks." And the Venerable Ānanda did as he was told.

Aśoka's Birth

Now at that time, King Bimbisāra was reigning in the city
35 of Rājagṛha. Bimbisāra's son was Ajātaśatru; Ajātaśatru's was Udāyin; the good Udāyin's son was Muṇḍa; Muṇḍa's was Kākavarṇin; Kākavarṇin's was Sahalin; Sahalin's was Tulakuci; Tulakuci's was Mahāmaṇḍala, Mahāmaṇḍala's was Prasenajit, Prasenajit's was Nanda; and Nanda's son was the king named Bindusāra who reigned in the city of Pāṭaliputra. King Bindusāra begot a son who was given the name Susīma.

Meanwhile, in the city of Campā, a certain Brahmin begot a fair, good-looking, gracious daughter, the most beautiful girl in the country. The fortunetellers predicted she would marry a king and bear two jewel-like sons: one would become a cakravartin ruling over one of the four continents, the other would wander forth and fulfill his religious vows.

The Brahmin was excited by what the soothsayers said. (The whole world desires good fortune.) He took his daughter to Pāṭaliputra. There, he had her put on all of her jewels, and he offered her in marriage to King Bindusāra, declaring her to be an auspicious and praiseworthy celestial maiden. King Bindusāra had her introduced into his harem.

Now the king's concubines were jealous of her. "This fair,
gracious girl," they thought, "is the most beautiful woman in
the country; if the king should ever make love to her, he would
36 no longer pay any attention to us!" They instructed her therefore in the barber's art, and soon she became an expert at
grooming the hair and the beard of the king. Indeed, whenever
she started to do this, he [would relax so much that he] would
quickly fall asleep. The king was very pleased with her and
decided to grant her one wish.

"What would you most desire?" he asked.

"That your majesty should have intercourse with me," she answered.

"But you are a barber girl," said the king, "I am a monarch, a consecrated kṣatriya [member of the warrior caste]—how can I have intercourse with you?"

"Your majesty," she replied, "I am not a barber girl but the daughter of a Brahmin; my father gave me to your highness as a wife!"

"Who then taught you the barber's art?" asked the king.

"The harem women," was her answer.

"Well, then, you won't do the work of a barber any more," King Bindusāra declared, and he installed her as his chief queen. Together they dallied, enjoyed each other, and made love; she became pregnant and, after a period of eight or nine months, gave birth to a son. When the prince's full birth festival was being celebrated, she was asked what his name should be. "When this baby was born, I became 'without sorrow' (*a-śoka*)," the queen replied, and so the child was given the name Aśoka.

Subsequently, the queen gave birth to a second son, and since he was born "when sorrow had ceased" (*vigate śoke*), he was given the name Vītaśoka.

One day, Bindusāra decided to test his sons so as to determine which one would best be able to rule after his death.

37 Accordingly he spoke to the wandering ascetic Piṅgalavatsājīva, asking him to examine the princes.

"Very well, your majesty," replied Piṅgalavatsājīva, "go with the princes to the Garden of the Golden Pavilion, and I will scrutinize them there." Bindusāra, therefore, summoned his sons and proceeded to that place.

Now Aśoka's body [had bad skin; it] was rough and unpleasant to the touch, and he was not at all liked by his father, King Bindusāra. His mother told him: "My son, the king wants to examine all the princes and has gone to the Garden of the Golden Pavilion to do so; you should go there as well."

But he retorted: "Why should I? The very sight of me is hateful to the king."

"Go nevertheless," she advised, and he finally consented. Asking his mother to send him some food later in the day, he departed forthwith.

As he was leaving Pāṭaliputra, Rādhagupta, the son of the prime minister, saw him and asked: "Aśoka, where are you going?"

"Today," he answered, "the king is going to examine the princes in the garden of the Golden Pavilion."

[When Rādhagupta heard this, he invited Aśoka to take][16] the old royal elephant on which he was mounted. It was a venerable beast, and Aśoka rode it out to the Garden of the Golden Pavilion. Once there, he got off and sat down on the ground in the midst of the other princes. Before long, food arrived for all of them; Aśoka's mother had sent him some boiled rice mixed with curds in a clay pot.

Then King Bindusāra said to the wanderer Piṅgalavatsājīva: "Master, please examine the princes; who will best be able to rule after my death?"

Piṅgalavatsājīva scrutinized the young men and realized that Aśoka would be king, but he thought: "Bindusāra does not like Aśoka; if I tell him he will be king, he will surely kill

[16] Added from the Chinese, see Przyluski, *La légende*, p. 231.

38 me!" So he said: "Your majesty, I will make my prediction without disclosing any names."

"Do so then," said the king, "predict without disclosure."

The wandering ascetic then declared: "He who has an excellent mount will become king."

All of the princes, of course, immediately thought that their mount was most excellent and they would become king, but Aśoka reflected: "I arrived on the back of an elephant; my mount is truly excellent! I shall be king."

Bindusāra then said: "Master, scrutinize the princes more than that!"

So Piṅgalavatsājīva declared: "Your majesty, he who has the best seat will become king."

And again, each of the princes thought his own seat was the best, but Aśoka reflected: "I am sitting on the ground; the earth is my seat! I shall be king."

In a similar fashion, Piṅgalavatsājīva examined the princes with regard to their vessels, food, and drink, and when he had finished he returned to Pāṭaliputra.

Later, Aśoka's mother asked him: "Who was predicted to become king?"

Aśoka responded: "The prediction was made without disclosure. The one who had the best mount, seat, drink, vessel, and food will become king. The back of an elephant was my mount, the earth was my seat, my vessel was made of clay, boiled rice with curds was my food, and water was my drink; therefore I know I shall be king."

Now the wanderer Piṅgalavatsājīva, knowing that Aśoka would ascend the throne, started honoring his mother. One day, she asked him which one of the princes would succeed her husband Bindusāra, and he told her it would be Aśoka.

"The king," she cautioned him, "may someday interrogate
39 you on this matter and press you for an answer. You had better go and seek refuge in the borderlands. When you hear that Aśoka has become king, it will be safe to return." And so he went into exile in a neighboring country.

Aśoka's Accession

Now it happened that the city of Takṣaśilā rebelled against King Bindusāra. He therefore sent Aśoka there, saying: "Go, son, lay siege to the city of Takṣaśilā." He sent with him a fourfold army [consisting of cavalry, elephants, chariots, and infantry], but he denied it any arms. As Aśoka was about to leave Pāṭaliputra, his servants informed him of this: "Prince, we don't have any weapons of war; how and with what shall we do battle?"

Aśoka declared: "If my merit is such that I am to become king, may weapons of war appear before me!"

And as soon as he had spoken these words, the earth opened up and deities brought forth weapons. Before long, he was on his way to Takṣaśilā with his fourfold army of troops.

When the citizens of Takṣaśilā heard that Aśoka was coming, they bedecked the road for two and a half yojanas, and with their vases full of offerings, went out to welcome him.

"We did not want to rebel against the prince," they explained upon greeting him, "nor even against King Bindusāra; but evil ministers came and oppressed us." And with great hospitality, they escorted him into the city.

Sometime later, Aśoka was welcomed in a similar fashion in the kingdom of the Khaṣas. There two great warriors entered his service; he provided for their livelihood, and they in return, marched ahead of him, cutting a path through the mountains. Everywhere they went the gods proclaimed: "Aśoka is to become a cakravartin ruler over one of the four continents; no one is to oppose him!" And eventually the whole earth, as far as the ocean, submitted to his rule.

Now one day when Prince Susīma happened to be returning to Pāṭaliputra from the royal park, he met King Bindusāra's prime minister who was just leaving the city. The prime minister was bald and Prince Susīma, in jest, slapped him on the head.

"Today he slaps me with his hand," the minister reflected,

"when he becomes king he'll let fall his sword! I had better take action now to insure that he does not inherit the throne."

He therefore sought to alienate five hundred ministers from Susīma, saying to them: "It has been predicted that Aśoka will become a cakravartin ruler over one of the four continents. When the time comes, let us place him on the throne!"

Shortly thereafter, it happened that the Takṣaśilans again rose in rebellion. This time the king sent Prince Susīma to quell the uprising; he, however, was not successful.

41 At the same time, King Bindusāra became very ill. He therefore recalled Susīma to Pāṭaliputra intending to install him as his successor, and ordered Aśoka to be sent to Takṣaśilā in his stead. The ministers, however, [thwarted his plan;] they smeared Prince Aśoka's body with turmeric, boiled some red lac in a spittoon,[17] filled other bowls with the boiled juice, and put them aside, saying "See, Prince Aśoka has become ill, [he cannot go to Takṣaśilā]."

Now Bindusāra was on his deathbed and about to breathe his last. The ministers, therefore, brought Aśoka to him adorned with all his ornaments. "Consecrate him as king for now," they urged, "we will install Susīma on the throne later when he gets back." This, however, only made the king furious.

Aśoka, therefore, declared: "If the throne is rightfully mine, let the gods crown me with the royal diadem!" And instantly the gods did so. When King Bindusāra saw this, he vomited blood and passed away.

As soon as Aśoka became king, his authority extended to the yakṣas as far away as a yojana above the earth, and to the nāgas a yojana beneath it. [As his first act] he appointed Rādhagupta prime minister.

Susīma too learned that Bindusāra had died and Aśoka had been installed on the throne. The news made him furious, and
42 he hastened to return to the capital.

Meanwhile, in Pāṭaliputra, Aśoka posted his two great war-

[17] Lohapātra: literally a copper (or iron) bowl, here used as a spittoon (or perhaps a chamber pot).

riors at two of the city gates and Rādhagupta at a third. He himself stood at the eastern gate. In front of it, Rādhagupta set up an artifical elephant,[18] on top of which he placed an image of Aśoka that he had fashioned. All around he dug a ditch, filled it with live coals of acacia wood, covered it with reeds, and camouflaged the whole with dirt. He then went and taunted Susīma: "If you are able to kill Aśoka, you will become king!"

Susīma immediately rushed to the eastern gate, intending to do battle with his half-brother, but he fell into the ditch full of charcoal, and came to an untimely and painful end. After he had been killed, his own great warrior, Bhadrāyuddha, was initiated into the Buddhist order and became an arhat along with his retinue of several thousand men.

Aśoka the Fierce

Once Aśoka had become king, many of his ministers began to look on him with contempt. In order to discipline them, he ordered them, [as a test of their loyalty], to chop down all the flower and fruit trees but to preserve the thorn trees.

"What is your majesty planning?" they asked, "should we
not rather chop down the thorn trees and preserve the flower
43 and fruit trees?" And three times they countermanded his
order. Aśoka became furious at this; he unsheathed his sword
and cut off the heads of five hundred ministers.

On another occasion, King Aśoka, together with his harem, went out to a park east of the city. It was springtime and the trees were in bloom or laden with fruit. Strolling through the park he came across an aśoka tree whose blossoms were at their peak, and thinking "this beautiful tree is my namesake," he became very affectionate. King Aśoka's body, however, was rough-skinned, and the young women of the harem did

[18] Yantramayo hastin: literally an "elephant made of yantras," that is, mechanical contrivances, apparatus, machines. Compare Przyluski, *La légende*, p. 234, "un éléphant mécanique."

not enjoy caressing him. So after he had fallen asleep, they, out of spite chopped all the flowers and branches off the aśoka tree.

After some time the king awoke; his eyes immediately fell on his dismembered tree.

"Who did this?" he asked his servants who were standing nearby.

"Your majesty's concubines," they answered.

On learning this, Aśoka flew into a rage and burned the five hundred women alive.[19] When the people saw all these vicious acts of the king, they concluded he was fearsome by temperament, and gave him the name "Aśoka the Fierce" (Caṇḍāśoka).

Rādhagupta, the prime minister, therefore, spoke to him: "Your majesty, it is not seemly for you yourself to do what is improper; why don't you appoint some royal executioners, men who will carry out the necessary killings for the king?"
44 So Aśoka told his men to go and find him an executioner.

Now, not too far away, in a small village at the foot of the mountains, there lived a weaver who had a son named Girika. Fearsome and evil-minded, the boy reviled his mother and father, and beat up the other boys and girls. With nets and hooks, he caught and killed ants, flies, mice, and fish. He was a ferocious youth and so people called him "Girika the Fierce" (Caṇḍagirika).

When the king's men saw him engaged in these wicked deeds, they asked him: "Are you able to be King Aśoka's executioner?"

"I could execute the whole of Jambudvīpa!" was his answer.

Aśoka was informed of this, and he ordered him brought to the capital. The king's men said to Girika: "Come, the king has summoned you."

[19] Literally, "he wrapped them in *kiṭika* and burned them." The meaning of kiṭika is very obscure, and is associated with both the notion of clothing and hot copper plates. It seems to have been some sort of covering used in torture. See Edgerton, *Dictionary*, s. v.

"You go along," he replied, "I must first go and see my mother and father."

He asked his parents for permission to leave, saying: "Mother, Father, I will become King Aśoka's executioner!" But they would not let him go. Therefore, he killed them both, and rejoined the king's men. When the latter asked him why he had been delayed, he told them everything that had happened.

Then they took Girika to King Aśoka. The first thing he did was to ask the king to have a building made for his purposes. Aśoka had one built immediately; it was lovely from the outside as far as the gate, but inside it was actually a very frightful place, and people called it "the beautiful gaol."

Caṇḍagirika then said: "Your majesty, grant me this wish—that whosoever should enter this place should not come out alive." And the king agreed to his demand.

Soon thereafter, Caṇḍagirika went to the Kukkuṭārāma where he heard a monk reciting the "Bālapaṇḍita Sūtra:"[20]

"There are beings who are reborn in hell, and the hell-guardians grab them, and stretch them out on their backs on a fiery floor of red-hot iron that is but a mass of flames. They pry open their jaws with an iron bar and pour fiery balls of red-hot iron into their open mouths. These sear their lips, scorch their tongue and throat and gullet, their heart and the area around it, and passing through their entrails and intestines, flow out down below. Truly, O monks, such are the sufferings of hell.

"There are other beings who are reborn in hell, and the hell-guardians grab them and stretch them out on their backs on a fiery floor of red-hot iron that is but a mass of flames. They pry open their mouths with an iron bar and pour boiling copper down their throats. It burns their lips; it scorches their

[20] The "Sūtra of the Fool and the Wise Man," one version of which can be found in the *Majjhima Nikāya*. See I. B. Horner, tr., *The Middle Length Sayings*, 3 vols., Pali Text Society Translation Series, nos. 29-31 (London: Luzac and Co., 1954-59), 3:209-23.

tongue and palate and throat and gullet and entrails and intestines, and finally flows out down below. Truly, O monks, such are the sufferings of hell.

"And there are beings who are reborn in hell whom the hell-guardians grab and throw on their faces on a fiery floor of red-hot iron that is but a mass of flames. They mark them with a chalk line of searing hot iron,[21] and with a burning, blazing, flaming, fiery axe, they hack and chop and chisel them from above and from below, with both powerful and soft strokes, and turn them into an octagon, a hexagon, a square,
46 an oval, and finally a circle. Truly, O monks, such are the sufferings of hell.

"Then there are beings who are reborn in hell whom the hell-guardians grab and throw on their faces on a fiery floor of red-hot iron that is but a mass of flames. They mark them with a chalk line of searing hot iron, and on an iron floor which is on fire but not a mass of flames, they hack and chop and chisel them from above and from below, with both powerful and soft strokes, and make them into an octagon, a hexagon, a square and a circle. Truly, O monks, such are the sufferings of hell.

"Finally, there are beings who are reborn in hell whom the hell-guardians grab, and stretch out on their backs on a fiery floor of red-hot iron that is but a mass of flames. Then they carry out the torture of the five-fold tether; they drive two iron stakes through their hands; they drive two iron stakes through their feet; and they drive one iron stake through their heart. Truly, O monks, hell is a place of great suffering."

"Such are the five great agonies," Caṇḍagirika reflected, and he began to inflict these same tortures on people in his prison.

[21] Ayomaya sūtra: literally "a cord made out of iron." On the hell of the black cord (kālasūtra) and the use of that cord as a carpenter's chalk-line, see Paul Mus, *La lumière sur les six voies*, Travaux et mémoires de l'Institut d'Ethnologie, no. 35 (Paris: Institut d'Ethnologie, 1939), p. 79.

Samudra and Aśoka's Conversion

Now in those days, there lived in Śrāvastī a merchant who, along with his wife, embarked on a journey across the great ocean. While at sea, his wife gave birth to a son and he was given the name Samudra ("Ocean"). When, after twelve years, the merchant returned from his travels, he was robbed and killed by five hundred brigands. His son, Samudra, then entered the Buddhist order, and wandering throughout the land
47 he arrived one day at Pāṭaliputra. Early in the morning, he dressed in his robes, took his bowl, and entered the city for alms. Unknowingly, he approached the mansion that was lovely from the outside—at least as far as the gateway. When he saw the terrifying interior like the abode of hell, he wanted to go right out again, but Caṇḍagirika stopped him.

"In this place," he said, "you will meet your doom; it is all over for you!"

Samudra was overcome by sorrow and started to cry.

"Why do you weep like a baby?" Caṇḍagirika demanded.

The monk answered:

Kind sir, I do not grieve
for the destruction of the body,
but I greatly mourn the disruption
of the elements leading to my liberation.
Having attained this hard-to-reach existence,
and entered the religious life that gives rise to bliss,
and had as my teacher the lion of the Śākyas,
I am now sadly going to lose them all again.

Caṇḍagirika said: "The king has given me the right to execute all those who enter here. You had better be steadfast because for you there won't be any emancipation!"

Then, pleading for compassion, Samudra begged for a month's stay of execution. He was granted seven days; and shuddering with the fear of death, he wrestled with the thought that in a week's time he would be no more.

Now early on the seventh day, King Aśoka happened to see one of his concubines conversing with and gazing lovingly at a youth with whom she was enamored. As soon as he saw
48 them together, he became furious and sent them both to the gaol. There they were ground with pestles in an iron mortar until only their bones remained.

Samudra was thoroughly shaken by the sight of this event and exclaimed:

Aho! The Great Sage, the compassionate Teacher
was right when he likened the body
to a bubble of foam, worthless and unstable.
Where now is that lovely face?
Where has that beautiful body gone?
Woe unto this inconstant world of suffering
wherein fools take their pleasure.
In this gaol I have come
to the fundamental realization
that today will enable me
to cross the ocean of existence.

And applying himself the whole night through to the Teaching of the Buddha, he broke the bonds of existence and attained supreme arhatship.

At dawn, Caṇḍagirika said: "Monk, the night has gone, the sun has risen, the time of your torture has come!"

And Samudra replied: "Indeed, my night has gone, and the sun that marks the time of highest favor has risen! You may do whatever you wish, my long-lived friend."

"I don't understand," said Caṇḍagirika, "please explain your words."

49 And Samudra said:

Gone from my heart is the dreadful night of delusion,
blanketed by the Five Obscurations,[22]

[22] The Five Obscurations (pañcāvaraṇa) are: sensuality, ill-will, torpor, worry, and wavering.

teeming with the thief-like defilements.
Risen is the bright sun of knowledge in the sky of my mind;
by its light I can see this three-fold world as it truly is.
I am following the practice of the Master;
this is for me the time of highest favor.
Do what you will to this body, O long-lived one!

Thereupon, that unmerciful monster, feeling no pity in his heart and indifferent to the other world, threw Samudra into an iron cauldron full of water, human blood, marrow, urine, and excrement. He lit a great fire underneath, but even after much firewood had been consumed, the cauldron did not get hot. Once more, he tried to light the fire, but again it would not blaze. He became puzzled, and looking into the pot, he saw the monk seated there, cross-legged on a lotus. Straightaway, he sent word to King Aśoka. Aśoka came to witness this marvel, and thousands of people gathered, and Samudra, seated in the cauldron, realized that the time for Aśoka's con-
50 version was at hand.

He began to generate his supernatural powers. In the presence of the crowd of onlookers, he flew up to the firmament, and, wet from the water like a swan, he started to display various magical feats.

As it is said:

From half of his body, water poured down;
from the other half, fire blazed forth.
Raining and flaming, he shone in the sky
like a mountain, whose streams flowed down
from the midst of fiery herbs.[23]

At the sight of the sky-walker, the king's mouth hung open in astonishment. Gazing upwards, making an añjali, he said in great wonderment:

[23] The association of herbs or grasses with fire is a commonplace of Indian poetic imagery.

I have something I wish to ask you, friend;
your form is like that of a man
but your magical powers are not human;
therefore I cannot decide what to call you,
O Mighty One, O Pure One, or what your nature is.
Please enlighten me now on this matter,
so that I may understand your power, and act as your disciple,
coming to know the might and qualities of your Dharma,
in so far as I am able.

Then the monk, realizing that Aśoka would completely comprehend the Teaching, would distribute the Blessed One's relics and assure the well-being of the multitudes, explained to him his qualities:

O king, I am a son of the compassionate Buddha,
that most eloquent of speakers,
who has cut through the tangles
of worldly inclinations.
A follower of Dharma,
51 I am detached from all modes of existence.
Subdued by the Subdued One, the best of men,
I was shown tranquility
by the One who found quietude.
I was released from the bonds of being
by the One who is free from the terrors of saṃsāra.

"Moreover, great king, with reference to you, the Blessed One predicted that one hundred years after his parinirvāṇa there would be in the city of Pāṭaliputra a king named Aśoka, a cakravartin ruling over one of the four continents, a righteous dharmarāja who would distribute his bodily relics far and wide, and build the eighty-four thousand dharmarājikās. But instead your majesty has built this place that resembles a hell and where thousands of living beings have been killed.

Your highness, you should give to all beings a promise of security and completely fulfill the wish of the Blessed One."

And he added:

O chief of men, grant security to all beings,
for they are attendant to compassion.
Fulfill the wish of the Lord and
distribute far and wide the dharma-bearers.[24]

Now the king's faith in the Buddha was aroused and cupping his hands together out of respect, he implored the monk Samudra, saying:

O son of the Daśabala, please forgive me this evil deed.
Today, I confess it to you and seek refuge
in that Sage, the Buddha, in the best of sects,
and in the Dharma that is taught by the Noble ones.

Furthermore:

Because of my faith in the Blessed One,
because of his venerability,
I resolve today to adorn the earth
with the chief of Jinas' caityas
that are as white as the conch, the moon, and the crane.

Then Samudra departed from that place by means of his supernatural powers. [Aśoka too made ready to leave] but just as he was about to go, Caṇḍagirika, making an añjali, said: "Your majesty, you granted me a wish—that no one at all should leave this place alive!"

52 "What?" said the king, "you want to put me to death too?"

"Just so," replied Caṇḍagirika.

"But which one of us," asked Aśoka, "entered this place first?"

"I did," admitted Caṇḍagirika.

[24] Dharmadhara, a word that usually is taken to mean missionary, but here probably indicates a stūpa, a relic holder. See Sujitkumar Mukhopadhyaya, ed., *The Aśokāvadāna* (New Delhi: Sahitya Akademi, 1963), p. 167.

Aśoka therefore summoned his guard. They seized Caṇḍagirika and took him away to the torture chamber where he was burned to death. And the beautiful gaol was then torn down, and a guarantee of security extended to all beings.

The 84,000 Stūpas

Then King Aśoka, intending to distribute far and wide the bodily relics of the Blessed One, went together with a fourfold army to the droṇa stūpa that Ajātaśatru had built. He broke it open, took out all the relics, and putting back a portion of them, set up a new stūpa. He did the same with the second droṇa stūpa and so on up to the seventh one, removing the relics from each of them and then setting up new stūpas as tokens of his devotion. Then he proceeded to Rāmagrāma. There the nāgas took him down to the nāga palace and told him: "We here pay homage to our droṇa stūpa." Aśoka, therefore, let them keep their relics intact, and the nāga king himself escorted him back up from the palace.

Indeed as it is said:

Today in Rāmagrāma the eighth stūpa stands
for in those days the nāgas guarded it with devotion.
The king did not take the relics from there
53 but left them alone and, full of faith, withdrew.

Then Aśoka had eighty-four thousand boxes made of gold,
54 silver, cat's eye, and crystal, and in them were placed the relics. Also, eighty-four thousand urns and eighty-four thousand inscription plates[25] were prepared. All of this was given to the yakṣas for distribution in the [eighty-four thousand] dharmarājikās he ordered built throughout the earth as far as the surrounding ocean, in the small, great, and middle-sized towns,

[25] Paṭṭa. Burnouf translates it literally as "cloth strips" (to hold on the lids of the urns), but see Monier Monier-Williams, *A Sanskrit-English Dictionary* (Oxford: Clarendon Press, 1899), s.v.

wherever there was a [population of] one hundred thousand [persons].[26]

Now in those days, in the city of Takṣaśilā, there were thirty-six hundred thousand [people]; they therefore requested thirty-six boxes of relics. Aśoka realized he could not agree to this if the relics were to be distributed far and wide. He was, however, a master of clever means; he announced that [since he could not give the Takṣaśilans more than one share of the relics], he would have to have thirty-five hundred thousand of them executed. [They quickly withdrew their demand.] Later, Aśoka formally proclaimed that no additional relics were to be given where there were more than one hundred thousand [people], and none at all where there were fewer than that.

Aśoka then went to the Kukkuṭārāma Monastery and spoke to the elder Yaśas: "This is my wish; I would like to complete the building of all eighty-four thousand dharmarājikās on the same day, at the same time."

"Very well," replied the elder, "when the moment comes,
55 I shall signal it by hiding the orb of the sun with my hand."
Then, not long thereafter, he eclipsed the sun with his hand, and all at once the eighty-four thousand dharmarājikās were completed.

As it is said:

From those seven reliquaries of old
the Mauryan took away the relics of the Sage,
and built on this earth in one day
eighty-four thousand stūpas,
resplendent as the autumn clouds.

[26] Burnouf (*Introduction*, p. 332) reads this as "wherever one hundred thousand *gold pieces* had been amassed," but the Chinese text and other sources make it clear that the figure refers to population and not to wealth. See Przyluski, *La légende*, p. 243, and Thomas Watters, *On Yuan Chwang's Travels in India*, 2 vols. (orig. pub., 1905; rpt. Delhi: Munshi Ram Manohar Lal, 1961), 2:92.

Now when King Aśoka had completed the eighty-four thousand dharmarājikās, he became a righteous dharmarāja, and thenceforth was known as "Dharmāśoka."

As it is said:

For the benefit of beings throughout the world
the noble Maurya built stūpas.
He had been known as "Aśoka the Fierce";
by this act he became "Aśoka the Righteous."

The Legend of Vītaśoka

56 Shortly after the completion of the eighty-four thousand dharmarājikās, in the days when King Aśoka had recently acquired faith in the Teaching of the Blessed One, he celebrated a quinquennial festival (*pañcavārṣika*) in which he provided food for three hundred thousand monks, one hundred thousand of whom were arhats, and two hundred thousand of whom were virtuous ordinary disciples. And by and large, throughout the world, as far as the surrounding ocean, people became favorably disposed toward the Buddhist order.

However, Aśoka's brother, whose name was Vītaśoka, was favorably disposed toward the heretics. They had prejudiced him, claiming: "There can be no liberation for the Buddhist monks for they delight in comfort and are averse to strenuous efforts."

Some time later when King Aśoka was hunting in the forest, Vītaśoka [who had accompanied him] came across a Brahmanical ascetic who knew the value of severe austerities and was performing the penance of the five fires.

He went up to the ṛṣi, prostrated himself at his feet, and asked: "Blessed One, how long have you been dwelling here in the forest?"

"Twelve years," was the reply.

"What do you eat?" Vītaśoka asked.

"Fruits and roots," said the ṛṣi.

"What is your dress?"

"A garment of grass."

"Where do you sleep?"

"On a layer of hay."

Then Vītaśoka asked: "Blessed One, are you disturbed by any suffering?"

57 "Yes," the ascetic answered, "the animals are now copulating in their time of rut; when I see them coupling I am consumed by passion."

Vītaśoka then declared: "If this sage, with all his severe austerities, is still harassed by sensuality, how much more so are the Buddhist monks who dote on comfortable seats and beds? How will they ever rid themselves of their passions?"

And he added:

Dwelling in this harsh, uninhabited forest
feeding on wind, water, and roots,
this ṛṣi has not even overcome the passions
though he has been here a long time.
How then can the Śākyas,
who enjoy quantities of meat with their rice
prepared with ghee and curds,
successfully suppress the senses?
Mount Vindhya would rather float in the ocean!

"King Aśoka has been completely deceived into paying homage to these Buddhist monks."

Aśoka came to hear about his brother's speech. Always the master of clever means, he said to his ministers: "Vītaśoka favors the heretics; by some expedient we should make him favorably disposed toward the Teaching of the Blessed One."

The ministers said: "What is your command, your majesty?"

"When I am taking my bath," Aśoka replied, "and have left my royal ornaments and diadem outside, you, in some way, must put the diadem on Vītaśoka's head and convince him to sit on the lion's throne."

The ministers agreed to this, and as soon as Aśoka had divested himself of his royal ornaments and his diadem and had entered the bathhouse, they approached Vītaśoka.

58 "When King Aśoka dies," they said to him, "you will become king. Let us dress you now in the royal ornaments, and place the diadem on your head, and seat you on the lion's throne so we can see how you will look!"

When they had done so, they sent word to the King Aśoka, who came forthwith and surprised his brother. [Pretending to be angry at seeing him] seated on the throne and wearing the royal ornaments and diadem, he cried: "Though I am still alive, you have become king?"

He called his guard; immediately, long-haired executioners dressed in blue and carrying bells arrived and fell at Aśoka's feet.

"What is your command, your majesty?" they asked.

"I am disowning my brother," the king declared, ["do with him what you will!"]. And swords in hand, the executioners approached Vītaśoka.

But the ministers, on cue, intervened and pleaded: "Your majesty, please forgive him; he is your highness's brother!"

"Very well," Aśoka said, "I will pardon him for a period of seven days, and since he is my brother, I will grant him the kingship for this one week—out of brotherly affection!"

And right away, hundreds of musical instruments were sounded; thousands of people saluted Vītaśoka with añjalis. There was rejoicing and cries of "Long live the king!" and he
59 was surrounded by hundreds of women.

But the executioners stood at the door, and when one day had passed, they went up to Vītaśoka and proclaimed: "Gone, Vītaśoka, is the first day; only six days more are remaining." And they did the same on the second and the following days. Finally, on the last day of the week, Vītaśoka, still bedecked with the royal ornaments, was brought before the king.

The latter said to him: "Well, Vītaśoka, how did you like

the pleasures of kingship—the singing, the dancing, and the concerts?"

Vītaśoka replied, "I could neither see them nor hear them," and he added:

You should get someone who heard the songs,
saw the dances, and tasted the flavors
to tell you how they were.

"But Vītasóka," Aśoka went on, "I gave you the kingship for seven days! Hundreds of instruments were sounded, there was rejoicing and cries of 'Long live the king,' and you were saluted with hundreds of añjalis, and surrounded by hundreds of women! How can you say you did not see or hear anything?"

Vītaśoka replied:

I did not see the dance, O king,
nor did I hear the sound of the music.
I did not smell the perfumes today
nor did I recognize any tastes.
I did not feel the touch of the women,
their bodies bedecked with gold
and necklaces of jewels,
for my mind was obsessed with dying.
Women, dance, song, palace,
beds, arrangement of seats,
youth, beauty, fortune, and
the whole earth with its many gems
were without joy and empty for me.
The choicest bed gave me no pleasure,
for I could see the executioners
dressed in blue standing at my door.
I could hear the ghastly sound of their bells,
and I became dreadfully afraid
of death, O chief of kings.
Hemmed in by the arrows of death,

I could not hear the wonderful songs,
I could not see the dances,
I could not find in my heart
any desire for food.
Feverish with the fear of death,
I could not sleep
and spent the whole night thinking
"I am going to die."

The king said: "Vītaśoka, can it be that the fear of death—in just one lifetime—kept you from all pleasures, even after you had obtained the privileges of a king? How then can you think that the Buddhist monks enjoy worldly pleasures—they who are afraid of death in hundreds of lifetimes and who see all the realms of rebirth and the sufferings which go with them?

"There are five sufferings, Vītaśoka, that characterize this Triple World: in hell, the suffering brought on by a blazing fire that causes great pain to the body; among the animals, the suffering coming from the fear of eating one another; among the pretas the suffering of hunger and thirst; among humans, the suffering of the practice of striving; among the gods, the suffering that marks their fall from the divine state. Hard pressed by these sufferings of mind and body, the monks conceive of the constituents of existence as executioners, of the sense-organs as deserted villages, of the sense-objects as thieves, and of the whole Triple World as being consumed by the fire of impermanence. How then can they become attached to worldly passions?"

And he added:

Constantly tormented by the fear of death
in but a single lifetime,
the pleasures of the senses
did not delight your mind.
How then could there be any delight
in food and other pleasures

in the minds of monks who meditate
61 on the fear of death in hundreds of future lives?
Those whose minds are set on liberation
cannot be attached to clothes, beds, seats, food.
They view the body as a deadly enemy,
and their lives as impermanent as a burning house.
And how could there not be liberation
for those who turn away from rebirth
and make liberation their goal?
Their minds part from all pleasures
as water slips from a lotus leaf.

By this clever means, then, King Aśoka succeeded in making his brother favorably disposed toward the religion of the Blessed One, and Vītaśoka, folding his hands out of respect, said: "Your majesty, I now take refuge in the wholly enlightened Blessed Tathāgata Arhat, and in the Dharma, and in the community of monks."

And he added:

I seek refuge in the dispassionate Jina,
who is honored by sages, gods, and men,
and whose eyes are like a pure, freshly opened lotus;
and I seek refuge in the sangha.

And King Aśoka, embracing his brother, said: "I did not really disown you, but simply used this means so as to make you favorably disposed toward the Buddha's Teaching."

From then on, Vītaśoka worshiped the caityas of the Blessed One with concerts and perfumes and garlands of flowers, and he listened to the true Dharma, and paid his respects to the sangha.

One day, he went to the Kukkuṭārāma in order to hear the Dharma and sat down at the feet of the elder Yaśas, an arhat who was endowed with the six supernatural faculties. The elder gazed down at him compassionately and saw that this was Vītaśoka's last existence; he had amassed the necessary

preconditions for enlightenment, and would attain arhatship
in this body. The elder therefore spoke to him in praise of the
62 religious life, and Vītaśoka, hearing this was delighted and
desired to enter the Blessed One's order.

He stood up, and, making an añjali, he said: "I would like to be initiated into the good Teaching of the Dharma and Vinaya, become ordained as a monk, and lead a saintly life in your sight."

"All right, my son," replied the elder, "but first you must go and get King Aśoka's permission."

So Vītaśoka approached the king, made an añjali, and said: "Your majesty, please grant me leave. I want to go forth from the home to the homeless life, and with complete faith embrace the good Teaching of the Dharma and Vinaya."

And he added:

I was as unruly as an elephant gone amuck
but now I have left restlessness behind;
under the powerful guidance of your wisdom,
I have been disciplined by the teachings of the Buddha.
Please O lord of princes, grant me one more favor:
Let me wear the distinctive signs
of a follower of the foremost Teaching
of the One who is the best in this world and beyond.

Hearing this, Aśoka embraced his brother and said, choking back his tears: "Vītaśoka, forego this resolution! The ascetic life results in a worsening of one's appearance; your garments will be rags from the dust-heap, and your cloak something that was thrown out by a servant; your food will consist of alms collected from strangers; your bed and your seat will be a layer of grass and a pile of leaves at the foot of a tree. When you are sick, food will not be easy to obtain, and urine will be your medicine; and you are very delicate and unable to endure the suffering of heat and cold, hunger and thirst; I beg you to change your mind."

63 "Your majesty," Vītaśoka replied,

I am absolutely certain
that I am not thirsty for sense-experiences
and will not be struck by fatigue.
One who desires to lead the religious life
will not have rogues take away his powers
nor thieves what little wealth he has.
I have seen this world afflicted by suffering,
desired by Death and encompassed by evil;
afraid of rebirth,
I am determined to follow
the auspicious and sure path.

Upon hearing these words, King Aśoka began to sob, and Vītaśoka, in order to comfort him, said:

Your majesty, saṃsāra
is like a swinging palanquin;
beings who get on it
must surely fall off.
Why are you so perturbed,
since we must all part someday?

"Vītaśoka," replied the king, "why don't you do your begging near at hand?" And he ordered a bed of leaves prepared for his brother within the royal palace in a grove of trees. Vītaśoka then went on his alms round and gathered food from the women of the harem. It was, however, a sumptuous meal that he received from them, and King Aśoka had to tell his concubines to offer him only food fit for one who was leading
64 an ascetic life. He was then given mashed rotten beans, and
he began to eat them.

Seeing his brother's resolve, Aśoka interrupted his meal and granted him permission to wander forth as an ascetic monk. "But," he added, "after leading the ascetic life, you must come back and show us your accomplishments."

Vītaśoka first went back to the Kukkuṭārāma, but he soon

realized that if he tried to lead the religious life there he would be bothered by the many crowds. So he went to the land of Videha, and leading there the life of a monk, he applied himself until he attained arhatship. When he had become an arhat and had experienced the pleasures and joys of liberation, he reflected: "I am now enlightened; my brother will want to see me," and he set out for Pāṭaliputra. He arrived at the palace gate and said to the porter: "Go and tell the king that Vītaśoka stands at his gate and would like to see him."

The gatekeeper went to Aśoka and said: "Good news, your majesty! Vītaśoka has arrived and is at this very moment at your gate wishing to see you."

"Go quickly," said the king, "and show him in."

Vītaśoka then entered the palace. As soon as he saw him, the king got down from his throne and fell full length at his feet like a tree felled at the root. Gazing at the Venerable Vītaśoka, he started weeping, and said:

Although you see me, you do not react
the way people usually do
when they meet after a long time.
It seems you have reached the state of aloofness
and are fully satisfied
65 by the exquisite taste of wisdom.

Now when Aśoka's prime minister, Rādhagupta, saw the Venerable Vītaśoka's robe of cast-off rags and his clay begging bowl into which both fine and coarse food had been indiscriminately thrown, he fell at the feet of the king and said, making an añjali: "Your majesty, since this man has so few desires and is perfectly content, he must surely have accomplished what he set out to do! You should therefore be happy, for:

How can there be any uncertainty
about one who lives on alms,
who dresses in dust-heap rags,

and dwells at the foot of a tree?
The world always rejoices
at one whose illustrious mind is without depravity,
whose healthy body is without illness,
and who accomplishes what he wants to in life."

And upon hearing this, the king's heart was filled with joy, and he declared:

I have seen an heir to the throne
give up pride, jealousy, and quarreling,
and forsake the Mauryan lineage,
the city of Magadha and all of its jewels,
but I feel as though my house had been highly honored
and the city filled with glory.
Expound, therefore, the noble Teaching
of the Daśabala.

And embracing his brother, King Aśoka led him to a seat
that he had spread for him, and served him fine food with his
66 own hand. When Vītaśoka had finished eating, he washed his
hands and put down his bowl, while the king sat down at his
feet in order to listen to the Dharma.

Then the Venerable Vītaśoka preached to his brother a dharmic sermon, and said:

You have established your sovereignty, O Lord.
Keep on ruling conscientiously
and always honor the precious Triple Gem.

After delighting the king with these words of Dharma, the Venerable Vītaśoka then departed. Aśoka, his hands folded in a gesture of respect, began to follow after him, together with his entourage of five hundred ministers, and accompanied by several thousand people from the city.

Truly, as it is said:

The brother was followed respectfully
by the king, his elder.

This, indeed, is a praiseworthy sign
of the fruits of the religious life.

Then the Venerable Vītaśoka, while all the people looked on, flew up into the air by means of his supernatural powers, thus making manifest his inherent qualities. And Aśoka, along with a hundred thousand other beings, stood with hands folded, staring up at the vault of heaven, his eyes fixed on the Venerable Vītaśoka.

He said:

Free from family ties, you go off like a bird
leaving us behind, we who are bound
67 by the shackles of worldly passions.
When a tranquil self-reliant man
roams through the air as a sign of his mental powers,
this is the result of his meditative trance,
unrealized by those who are blinded by infatuation.

Furthermore:

Haughty about our own accomplishments,
we are humbled by your great magical power.
Your wisdom makes us bow the heads we held high,
conceited about our knowledge.
We who blindly thought we knew about fruits,
have been shaken by One
who has truly attained the goal.
In short, on this occasion,
we shed a flood of tears.

Vītaśoka's Death

Upon leaving the capital, Vītaśoka set out for the borderlands, where he established a seat and a bed for meditation. Soon, however, he became very ill. King Aśoka, learning of his condition, sent him some medicine and some servants to look after him. Now prior to his illness, Vītaśoka had kept his head tonsured, but by the time he recovered, his hair had grown long. He no longer needed the servants who were skilled in the art of healing and sent them back, but he continued to take medicinal food such as cow's milk, frequenting a cattle station on his alms rounds.

In the meantime, in the city of Puṇḍavardhana, a lay follower of Nirgrantha Jñātiputra[27] drew a picture showing the Buddha bowing down at the feet of his master. A Buddhist devotee reported this to King Aśoka, who then ordered the
68 man arrested and brought to him immediately. The order was heard by the nāgas as far as a yojana underground, and by the yakṣas a yojana up in the air, and the latter instantly brought the heretic before the king. Upon seeing him, Aśoka flew into a fury and proclaimed: "All of the Ājīvikas[28] in the whole of Puṇḍavardhana are to be put to death at once!" And on that day, eighteen thousand of them were executed.

Sometime later, in Pāṭaliputra, a different devotee of Nirgrantha drew yet another picture of the Buddha bowing down in front of his master. When Aśoka heard about this, he was without mercy. He forced the man and his whole family to enter their home and burnt it to the ground. He then issued a proclamation that whoever brought him the head of a Nirgrantha heretic would be given a reward of one dīnāra.[29]

Now around that time, the Venerable Vītaśoka decided to spend the night in the house of a cowherd. Because of his illness, his clothes had become tattered and his nails, hair and beard had grown long; and the cowherd's wife thought it was a Nirgrantha who had come to spend a night in their house. So she said to her husband: "My lord, that dīnāra is as good as ours; let's kill this Nirgrantha and present his head to King

[27] Nirgrantha Jñātiputra, one of the six heretic masters often listed in Buddhist texts, whose followers were Jains. He is most probably identical with Mahāvira.

[28] Interestingly, the text here confuses the Ājīvikas with the Jains.

[29] The reference to this gold coin, first minted during the period of the Kuṣāṇas, has been used to date the text as posterior to the first century A.D.

Aśoka." The cowherd, unsheathed his sword and approached the venerable monk. Vītaśoka just sat there. He accepted the facts of karma, and calling upon his knowledge of his past lives, he realized that the time had come for him to reap the fruit of some of his own previous misdeeds. The cowherd then cut off his head, took it to King Aśoka and asked for his
69 dīnāra reward.

Aśoka did not immediately realize whose head it was for the unusual amount of hair prevented him from recognizing his brother. But the servants who had attended Vītaśoka were called in and upon seeing it, they proclaimed: "Your majesty, this is Vītaśoka's head!"

And hearing this, the king collapsed in a faint. He was revived by his ministers who splashed some water in his face.

"Your majesty," they declared, "this is an example of the suffering that is being inflicted even on those who are free from desire; you should guarantee the security of all beings!"

Aśoka followed their advice, and thenceforth, no one was ever condemned to death again.

Vītaśoka's Past Life

Now a number of monks were unclear about certain points of this story, so they questioned the Venerable Upagupta, knowing that he could remove all their doubts.

"What deed," they asked, "did Vītaśoka do that resulted in his being killed by the sword?"

"Venerable sirs," the elder replied, "let me tell you about the deeds he did in previous lifetimes. Long ago, O monks, in days gone by, there was a hunter who made a living killing wild animals. In the forest there was a pool where this hunter used to go to set up his snares and catch game. Now when there is no Buddha alive in the world, pratyekabuddhas are born. And at that time, one of these pratyekabuddhas stopped by the pool to eat his meal. When he had finished, he wandered
70 off and sat down to meditate at the foot of a tree, but because

of his lingering scent the animals did not come to the water to drink.

"Not long thereafter the hunter arrived. He saw that no animals at all had come, and following the trail of the pratyekabuddha, he soon found him at the foot of the tree. 'This is all his fault,' he thought, and unsheathing his sword, he killed him on the spot.

"Do you understand, venerable sirs? Vītaśoka was that hunter. Because he killed wild animals, he, as a result, became very ill. Because he killed the pratyekabuddha with his sword, he, as a result, suffered many thousands of years in hell, and then was reborn five hundred times as a man, only to die each time by the sword. Now, as the final effect of that deed, he has once again perished by the sword, even after attaining arhatship."

"And what deed," the monks asked, "did Vītaśoka do that resulted in his being born in a prominent family and in his becoming an arhat?"

"At the time of the completely enlightened Buddha Kāśyapa," the elder replied, "a man named Pradānaruci entered the religious life. He inspired generous donors to supply the community with food, and to invite the monks to receive refreshing drinks of rice-milk. Because of him, umbrellas were raised over stūpas that were then venerated with offerings of flags, banners, perfumes, garlands, flowers, and concerts. The fruit of this deed was that he was born into a prominent family. Then, after he had led a saintly life for ten thousand years, he made a resolute wish (praṇidhāna). The fruit of that act was that he attained arhatship.

Aśoka and His Minister Yaśas

71 Not long after King Aśoka had come to have faith in the Teaching of the Buddha, he started honoring Buddhist monks, throwing himself at their feet wherever he saw them, in a crowd, or in a deserted place.

Now Aśoka had a minister named Yaśas, and although he had the utmost faith in the Blessed One, he said, one day, to the king: "Your majesty, you ought not to prostrate yourself before wandering mendicants of every caste, and the Buddhist monks do come from all four castes."

To this Aśoka did not immediately respond. Sometime later, however, he told all his ministers that he needed to have the heads of various sorts of creatures, and he asked one of them to bring him the head of such and such an animal, and another to bring him the head of another animal, and so on. Finally, he ordered Yaśas to bring him the head of a human being.

Now when the ministers had gathered all these heads, Aśoka
ordered them to go to the market place and sell them. Soon,
all of the heads had been sold, except Yaśas's human head
72 that no one would buy. Aśoka then told Yaśas to give his
head away, but, even though it was gratis, still no one would
take it.

Ashamed at his lack of success, Yaśas came back to Aśoka and said:

> O king, the heads of cows, asses, sheep, deer, and birds—
> all were sold to people for a price;
> but no one would take this worthless human head,
> even free of charge.

"Why is that?" Aśoka asked his minister, "why wouldn't anyone accept this human head?"

"Because it disgusted them," Yaśas replied.

"Oh?" said the king, "is it just this head that is disgusting or the heads of all human beings?"

"The heads of all humans," answered Yaśas.

"What?" said Aśoka, "is my head disgusting as well?"

Out of fear, Yaśas did not want to tell him the real fact of the matter, but the king ordered him to speak the truth, and finally he answered: "Yes."

After forcing this admission out of his minister, Aśoka then revealed to him his purpose in doing so: "You, sir, are obsessed with matters of form and superiority, and because of this attachment you seek to dissuade me from bowing down at the feet of the monks."

But if I acquire some merit
by bowing down a head so disgusting
that no one on earth would take it,
even free of charge,
73 what harm is there in that?
You, sir, look at the caste (jāti)
and not at the inherent qualities of the monks.
Haughty, deluded, and obsessed with caste,
you harm yourself and others.
When you invite someone,
or when it is time for a wedding,
then you should investigate the matter of caste,
but not at the time of Dharma.
For Dharma is a question of qualities,
and qualities do not reflect caste.
If a man of prominent family
happens to resort to vice,
the world censures him.
How then should one not honor virtue
when displayed by a man of low birth?
It is on account of men's minds
that their bodies are reviled or honored;
the minds of the Buddhist monks are pure,
therefore I honor them.
If a twice-born man is devoid of virtue,
he is known as fallen, and is held in contempt.
But one should bow down and honor
a man who is honorable
even if he comes from a poor family.

Furthermore:

Have you not heard that saying
of the compassionate leader of the Śākyas

that the wise are able to grasp the essence
of this world's empty constructs?
His word is certain,
and if I wish to follow his advice
and you then seek to prevent me,
that is not a sign of friendship.
When my body lies in the ground,
discarded like the pulp of sugarcane,
it will be of no use for merit making;
it won't be able to perform strenuous activities:
getting up, bowing down, and making añjalis.
Therefore, right now, I should endeavor to save
74 my meritorious essence from perishing in the grave.
Those who do not extract the essence
from this body that must inevitably perish
are like those who fail to save a chest of jewels
from a burning house or a ship sinking at sea.
Unable to distinguish essence from non-essence,
they never see the essence at all,
and are totally distraught
when they enter the jaws of Death.
Once one has enjoyed curds,
ghee, fresh butter, and buttermilk,
the best part of the milk—its essence—is gone.
If the jar is then accidentally broken,
it is hardly something to get upset about.
So too there should be no sorrow at death
if one has already extracted from one's body,
its essence—good conduct.
But when, in this world, conceited men
turn away from good conduct,
and Death smashes the jar of their body,
then their hearts are consumed
by the fires of sorrow,
just as when a jar full of curds
is broken before it has been enjoyed.
You should not therefore seek to prevent me

from prostrating my body before these monks.
You have not examined the matter,
are always reckoning "I am the best,"
and have become blind with delusion.
A wise man who considers the body
in the light of the Buddha's Teachings
does not perceive any bodily differences
between a prince and a slave.
Skin, flesh, bones, head, and liver,
as well as the other organs,
are common to all men.
Only removable ornaments make
one body "better" than another.
The wise in this world make merit
by getting up, bowing down, and performing
other acts of obeisance,
relying on this most vile body,
hoping for the essence.

The Meeting of Aśoka and Upagupta

Now King Aśoka knew that although the body was even more worthless than ground-up eggshells mixed with sand, the rewards of prostration and other bodily acts of worship were greater than dominion for many aeons over the whole
75 world from Mount Meru to the outer ocean.

He therefore wished to prepare himself in order to pay even greater honors to the stūpas of the Blessed One. With his entourage of ministers, he went to the Kukkuṭārāma, and, standing before the elders, he made an añjali and asked:

Did the All-Seeing Buddha make
a prediction about anyone else
just as he made one about me,
at the time of my gift of dirt?

Yaśas, the elder of the community, answered: "Yes, he did, great king. Around the time of his parinirvāṇa, after he had converted the nāga Apalāla, the potter, the outcaste woman, Gopālī, and the snake, the Blessed One went to Mathurā. There he said to the Venerable Ānanda: 'Ānanda, right here in Mathurā, one hundred years after the Tathāgata has gone to parinirvāṇa, there will live a perfumer named Gupta. He will have a son named Upagupta who, in those days, will become the best of preachers, a Buddha without the marks who will carry on the work of a Buddha.'

And he asked Ānanda: 'Do you see over there that dark line on the horizon?'

'Yes, your reverence.'

'That, Ānanda, is the mountain called Urumuṇḍa where one hundred years after the Tathāgata has gone to parinirvāṇa
76 there will be a forest hermitage called the Naṭabhaṭika. Of all the places where the beds and seats are conducive to meditation, Ānanda, it will be the best.' "

As it is said:

The most excellent of preachers—
glorious Upagupta—
the Lord of the World has predicted
he will do the work of a Buddha.

Aśoka then said to Yaśas: "Tell me, is this saintly being, this Upagupta, alive today, or has he not yet been born?"

"He is alive," the elder replied, "this magnanimous being who has triumphed over the defilements. For the sake of this world in need of compassion, he resides even now on Mount Urumuṇḍa, at the head of a circle of arhats. Furthermore, your majesty:

This pure being who enjoys omniscience
now preaches the most excellent Dharma
to the best of flocks,
guiding gods, demon-chiefs, snakes, and men
by the thousands to the city of liberation."

Indeed, at that time, the Venerable Upagupta was dwelling at the Naṭabhaṭika hermitage with a following of eighteen thousand arhats. Upon learning this, Aśoka summoned his ministers and said:

Equip an escort of elephants, chariots, and horses,
and I will go quickly to Mount Urumuṇḍa
to see with my own eyes the noble arhat Upagupta
who is free from all evil inclinations.

Aśoka's ministers, however, said: "Your majesty, you ought [not to go yourself, but] send a messenger to Mount Urumuṇḍa and ask the sage who lives there to come and see you!"

To this Aśoka replied: "He is not someone who should
77 have to come to us, but we should go to him! "Moreover:

I think that Upagupta's body is made of vajra,
harder than a rock.
He is a man like the Master,
and could well refuse an order."

And without further ado, Aśoka sent a messenger to the elder Upagupta to tell him he was coming to see him.

The elder, however, reflected that if the king did come, it would be difficult to find provisions for the large number of men in his escort; he therefore announced that he would go to the capital himself.

Aśoka, thinking Upagupta would come by boat, then provided a ferry for his passage from Mathurā to Pāṭaliputra. As a favor to the king,[30] the elder agreed to board the boat, and accompanied by eighteen thousand arhats, he soon reached the capital.

The king's men then announced this to Aśoka: "Rejoice, your majesty! As a favor to you, that master of the mind, that helmsman of the Teaching, Upagupta, has arrived standing at the head of his followers who have all crossed over to the other shore of the stream of existence."

[30] It is a favor because Upagupta enables Aśoka to make merit when he could just as easily have come through the air by means of his magical powers.

Upon learning this Aśoka was very pleased and took off
his string of pearls worth a hundred thousand pieces of gold,
and gave it to the man who had brought him the good news.
He then called the town crier and said: "Sound all the bells
in Pāṭaliputra! Announce the arrival of the elder Upagupta!
78 And proclaim:

If you want to leave behind poverty
which is the root of worthlessness,
and would like to prosper magnificently in this world,
go see the compassionate Upagupta
who can bring you heaven and release.
If you never saw the foremost of men,
the greatly compassionate self-existent Master,
go see the elder Upagupta who is like the Master,
a bright light in this Triple World."

Aśoka then had the city decorated [for the elder's arrival]. Along with all the citizens and his officers of state, he went two and a half yojanas out of town to meet him and to welcome him with every kind of musical instrument and every variety of garland, perfume, and blossom.

While still a way off, Aśoka saw the elder with his eighteen thousand arhats gathered around him in a semi-circle. Forthwith, he alighted from his elephant and proceeded to the riverbank on foot. There, he stood with one foot on shore and the other on board the boat, and, clasping the elder in his arms, he lifted him from the ship on to the dry land.

He then fell full-length in front of Upagupta like a tree felled at the root. He kissed his feet, got up, and then knelt down on the ground again. Making an añjali and gazing up at the elder, he said:

When I had cut down the enemy hosts
and placed the earth and its mountains ringed by the sea
under a single umbrella of sovereignty,
my joy was not then what it is now

79 that I have seen you, O elder.
The sight of you has doubled my faith
in this most excellent order.
Looking at you today I see in you
the incomparable Self-Existent Pure One,
eventhough he is gone beyond.

Furthermore:

Now that the compassionate Jina has gone to rest,
you carry on the work of a Buddha in this Triple World.
Now that he has disappeared and closed his eyes
on this world of delusion,
you, like the sun, shine with the light of knowledge.
You are like the Master, the one eye of the world,
the foremost of preachers, a refuge.
O mighty one, tell me what to do and I will quickly,
this very day, carry out your command, O pure being.

Then the elder Upagupta blessed the king with his right hand, and said:

You have established your sovereignty, O lord,
keep on ruling conscientiously,
and always honor the precious Triple Gem.

"Furthermore, great king, the Blessed Tathāgata Arhat, the completely enlightened Buddha, that most excellent charioteer of beings, has entrusted us—you and me—with the safe keeping of his Teaching which we are to maintain diligently in the midst of his flock."

"Elder," said Aśoka, "I have carried out everything that the Blessed One foretold I would do:

I distributed his reliquaries
and beautified the earth everywhere
with mountain-like stūpas of many colors,
80 with lofty banners and bejewelled parasols.

Moreover:

My son, myself, my house, my wives
The whole earth, even the royal treasure—
there is nothing whatsoever that I have not given up
for the Teaching of the Dharma King."

The elder Upagupta said: "Excellent, great king! You have done well, for:

Those who serve the Dharma
with their bodies, their wealth, and their lives,
do not grieve when they die
but go to the desired abode of the gods."

Then the king led Upagupta into the palace, with great pomp and ceremony, and clasping him in his arms, he had him sit down on the seat expressly provided for him.

Now Upagupta had very soft skin, as soft as cotton. Having noticed this when he touched him, Aśoka made an añjali and said:

O exalted being, your limbs are smooth
and your skin like cotton or Benares silk.
But I am unfortunate; my body is not soft,
my limbs are hard and coarse,
and my rough skin unpleasant to touch.

"That is because," the elder answered,

The gift I gave to that peerless Person
was very pure and pleasing.
I did not offer the Tathāgata
a gift of dirt like you!

"But elder," the king replied,

It was because I was a child that long ago,
encountering an incomparable field of merit,
I planted a gift of dirt therein.
81 This is the result of that act.

Then the elder, in order to cheer up the king, said:

Great king, behold the greatness of the field
in which the dirt was planted!
It brought you royal splendor
and unsurpassed sovereignty!

Hearing this, Aśoka's eyes grew wide with amazement. He called his ministers and said:

I was rewarded with the kingship of a balacakravartin
simply because of a gift of dirt!
You should spare no effort, sirs,
in honoring the Blessed One.

Aśoka's Pilgrimage

The king then fell at the feet of the elder Upagupta and said: "Elder, I want to honor the places where the Blessed One lived, and mark them with signs as a favor to posterity."

"Excellent, great king," Upagupta replied, "your intention is magnificent. I will show you the sites this very day."

[And he added:]

The places where the Blessed One lived
we will honor with folded hands,
and mark them with signs
so that there will be no doubt.

Then Aśoka equipped a fourfold army, procured perfumes, garlands, and flowers, and set out with the elder Upagupta.

First, Upagupta took him to the Lumbinī Wood, and stretching out his right hand he said: "In this place, great king, the Blessed One was born."

And he added:

This is the first of the caityas
of the Buddha whose eye is supreme.
Here, as soon as he was born,

82 the Sage took seven steps on the earth
looked down at the four directions,
and spoke these words:
"This is my last birth
I'll not dwell in a womb again."

Aśoka threw himself at Upagupta's feet, and getting up, he said, weeping and making an añjali:

They are fortunate and of great merit
those who witnessed
the birth of the Sage
and heard his delightful voice.

Now for the sake of further increasing the king's faith, the elder asked Aśoka whether he would like to see the deity

who witnessed in this wood the birth
of the most eloquent Sage,
saw him take the seven steps,
and heard the words he spoke.

Aśoka replied that he would. Upagupta, therefore, stretched out his right hand toward the tree whose branch Queen Mahāmāyā had grasped while giving birth, and declared:

Let the divine maiden who resides in this aśoka tree
and who witnessed the birth of the Buddha
make herself manifest in her own body
so that King Aśoka's faith will grow greater still.

And immediately, the tree spirit appeared before Upagupta in her own form, and said, making an añjali:

Elder, what is your command?

The elder said to Aśoka: "Great king, here is the goddess who saw the Buddha at the time of his birth."

Aśoka said to her, making an añjali:

You witnessed his birth and saw
his body adorned with the marks!
You gazed upon his large lotus-like eyes!
You heard in this wood
the first delightful words
83 of the leader of mankind!

The tree spirit replied:

I did indeed witness the birth of the best of men,
the Teacher who dazzled like gold.
I saw him take the seven steps,
and also heard his words.

"Tell me, goddess," said Aśoka, "what was it like—the magnificent moment of the Blessed One's birth?"

"I cannot possibly fully describe it in words," answered the deity, "but, in brief, listen:

Throughout Indra's three-fold world,
there shone a supernatural light,
dazzling like gold and delighting the eye.
The earth and its mountains,
ringed by the ocean,
shook like a ship being tossed at sea."

Hearing this, Aśoka made an offering of one hundred thousand pieces of gold to the birthplace of the Buddha, built a caitya there, and went on.

The elder Upagupta then took him to Kapilavastu. "Great king," he declared, stretching out his right hand, "in this place here, the bodhisattva was brought before his father, King Śuddhodana. Seeing that his son's perfect body was adorned with the thirty-two marks of the Great Man, he prostrated himself full length at his feet.

"And this, great king, is the ancestral temple of the Śākya clan, called the Śākyavardha. The bodhisattva was brought here soon after his birth so that he could worship the gods, but instead all the deities fell at the bodhisattva's feet. King Śuddhodana declared that his son was a god even for the gods, and so gave him the name: 'Devātideva.'

"In this place, great king, the bodhisattva was shown to
the learned Brahmin fortunetellers; and over here, the sage
84 Asita predicted that he would become a Buddha in this world.

"In this place, great king, he was reared by Mahāprajāpatī; here he was taught how to write; and here he became a master of the arts appropriate to his lineage such as riding an elephant, a horse, or a chariot, handling a bow, grasping a javelin, and using an elephant hook. And this was the gymnasium where the bodhisattva trained. And in this place, great king, the bodhisattva, surrounded by a hundred thousand deities, pursued pleasure with sixty thousand women.

"In this place, upset over the sight of an old man, a sick man and a corpse, the bodhisattva went out to the woods; and over here he sat down in the shade of a jambu tree, and ridding himself of evil and negative elements, he attained the first level of trance, a joyful and blissful state free from evil inclinations, born of discrimination, and characterized by reason and reflection. And when it was afternoon and the mealtime was past, the lengthening shadows of the trees slanted towards the east, but the shadow of the jambu tree did not leave the body of the bodhisattva. And witnessing this, King Śuddhodana once again fell full length at the bodhisattva's feet.

"Through this gateway over here, the bodhisattva left Kapilavastu at midnight, surrounded by a hundred thousand deities; and here he sent his horse and his ornaments back with Chandaka."

And he added:

In this place he made Chandaka return
with the horse and the ornaments,
and all by himself, without an attendant,
85 he entered the forest of asceticism.

"In this place, the bodhisattva gave his clothes of Benares silk to a hunter in exchange for a yellow robe, and began his ascetic practice. Here the potter invited the bodhisattva to his hermitage; here King Bimbisāra offered him half of his kingdom; and here he met Ārāḍa and Udraka."[31]

As it is said:

In the forest of asceticism,
the Noble Being, that Indra among men,
studied and practiced austerities
under the ṛṣis Udraka and Ārāḍa.

"In this place, the bodhisattva practiced self-mortification for six years."

And he added:

For six long years, the great Sage
undertook fierce austerities,
and then gave them up realizing
this was not the way to highest knowledge.

"In this place, Nandā and Nandabalā, the daughters of a village headman, offered the bodhisattva sweetened milk-rice which had been condensed sixteen times."[32]

And he added:

Here the most eloquent Great Hero
enjoyed Nandā's sweetened milk-rice,
and then set out
for the seat of enlightenment.

[31] For the story of Ārāḍa and Udraka, see André Bareau, *Recherches sur la biographie du Buddha dans les sūtrapiṭaka et les vinayapiṭaka anciens*, Publications de l'Ecole Française d'Extrême-Orient, vol. 53 (Paris: Ecole Française d'Extrême-Orient, 1963), pp. 13-28. On the stūpa at the site of the exchange of robes with the hunter, see W. Woodville Rockhill, *The Life of the Buddha* (London: Kegan Paul, Trench, Trübner and Co., 1907), p. 26. For the potter's hermitage, see Edgerton, *Dictionary*, s.v. "Bhārgava."

[32] Apparently these two daughters are the same as Sujātā, who is usually portrayed as the one offering the milk-rice. See Edgerton, *Dictionary*, s.v. Nandabalā.

"In this place, the bodhisattva, on his way to the Bodhi
86 tree, was praised by the nāga king, Kālika."

And he added:

Coming along this path toward the seat of enlightenment
where he sought immortality,
the most eloquent of men was praised
by Kālika, chief of serpents.

Then Aśoka fell at the elder Upagupta's feet, and making an añjali, he said:

I would like to meet the nāga king
who saw the Tathāgata
walking along this path
as unstoppable as an elephant bull in rut.

And immediately, Kālika the nāga king appeared before Upagupta and said, making an añjali: "Elder, what is your command?"

Upagupta said to King Aśoka: "This, your majesty, is Kālika, the nāga king who praised the Blessed One while he was heading along this path toward the Bodhi tree.

Aśoka said to the nāga, making an añjali:

You saw my peerless Master,
his complexion like blazing gold
and his face like the autumn moon.
Recount for me some of the Buddha's qualities;
tell me what it was like—
the splendor of the Sugata.

"I am unable fully to describe it in words," replied Kālika, "but, in brief, listen:

Beneath his feet, the whole earth
and its mountain ranges trembled
in six different ways.
The Sugata shone on the world of men

like a beautiful never-waning moon,
87 surpassing the sun in splendor."

Now when the king had built a caitya at that spot, the elder Upagupta led him to the foot of the Bodhi tree, stretched out his right hand and said: "In this place, great king, the bodhisattva first defeated the forces of Māra with the power of his loving kindness, and then completely realized total unsurpassed enlightenment."

And he added:

Here at the seat of enlightenment
the greatest of sages dispersed
and quickly repelled the forces of Namuci [Māra]
And here that peerless individual
attained everlasting, exalted,
supreme enlightenment.

And hearing this the king made an offering of one hundred thousand pieces of gold to the Bodhi tree and built a caitya there.

They went on, and after a while the elder Upagupta stopped and said to Aśoka: "In this place, the Blessed One received from the celestial guardians of the four quarters four stone begging bowls which he joined into a single bowl. Over here, the merchants Trapuṣa and Bhallika made him an offering of alms food. And here the Blessed One, on his way to Benares, was praised by the Ājīvika Upaga."[33]

Then Upagupta led Aśoka to Ṛṣipatana, and stretching out his right hand he declared: "In this place, great king, the Blessed One set in motion the holy Wheel of the Dharma, which in three turns thrice teaches the Four Noble Truths."[34]

[33] The text has Upagaṇa, but see Edgerton, *Dictionary*, s.v. Upaga. For the story, see Bareau, *Recherches*, pp. 155-60.

[34] Triparivarta dvādaśākāra dharmacakra. The Wheel of Dharma is turned three times, on each occasion teaching the Four Noble Truths at a higher stage of knowledge. See Edgerton, *Dictionary*, s.v. parivarta. For a full account of this the Buddha's first sermon, see Bareau, *Recherches*, pp. 172-82.

And he added:

Here the Lord set in motion
the unstoppable most splendid Wheel of Dharma
in order to bring
saṃsāra to a standstill.

"In this place, over here he initiated a thousand long-haired ascetics into the religious life. In this place, he taught the
88 Dharma to King Bimbisāra, and the king along with eighty-four thousand deities and several thousand Magadhan Brahmin householders perceived the Noble Truths.[35] In this place, he taught the Dharma to Śakra, Indra of the gods, and Śakra, along with eighty-four thousand other deities perceived the Truths. In this place, the Blessed One performed a great miracle.[36] Over here, surrounded by a host of gods, he descended from the Trāyastriṃśa Heaven after spending a rains retreat there teaching the Dharma to his mother."

Finally, the elder took King Aśoka to Kuśinagarī. Stretching out the palm of his right hand, he said: "In this place, great king, the Blessed One, having finished doing the work of a Buddha, entered the state of complete nirvāṇa without any remaining attributes."

And he added:

The great, wise, most compassionate Sage
converted everyone to the eternal Dharma and Vinaya—
gods, men, asuras, yakṣas, and nāgas.
Then he went to rest, his mind at ease,
because there was no one left for him to convert.

Hearing these words, Aśoka collapsed on the ground in a faint. His attendants splashed some water in his face, and as soon as he had somewhat regained consciousness, he made an offering of a hundred thousand pieces of gold to the site of the parinirvāṇa, and built a caitya there.

[35] On this episode, see ibid., pp. 331-42.
[36] Most certainly the great miracle of Śrāvastī.

The Stūpas of the Buddha's Disciples

He then fell at Upagupta's feet and said: "Elder, I wish also to pay homage to the bodily relics of those disciples whom the Blessed One declared to be foremost [in some quality]."[37]

"Excellent, great king," the elder replied, "your intention is splendid!" And he took Aśoka to the Jetavana. There, he stretched out his right hand and said: "This, great king, is the stūpa of the elder Śāriputra who is worthy of praise."

"What were his virtues?" asked Aśoka.

"The Blessed One," replied Upagupta, "called him the foremost of the wise, a second master, commander of the army
89 of Dharma who keeps the Dharma Wheel rolling. No one in the whole world, excepting the Tathāgata, has as much as a sixteenth of Śāriputra's wisdom."

And he added:

The supreme Wheel of the Good Dharma
which the Jina set in motion
was kept rolling
by Śāriputra the Wise.
Who in this world, other than the Buddha,
would ever know how to count the virtues
of the son of Śāradvatī
and be able to describe them completely?

Aśoka then, with heartfelt joy, made an offering of one hundred thousand pieces of gold to the stūpa of the elder Śāradvatīputra and, making an añjali, he said:

Devoutly I praise great Śāradvatīputra,
the wisest of the wise,
who is free from attachment to existence,
and whose glory lights up the whole world.

[37] The list of these may be found in the *Aṅguttara Nikāya*. See F. L. Woodward and E. M. Hare, tr., *The Book of Gradual Sayings (Anguttara Nikāya)*, 5 vols., Pali Text Society Translation Series, nos. 22, 24-27 (London: Pali Text Society, 1932-36), 1:16-22.

Then the elder Upagupta pointed out the stūpa of Mahāmaudgalyāyana and declared: "This, great king, is the stūpa of the elder Mahāmaudgalyāyana who is worthy of praise."

"What were his virtues?" asked Aśoka.

"The Blessed One," replied Upagupta, "called him the foremost of those who have supernatural powers. He subdued the nāga kings Nanda and Upananda, and with the big toe of his right foot he shook Vaijayanta, the palace of Śakra, Indra of the gods."

And he added:

Zealously honor Kolita,
the best of the twice-born,
who set a-trembling Śakra's abode
with his big right toe.
Who in this world could ever fathom
the ocean of merits of the pure-minded One
who subdued the fearful snake lords
most difficult to tame?

Then Aśoka made an offering of one hundred thousand pieces of gold to the stūpa of the elder Mahāmaudgalyāyana,
90 and making an añjali, he said:

Head bowed, I honor the celebrated Maudgalyāyana,
foremost of those who have supernatural powers.
He has escaped from birth,
old age, sorrow, and suffering.

Then the elder Upagupta pointed out the stūpa of Mahākāśyapa, and declared: "This, great king, is the stūpa of the elder Mahākāśyapa who is worthy of praise."

"What were his virtues?" asked Aśoka.

"The Blessed One," replied Upagupta, "called this magnanimous disciple the foremost of those who have few desires, are quite contented and advocate the qualities of the purified.[38]

[38] For a list of these qualities, see Edgerton, *Dictionary*, s.v. dhūta-guṇa.

Furthermore, he invited him to share his seat, and clothed him in his faded robe. Accepting misery and poverty, this disciple held the community together."

And he added:

A lofty field of merit,
a kindly sage who welcomes misery and poverty,
who wore the robe of the Omniscient One
and united the community—
who is able to describe fully
the qualities of this guru
with whom the benevolent Jina
shared the best of seats?

Then Aśoka made an offering of one hundred thousand pieces of gold to the stūpa of the elder Mahākāśyapa, and said, making an añjali:

I honor the elder Kāśyapa
who dwells hidden inside the mountain;[39]
serene, his face turned away from strife, devoted to
  tranquility,
he has fully developed the virtue of contentedness.

Then the elder Upagupta pointed out the stūpa of Batkula,[40] and declared: "This, great king, is the stūpa of the elder Batkula, who is worthy of praise."

91 "What were his virtues?" asked Aśoka.

"The Blessed One," replied Upagupta, "called this magnanimous disciple the foremost of those who seldom get sick.

[39] A reference to the legend that Mahākāśyapa disappeared at death into a mountain where he remains in a meditative trance and from where he will emerge at the time of the future Buddha Maitreya. See Lamotte, *Histoire*, p. 778.

[40] Less known than the other disciples mentioned, Batkula figured along with Piṇḍola among the sixteen great arhats (*lohan*). See Gustav Ecke, "Ānanda and Vakula in Early Chinese Carvings," *Sino-Indian Studies* 5 (1957): 40-46.

Moreover, [he was so aloof that] he never preached so much as a single two-line stanza to anyone."

Aśoka said: "Make an offering of a penny here."

Hearing this, his ministers immediately asked: "Your majesty, why have you changed the pattern you established by your offerings to the other stūpas and given only a penny to this one?"

"Let me tell you the reason," the king answered.

Even though he managed,
with the lamp of perfect knowledge,
completely to dispell the darkness
housed in his mind,
he had so few desires that he did not act
as others did for the benefit of all mankind.

The ministers were amazed. They fell at Aśoka's feet and said in awe: "Aho! Although this magnanimous being lacked desires, he unfortunately also lacked purpose."

Finally, the elder Upagupta pointed out the stūpa of Ānanda and declared: "This, great king, is the stūpa of the elder Ānanda, who is worthy of praise."

"What were his virtues?" asked Aśoka.

"He was," replied Upagupta, "the Blessed One's personal attendant. He was the foremost of those who had listened to the Teaching a great deal and was the preserver of the Buddha's word."

And he added:

Diligently guarding the bowl of the Sage,
firm in his recollection, his resolution and reflection,
an ocean of oral tradition is good Ānanda.
His sweet words are perfectly clear,
and he is honored by gods and men.
Thoroughly familiar with the thoughts of the Buddha,
clearsighted, a basket of virtues,
praised by the Jina is good Ānanda.

Victorious over evil inclinations,
92 he is honored by gods and men.

Then Aśoka made an offering of ten million pieces of gold to Ānanda's stūpa.

"Your majesty," his ministers asked, "why do you honor this disciple above all others?"

"Let me tell you the reason," said the king:

He whose name means "the cessation of sorrow"[41]
should be honored in a special way,
because he attended to the dharmic body
of the most eloquent master who himself is the Dharma.
It is because of this son of the great Sugata
that the lamp of Dharma still burns today
and dispells the darkness of defilements in all beings.
The waters contained in the ocean
would never have fit in a cow's hoofprint;
it was after recognizing this elder's dharmic capacity
that the Lord consecrated him as sūtra-master.

Now after honoring the stūpas of all the elders, Aśoka fell at Upagupta's feet and said, with heartfelt joy:

I have profited from the human condition I attained
by making hundreds of offerings.
With the vacillating powers of royal sovereignty,
I have grasped the supreme essence (sāra).
I have ornamented this world with hundreds of caityas
resplendent as cumulus clouds.
In fulfilling today the Teaching of the peerless Master
93 have I not done the difficult to do?

And after saying this, Aśoka took his leave of the elder Upagupta.

[41] "Ānanda" more literally refers to bliss or happiness. "Cessation of sorrow" is a better etymology for "Aśoka!"

The Worship of Bodhi

Now although King Aśoka had given a hundred thousand pieces of gold to the places marking the Buddha's birth, his enlightenment, his setting in motion the Wheel of Dharma, and his parinirvāṇa, his faith was particularly roused by the Bodhi tree, since that was where the Blessed One had realized complete unsurpassed enlightenment. He therefore sent to the place of Bodhi an offering of the most precious jewels.

Now Aśoka's chief queen was named Tiṣyarakṣitā. [She was a very jealous woman] and she thought: "Although the king pursues his pleasure with me, he sends all the best jewels to Bodhi's place!" She therefore asked a Mātanga woman to bring about the destruction of "Bodhi, her rival." The sorceress said she would do it, but first demanded some money. When she had been paid, she muttered some mantras and tied a thread around the Bodhi tree; soon it began to wither.

The king's men quickly informed Aśoka of this fact. "Your majesty," one of them said, "the Bodhi tree is drying up."

And he added:

The place where the seated Tathāgata
obtained omniscience and understood
the whole world just as it is—
the Bodhi tree, O chief of men, is dying!

The news made Aśoka collapse on the ground in a faint, His attendants splashed some water in his face, and when he had somewhat regained consciousness, he said, sobbing:

When I looked at the king of trees, I knew
that even now I was looking at the Self-Existent Master.
If the tree of the Lord comes to die,
94 I too shall surely expire!

Now Tiṣyarakṣitā saw the king afflicted with sorrow and said: "My lord, if Bodhi should happen to die, I will bring about your pleasure!"

"Bodhi is not a woman," said the king, "but a tree; it is where the Blessed One attained complete unsurpassed enlightenment."

Tiṣyarakṣitā [now realized her mistake]. She summoned the Mātanga woman and asked whether it was possible to restore the Bodhi tree to its previous healthy condition.

"If there is still some life left in it," said the sorceress, "I shall be able to revive it." She then untied the thread, dug up the ground all around the tree, and watered it with a thousand pitchers of milk a day. After some time, it grew to be as it was before.

The king's men quickly told Aśoka: "Rejoice, your majesty, the tree has returned to its previous state!"

The king was so overjoyed that, gazing at the Bodhi tree, he proclaimed:

I will do something that Bimbisāra
and all the other resplendent royal lords never did.
I will twice perform the highest honors;
I will bathe the Bodhi tree
with jars full of fragrant waters,
and I will undertake to honor the sangha
with a great quinquennial festival.

The king then had a thousand jars of gold, silver, cat's eye, and crystal filled with fragrant water. He had much food and drink prepared, and collected a pile of perfumes, garlands, and flowers. He bathed, put on clean clothes that had never been worn and still had long fringes on them, and he observed the fast day by maintaining the eight precepts. Then, holding
95 a small spoon of incense, he went up to the roof of his dwelling, turned in all four directions, and began to implore the disciples of the Buddha to assemble, as a favor to him:

Ye students of the Sugata whose conduct is correct,
who have quieted your senses and conquered your
faults and fancies

who are worthy of worship and honored by gods and
  men,
draw near out of compassion for me!

Ye distinguished sons of the King of Dharma, the Sugata,
who, free from all bonds, delight in tranquility and
  self-control,
who as āryas are praised by asuras, gods, and men,
approach as a favor to me!

Ye resolute āryas who dwell
in the delightful city of Kāśmīrapura,
and ye who live in Mahāvana and Revataka,[42]
come here so as to favor me!

Ye sons of the Jina who reside at Lake Anavatapta,[43]
and those of you who dwell by mountain streams,
or in caves along a cliff,
gather here today impelled by compassion!

Ye sons of the most eloquent of teachers,
who dwell in Śairīṣaka, the supreme celestial mansion,
who are free from sorrow and full of compassion,
come as a favor to me!

Ye disciples of great vigor,
who dwell on Mount Gandhamādana,[44]

[42] Kāśmīrapura: the city of Kashmir, i.e., Śrinagar. On Mahāvana and Revataka, see Edgerton, *Dictionary*, s.v.

[43] Lake Anavatapta (Pali: Anotatta): A lake, sometimes identified with Mānasa Sarovara, and famous as the site of a great congress of Buddhist elders. See Marcel Hofinger, *Le congrès du lac Anavatapta (vies de saints bouddhiques) extrait du Vinaya des Mūlasarvāstivāda Bhaiṣajyavastu*, Bibliothèque du Muséon, vol. 34 (Louvain: Institut Orientaliste, 1954).

[44] Mount Gandhamādana: Said to be located to the north of Anavatapta, the mountain is famous in Indian mythology, and well known in Buddhism as the repair of pratyekabuddhas. See Ria Kloppenborg *The Paccekabuddha, A Buddhist Ascetic* (Leiden: E. J. Brill, 1974), p. 14.

I invite you to draw near,
96 your compassion aroused.

Piṇḍola Bhāradvāja

Before Aśoka had even finished speaking, three hundred thousand monks had gathered around him. One hundred thousand of them were arhats and the rest were virtuous ordinary disciples; not one of them, however, sat down on the senior monk's seat.

Aśoka inquired why this was so, and Yaśas, the old abbot who was endowed with the six supernatural insights, replied: "Great king, that is the seat of the senior monk."

"Elder," Aśoka asked, "is there anyone who is more senior than you?"

"There is, great king," Yaśas replied, "this seat of honor belongs to Piṇḍola Bhāradvāja, whom the most eloquent of sages described as the foremost of lion-roarers."

"What?" cried the king, so thrilled that his hair stood on end and shivered like the blossoms of a kadamba tree, "is there a monk still alive who has seen the Buddha?"

"Indeed there is, great king," replied Yaśas, "Piṇḍola Bhāradvāja was with the Buddha, and he still lives."

"Would it be possible," Aśoka enquired, "for me to see him?"

"Great king," the elder replied, "you will meet him presently, for the time of his arrival has come."

"Ah!" exclaimed the king, rejoicing in his heart,

Great would be my gain,
and unprecedented my great bliss
unsurpassed here on earth,
were I to see with my own eyes
that exalted being of the Bhāradvāja clan.

And folding his hands in reverence, Aśoka stood with his eyes fixed on the vault of heaven.

Then the elder Piṇḍola Bhāradvāja, in the midst of several thousand arhats who formed a crescent moon around him,
97 flew down from the heavens like a royal goose, and took his place on the seat of honor. Instantly those several hundred thousand monks rose to greet him, and Aśoka too could see Piṇḍola Bhāradvāja—his body that of a pratyekabuddha, his hair very white, and his eyebrows so long that they hung down and covered his eyes. The king immediately fell full-length in front of the elder like a tree felled at the root. He kissed his feet, got up, and then knelt down again on the ground. Making an añjali, gazing up at the elder, he said, choked with emotion:

When I had cut down the enemy hosts
and placed the earth and its mountains ringed by the sea
under a single umbrella of sovereignty,
my joy was not then what it is now
that I have seen you, O elder.

"By looking at you, I can, even today, see the Tathāgata. You show yourself out of compassion, and that redoubles my faith. O elder! You saw him, the Lord of the Triple World, the Blessed Buddha, my Guru!"

Piṇḍola then lifted up his eyebrows with his hands and looking straight at the king, he replied:

Indeed I saw him many times—
that great incomparable Sage,
whose brilliance matched that of the best polished gold,
whose body bore the thirty-two marks,
whose face was like the autumn moon,
whose voice carried more authority than Brahmā's
98 who dwelt ever free from passion.

"Elder," said the king, "where did you see the Blessed One and how?"

"Great king," replied the elder, "I saw him first after he had conquered Māra's hosts and was spending the rains retreat in Rājagṛha together with five hundred arhats. I was there at the time and could see him perfectly, he who is worthy of veneration."

And he added:

When the great Sage, the Tathāgata,
who is free from passion
and surrounded by others equally free from passion,
was spending the rains-retreat in Rājagṛha,
I was then right there
in front of the enlightened Sage,
and I saw him face to face
just as you see me now with your own eyes.

"Then again, great king, I was there when the Blessed One performed a great miracle at Śrāvastī, magically creating a large number of Buddha images in mid-air as far up as the Akaniṣṭha heaven in order to outdo the heretics. At that time I witnessed that Buddha show."

And he added:

When the Blessed One used his supernatural powers
to subdue the heretics gone astray,
I saw, my lord, his lofty sport
that delighted all creatures.

"Then again, great king, I was right there when the Blessed
One surrounded by a host of deities came down into the city
of Sāṃkāśya from the Trāyastriṃśa Heaven where he had
spent the rains retreat among the gods preaching the Dharma
to his mother. At that time, I saw the achievements of both
99 gods and men, including Utpalavarṇā's magical creation of a
cakravartin."[45]

[And he added:]

[45] Utpalavarṇā: A Buddhist nun who, wishing to be first in honoring the Buddha upon his descent from the Trāyastriṃśa Heaven, took on the form of a cakravartin to pay her respects to him.

When the most eloquent of teachers descended
from the divine realm where he had spent the rains,
I was there, close by,
and I saw him, the supreme Sage.

"Furthermore, great king, when the Blessed One accepted an invitation from Anāthapiṇḍada's daughter Sumāgadhā, and flew, together with five hundred arhats, to Puṇḍavardhana by means of his supernatural powers, I, at that time, used my own supernatural powers and grabbed a mountain boulder and flew with it to Puṇḍavardhana.[46] On account of that, the Blessed One forbade me from entering parinirvāṇa until the Dharma dies out."

And he added:

When the Guide, my Guru,
invited by Sumāgadhā,
went off by supernatural means,
I tore off a mountain top
and followed him quickly to Puṇḍavardhana.
There the compassionate scion of the Śākya clan
gave me an order:
"You shall not enter into nirvāṇa
as long as the Dharma has not disappeared."

"Finally, great king, I was right there when, long ago, as a child, you threw a handful of dirt into the bowl of the Blessed One who had come to Rājagṛha for alms, thinking that you would offer him some ground meal. Rādhagupta approved of your act, and the Blessed One predicted that one hundred years after his parinirvāṇa, you would become a king named Aśoka in the city of Pāṭaliputra, that you would be a righteous dharmarāja, a cakravartin ruling over one of the four conti-

[46] A famous episode in the legend of Piṇḍola. See Tsurumatsu Tokiwai, *Studien zum Sumāgadhāvadāna*, (Darmstadt: G. Ottos, 1898), and Sylvain Lévi and Edouard Chavannes, "Les seize arhat protecteurs de la loi," *Journal asiatique* 8 (1916): 266.

nents, and that you would distribute his reliquaries far and wide and build the eighty-four thousand dharmarājikās."

And he added:

When you with childish faith
put a handful of dirt
in the Buddha's dish
I too was there at that time.

Aśoka then asked Piṇḍola: "Elder where are you living now?"

He replied:

O king, I dwell on Mount Gandhamādana
to the north of the best of lakes
with fellow followers of the religious life.

The king asked:

How large is your following?

The elder answered:

O chief of men, I live with an entourage
of sixty-thousand saints.
They are free from longing
and have conquered sin.

"However, great king, why ask all these questions? Let the community of monks be served, then when they have finished eating, I will say a few words of greeting to them."

"So be it," said the king, "however, with the recollection of the Buddha fresh in my mind, I first want to bathe the Bodhi tree; then, immediately afterwards I will offer a pleasing meal to the community."

Aśoka then summoned Sarvamitra, the crier, and told him: "I want to make an offering of a hundred thousand pieces of gold to the community of āryas, and bathe the Bodhi tree with a thousand pots of scented water. Proclaim in my name a great quinquennial festival!"

The Quinquennial Festival

Now at that time Kunāla's eyes had not yet been put out. He was standing a bit to the right of the king, [his father. When Aśoka announced his offering] he said nothing but threw up two fingers, declaring by this gesture that he would give twice that amount. Seeing Kunāla thus increasing the size of the offering by a hand signal, the whole crowd roared with laughter.

The king too burst out laughing and said "Aho! Rādhagupta, who brought about this increase?"

Rādhagupta answered: "Your majesty, there are many liv-
101 ing beings who want to make merit; you were outbid by one
of them."

"Well then," said the king, "I will give three times a hundred thousand pieces of gold to the community of āryas, and will bathe the Bodhi tree with three thousand pots of scented water. Proclaim in my name a great quinquennial festival!"

But then, Kunāla put up four fingers. Thereupon, King Aśoka became irritated.

"Aho, Rādhagupta," he said to his minister, "who is it who is so ignorant of the ways of the world as to contend with me?"

Realizing that Aśoka was angry, Rādhagupta fell at his feet, and said: "Your majesty, who possibly would have enough power to vie with the chief of men? It is the virtuous Kunāla who is playfully rivalling his father."

Aśoka then turned around to the right and saw Kunāla standing there. "Elder," he then declared to Piṇḍola, "except for the state treasury, I now present to the noble community my kingship, my harem, my state officials, my self, and Kunāla. And I will bathe the great Bodhi tree with milk scented with sandalwood, saffron, and camphor [pouring it from] five thousand pitchers of gold, silver, crystal, and cat's eye, filled with different kinds of perfumes. And in front of the Bodhi tree, I will offer a hundred thousand flowers to the noble community. Proclaim in my name a great quinquennial festival!"

And he added:

My flourishing kingship
my harem, my officials, my self,
and my own virtuous Kunāla—
all of these (except for the treasury)
I offer to the sangha
that is a bowl of merit.

After making this present to the community of monks headed by Piṇḍola Bhāradvāja, the king himself mounted a platform that he had had built on all four sides of the Bodhi tree, and there he bathed the tree with four thousand pitchers [of milk].[47] As soon as the Bodhi bath was finished, the tree returned to its previous condition.[48]

102 As it is said:

As soon as the king had given the Bodhi tree
this most excellent bath,
tender, pale green sprouts appeared;
the tree was soon covered with green leaves,
delicate buds and shoots,
and the king and his court and the townspeople
greatly rejoiced at the sight.

After he had bathed the Bodhi tree, it was time for Aśoka to start waiting on the community of monks.

"Great king," the elder Yaśas announced, "this great noble community, which is worthy of the highest veneration, has assembled; you may now wait upon it in the correct manner."

The king therefore began to serve the monks with his own hand. [Starting with the senior monks] he went on until he reached the novices' seats. There he saw two young novices

[47] Probably should read five thousand.

[48] This statement seems out of place here and is perhaps an interpolation from the story of Tiṣyarakṣitā and Bodhi.

who were carrying on a friendly game of give-and-take. One would give some ground meal to the other who, in turn, would give some back. One would then offer cakes to his friend who would offer them back. Then sweetmeats would be given by one and returned by the other.

The king laughed. "These two novices are playing the games of children," he observed and having now finished serving the entire community, he returned to the elders' end.

There, Yaśas asked him: "Did your majesty see anything at all that raised doubts in his mind about the community?" "No," replied the king, "however, I did see two novices who were playing children's games. Just as young boys play at building houses in the dirt, so these two were playing at games of ground meal and cakes."

"Say no more, great king," said the elder, "both of these novices are arhats who are free from both physical and mental
103 defilements!"

Upon hearing this, Aśoka rejoiced in his heart and resolved to present to these two novices his offering of cloth for the community. The novices immediately divined the king's intention and said: "Let us make his merits even more numerous." One of them therefore set up a cauldron and the other began to prepare dye.

"What is this you are undertaking?" the king asked them.

"Your majesty," they answered, "has approached us with the desire of presenting an offering of cloth to the community of monks; we will dye that cloth."

"I never said anything about this," Aśoka reflected, "but only thought it. These two can read other people's minds!"

And immediately he fell full length at their feet, made an añjali and said:

The Mauryan, who sacrificed
what it was good to sacrifice
in order to attain what it is good to attain,
today has such faith in you, good people,

that he resolutely makes this offering
along with his servants, his court,
and the citizens of his capital.

And he said to the two novices: "Before you, I would like to present the three kinds of robes to the community of monks."

Aśoka then brought the great quinquennial festival to a close. After presenting the triple robe to all of the monks, he made an offering of four hundred thousand pieces of gold to
104 the community and redeemed from it the earth, his harem, his cabinet, himself, and Kunāla. His faith in the Teaching of the Blessed One reached even greater heights.[49]

The Birth of Kunāla

105 On the very same day on which King Aśoka built the eighty-four thousand dharmarājikās, his queen Padmavatī gave birth to a son who was handsome, good-looking, and gracious, and whose eyes were very bright.

"Rejoice, your majesty!" the king was told by those who came to announce the birth, "a son has been born to you!"

Aśoka was overjoyed by this good news, and declared:

I am filled with supreme delight
for the greatness of the Mauryan line has been assured.
A son has been born to me.
I ruled through Dharma, may he increase Dharma!

And so the boy was given the name Dharmavivardhana ("Dharma-increasing").

When the prince was brought to Aśoka, he looked at him and said with heartfelt joy:

My son's eyes are beautiful and very auspicious;
they resemble a fully blossomed blue lotus.

[49] The text then adds: "He built the eighty-four thousand dharmarājikās." This is probably an interpolation for the sake of transition to the opening line of the next episode.

His face, adorned by them,
shines and glows like the full moon.

And he asked his ministers: "Have you ever seen anyone with eyes such as these?"

"Your majesty," his ministers replied, "we have never seen a human being with such eyes, but there is a bird called the kunāla that lives in the great Himālaya mountains; its eyes are similar to these."

106 And they added:

On King of Snows, the mountain peak,
where streams abound, new leaves sprout,
and flowers bud,
there dwells a bird called the kunāla,
and its eyes are like those of your son.

The king then ordered a kunāla bird to be brought to him. His command was heard by the nāgas as far as one yojana underground, and by the yakṣas as much as one yojana up in the air; and the latter instantly fetched a kunāla for the king. Aśoka examined the bird's eyes thoroughly, and finding them no different from those of his son, he declared: "The prince's eyes are like those of a kunāla, let him therefore be called 'Kunāla!' "

As it is said:

Enamored with his eyes, the lord of the earth
then called his son "Kunāla."
Thus throughout the world, that noble being,
the king's son, was known by that name.

By and by, the prince grew up, and was married to a girl named Kāñcanamālā. One day, Aśoka went with Kunāla to the Kukkuṭārāma Monastery. There the elder of the community, Yaśas, an arhat endowed with the six supernatural faculties, realized that Kunāla's eyes would soon be destroyed.

He thereupon said to the king: "Why has Kunāla not been pushed to perform his religious practices?"

Aśoka [did not answer] but told Kunāla to carry out whatever the elder ordered him to do. The boy, falling at Yaśas's feet, then asked: "Elder, what is your command?"

"Kunāla," Yaśas replied, "you must practice this saying: 'The eye is impermanent.' "

107 And he added:

O prince, you should constantly examine the eye.
It is fickle by nature and yokes you to a thousand
sufferings.
Many common folk who are attached to it
commit acts that lead to misfortune.

Thereafter Kunāla made it a habit always to keep this teaching in mind. Delighting in solitude, he sought a tranquil hermitage; seated in a secluded spot in the royal palace, he examined the eye and all the other senses, seeing them as impermanent, empty, and characterized by suffering.

One day, Tiṣyarakṣitā, Aśoka's chief queen, happened to come to the place where he was meditating. She was enamored with Kunāla's beautiful eyes, and seeing him all alone, she embraced him and said:

When I see your handsome, glorious body
and your beautiful eyes,
I get a burning feeling inside
as though a forest fire were consuming a dry wood.

Hearing this, Kunāla put his hands over his ears, and said:

It is not proper for you
to say such things in front of your son;
you are a mother to me!
Shun this non-dharmic path,
for it will lead to a lower rebirth.

Now Tiṣyarakṣitā, seeing that her opportunity would come to nought, said angrily:

I came here longing for love,
but you didn't want me.
You fool! You won't live long,
108 I guarantee it!

"Mother," Kunāla replied,

I would rather die,
abiding by the Dharma and remaining pure,
than lead a life open to reproach by good people.
Such a life would be condemned by the wise
and violate the Dharma which leads to heaven,
and bring about my death.

Thereafter, Tiṣyarakṣitā was always seeking to find fault with Kunāla.

The Takṣaśilā Uprising and Aśoka's Illness

Now it came to pass that the city of Takṣaśilā, which is in the north country, rose in rebellion against the rule of King Aśoka. Learning this, the king wanted to go there himself, but his ministers advised him to send Kunāla instead.

Aśoka, therefore, called the prince and said: "Kunāla, my son, I want you to go and subdue the uprising in the city of Takṣaśilā."

"I will go there, my lord," Kunāla replied.

As it is said:

Then, understanding the ambition
of the one he called his son,
and realizing how he was bound by affection,
the king ordered him to go on the expedition,
while he himself stayed at home.

Aśoka then had the city and the highway beautified; he cleared the road of all old, sick, and poor people, got into the same chariot with his son, and accompanied him some ways out from Pāṭaliputra. When the time came for him to turn back, he embraced Kunāla, looked into his eyes and said, filled
109 with emotion:

Auspicious are the prince's eyes;
men who are endowed with sight
will always look
at his lotus-like face.

But at that time a Brahmin fortuneteller realized that it would not be long before the prince's eyes would be destroyed. And seeing that King Aśoka was too attached to his son's eyes, he said:

The eyes of the prince are pure,
and the lord of the earth is fond of him.
Today, I see those eyes,
that abound with beauty and lead to bliss,
being destroyed!
I see this city, which is happy as heaven
and rejoicing at the sight of the prince,
filled with sorrow
once those eyes have been put out.

Before very long, Kunāla reached Takṣaśilā. Hearing that he was coming, the inhabitants of the city bedecked the town and the road along two and a half yojanas, and went out to welcome him with their vases full of offerings.

As it is said;

At the news the Takṣaśilans took
their vases full of gems,
and went out to meet
the highly esteemed son of the king.

Welcoming him, they said, making an añjali: "We did not want to rebel against the prince, nor against King Aśoka—but evil-minded ministers came and were contemptuous of us." And they escorted Kunāla into the city with great respect.
110 Now it happened that King Aśoka became very ill; excrement began to come out of his mouth, and an impure substance oozed out of all his pores. No one was able to cure him.

"Have Kunāla come back," he declared, "and I will set him on the throne; what is the purpose in a life such as this?"

Now when Tiṣyarakṣitā heard this, she was afraid that if Kunāla were to become king, he would soon have her killed. She therefore said to Aśoka: "I will make you well, but first you must forbid all the doctors from coming in to see you."

When this had been done, Tiṣyarakṣitā said to the doctors: "If any man or woman should come to you suffering from a disease similar to that of the king, I would like to see him immediately."

Before long, it happened that a certain Abhīra man was stricken with just such a disease. His wife went to see a doctor and described the illness to him. "Bring him in," said the doctor, "I will examine him and then prescribe some medicine." However, as soon as the Abhīra was brought to him, he took him straight to Tiṣyarakṣitā. She, in secret, had him killed, and when he was dead, she split open his belly and examined the stomach. She found inside it a large worm; when it moved up, excrement would ooze out of the man's mouth, and when it went down, it would flow out down below.

The queen then ground some peppercorns and gave them to the worm, but it did not die. She tried long peppers and ginger, but again with no success. Finally, she gave some onion
111 to the worm; immediately it died and passed out through the intestinal tract.

She then went to Aśoka and prescribed this treatment "My lord, eat an onion and you will recover."

"Queen," the king objected, "I am a kṣatriya; how can I eat an onion?"

"My lord," she replied, "this is medicine; take it for the sake of life!"

Aśoka then ate it; the worm died, and passed out through his intestines, and he fully recovered. He was so pleased with Tiṣyarakṣitā that he granted her a boon.

"I will give you whatever you desire," he said to her.

"Then grant me the kingship," she replied, "for a period of seven days."

"And what will become of me [during that time]?" he asked.

"[Nothing,] my lord," she replied. "After seven days, you will become king again."

Aśoka thereupon agreed to cede the throne to Tiṣyarakṣitā for a period of seven days. [Once installed as ruler], her first thought was that she could now take her revenge on Kunāla. She composed, in Aśoka's name, a false letter to the people of Takṣaśilā, telling them to destroy Kunāla's eyes.

It said:

Truly, the powerful and fearsome King Aśoka
has ordered the people of Takṣaśilā
to gouge out the eyes of this enemy
who is a stain on the Mauryan lineage.

Now when Aśoka wanted something to be accomplished quickly, he always sealed the orders with his teeth. Therefore, that night, Tiṣyarakṣitā went to Aśoka, thinking she would get him to [bite the letter in his sleep and so] seal it with his
112 teeth. But something startled the king, and he woke up.

"What is it, my lord?" asked Tiṣyarakṣitā.

"Oh, queen," Aśoka replied, "I have just had a nightmare! I saw two vultures trying to pluck out Kunāla's eyes!"

"May the prince be well!" said Tiṣyarakṣitā, [and the king went back to sleep].

But then a second time he awoke, frightened, and said, "Queen, once again, I have not had a good dream."

"What was it like?" she asked.

"I saw Kunāla," he replied. "He was entering the city with a beard and long hair and long nails."

"May the prince be well!" said Tiṣyarakṣitā, [and again the king went back to sleep]. This time, he did not awaken. Tiṣyarakṣitā managed to get the letter sealed with his teeth, and she sent it immediately to Takṣaśilā. Aśoka, still asleep, dreamt that his teeth were falling out.

When the night passed, the king called his soothsayers and asked them to interpret these dreams.

"Your majesty," they replied, "one who sees such dreams will see the eyes of his son destroyed."

And they added:

One whose teeth decay
and fall out in a dream
will see his son's eyes destroyed
and the death of his son as well.

Hearing these words, Aśoka quickly got up from his seat, made añjalis in all four directions, and began to implore the deities:

May the gods who are well disposed
toward the Master, and toward the Dharma,
and toward the sangha, that most excellent assembly,
protect my son Kunāla!
And may all the best ṛṣis
in the world do likewise!

Kunāla's Blinding and Enlightenment

113 Now in due time Tiṣyarakṣitā's letter reached Takṣaśilā. The cityfolk and the people of the area read it, but they greatly appreciated Kunāla's many virtues, and could not immediately bring themselves to reveal to him its contents. In time, however, they reasoned that if Aśoka was so fierce and vicious that he would not exempt his own son from punishment, he

was even less likely to exempt them [for failing to carry out his orders]. And they said:

Whom will he not hate
if he hates the prince
who is a tranquil and accomplished sage
desiring the welfare of all beings?

Finally, then, they spoke to Kunāla and brought him the order. Kunāla had it read out aloud, and calmly told them to carry out fully the royal command. [Reluctantly,] they summoned the caṇḍalas (untouchables) and ordered them to gouge out Kunāla's eyes.

But the caṇḍalas made añjalis and said: "We can't do it, because:

Only a deluded man who would try
to take the beauty from the moon
could pluck out the eyes
from your face which is like the moon."

Kunāla then offered them, [as payment, his costly] diadem, and asked them to tear out his eyes in exchange for it, but they protested, saying: "Such an act will inevitably result in bad karma."

114 Finally, a disfigured man, endowed with the eighteen uglinesses, came forward and offered to pluck out the prince's eyes; he was taken right up to Kunāla.

At that moment, the words of the elders came to Kunāla's mind, and remembering them he said:

They divined this disaster and spoke the truth,
those who said to me:
"See, all of this is impermanent;
there is nothing which abides forever."
They were spiritual friends
who hoped for my happiness,
those magnanimous beings

who taught me this Dharma.
They were free from the defilements
and wished my well-being.
When I consider impermanence
and set my mind on the teachings of the gurus,
I do not fear this gouging, my friend,
for I can see the transient nature of my eyes.
Do whatever the king wishes
for whether my eyes are ripped out or not
I have already grasped the essence of my eye,
basing myself on the teachings of impermanence,
suffering, and emptiness.

Kunāla then said to the disfigured man: "Sir, first tear out one eye only and put it in my hand."

The man proceeded to do so. Instantly, hundreds of thou-
115 sands of beings cried out:

Oh! Woe! The brightly shining moon
has fallen from heaven,
the most beautiful of blossoms
is torn from the lotus pond.

And while these hundreds of thousands of beings continued their lamentations, the man placed the eye he had plucked out in Kunāla's hand.

Kunāla grasped it and said:

Why do you not see forms as before,
O lump of fashioned flesh?
They are fools, those who depend on you.
They are reprehensible and deceived
into thinking "This is the self!"
But those who are always attentive,
who regard you just as a composite whole,
a bubble that is hard to hold,
that is dependent and has no resting place—
they do not chase after suffering!

And reflecting thus on the impermanence of all existence Kunāla attained the fruit of entering the stream while the crowd of people looked on.

Having perceived the truth, Kunāla then calmly said to the man: "Now pluck out my other eye."

The man did so and put it in Kunāla's hand. Now when both of Kunāla's eyes of flesh had been torn out, his eye of wisdom was purified.

And he said:

Though my eye of flesh, difficult to come by,
has been plucked out,
I have obtained the pure
116 and virtuous eye of wisdom.
Though rejected by the king whose son
I am said to be,
I have become the son
of the magnanimous King of Dharma.
Though fallen from the sovereignty
that is bound to suffering and sorrow
I have obtained the sovereignty of Dharma
that puts an end to suffering and sorrow.

Sometime later, Kunāla found out that what had happened had not been his father's deed[50] but Tiṣyarakṣitā's undertaking. Upon learning this, he said:

May the queen called Tiṣya
have a long and happy life!
May she be healthy and strong,
for she brought about
the turn of events that resulted
in my achieving my aim.

When Kañcanamālā, who was devoted to her husband, heard that Kunāla's eyes had been plucked out, she plunged through

[50] I here follow P. L. Vaidya's edition of the text in reading "karmā" instead of "ādeśaḥ."

the crowd and made her way to him. Seeing him with his eyes gouged out and his body smeared with blood, she fainted and fell on the ground. They revived her by splashing water in her face; as soon as she regained consciousness, she cried out, sobbing:

> Those beautiful, captivating eyes
> that gazed at me and brought me joy
> are gone!
> They can no longer regard my body;
> dear to me as life, they have left me!

But Kunāla, seeking to console his wife, said: "Enough with this crying! You should not succumb to sorrow; one always reaps the fruit of one's own actions in this world."

And he added:

> Knowing this world to be constituted by karma
> and considering man to be made up of suffering
> and separation from dear ones to be the way of the
> world,
> you should not shed these tears, my dear.

Kunāla's Return

117 Soon Kunāla and his wife had to leave Takṣaśīla. Now from the time of his conception in his mother's womb, Kunāla had had a very delicate constitution. Unable to do any hard physical labor, his only occupation was to play the vīṇā and sing; so in this manner he collected alms and shared them with his wife. Following the same road by which they had come from Pāṭaliputra, Kañcanamālā led her husband back to the capital. There they tried to enter Aśoka's palace, but the gatekeeper stopped them, and they had to stay in the coach house. When the night had passed, Kunāla began to play the vīṇā, and sang a song about how his eyes had been ripped out, and how he had attained a vision of the truth and so salvation.

And he added:

The wise man who sees the eye and the other senses
by the light of the pure lamp of knowledge
is released from saṃsāra.
If your mind is afflicted by the suffering of existence
and settled on wickedness,
but you yearn for happiness in this world,
then quickly and resolutely relinquish
118 the field of your senses.

Now King Aśoka heard the sound of Kunāla's song and it pleased him.

It must be Kunāla who is singing this for me;
I recognize from long ago the sound of his vīṇā.
He must have come back and is now here at home,
but does not want to see anyone yet!

Aśoka then called one of his men, and said, "Listen:

Is the sound of that song not like Kunāla's?
It seems to be pointing out the inconstancy of acts.
I am greatly moved by the sound of it,
like an elephant who has found her long lost calf.

Go, and bring Kunāla here."

Accordingly, the servant went to the coach house, but he did not recognize Kunāla with his eyes torn out and his skin burnt by the wind and the sun. He therefore went back to Aśoka and said: "Your majesty, that is not Kunāla, but a blind beggar who is staying with his wife in your majesty's coach house."

Hearing this, Aśoka was very upset, for he remembered the unpleasant dreams he had had and thought "surely these must be the blinded eyes of Kunāla."

And he said:

In a dream, long ago,
I saw certain signs;
there can be no doubt now,
Kunāla's eyes have been destroyed.

And with tears in his eyes, he added:

Quickly bring
that beggar before me,
for my mind cannot rest
thinking of the fate of my son.

The man then went to the coach house and said: "Whose son are you and what is your name?"

119 "O servant," Kunāla replied,

The king they call Aśoka,
increaser of the house of Maurya,
under whose rule rests the entire world—
I am his son, known as Kunāla.
But I am also the son of the righteous Buddha,
a kinsman of the sun.

Kunāla and his wife were then taken to King Aśoka, but Aśoka did not recognize him with his eyes torn out, his skin burned by the wind and the sun, and his loins barely covered by a garment less honorable than a rag tossed out on the dust heap.

Perceiving only a human form, he asked: "Are you Kunāla?"

"Yes, my lord," came the answer, "I am Kunāla."

And hearing these words, Aśoka fainted and collapsed on the ground.

And it is said:

When King Aśoka saw the face
of Kunāla whose eyes had been torn out,
his senses were carried away by the pain;
he fell on the ground crying:
"O my son, my heart is consumed by sorrow!"

Then they revived him by splashing water in his face, and they sat him down on a seat. And when he had recovered his senses, he embraced his son.

As it is said:

Presently the king recovered
and embraced Kunāla around the neck,
his own cheeks wet with tears.
He stroked his face again and again
and then began to cry:
"Long ago, when I saw that your eyes resembled
those of the kunāla bird,
I called you 'Kunāla' my son;
But how can I say 'Kunāla' now
to my son whose eyes have been destroyed?"

And he added:

Tell me, tell me, saintly son,
120 how your face with its beautiful eyes
came to be like the sky
darkened and deprived of beauty
by the fall of the bright moon.
Only a man with a pitiless heart
could have done such a thing, my boy,
to the eyes of the best of men
whose saintly mind is like the Sage's.
This evil act of enmity
to one who knew no hatred
is for me a source of much sorrow.
Tell me quickly the reason for this,
you whose face was so handsome.
Consumed by sorrow over the loss of your eyes,
my body will soon come to nought
like a forest burned down
by the lightning the nāgas let loose.

Then Kunāla bowed down to his father and said:

O king, do not grieve so over what is past,
Have you not heard the saying of the Sage
that even Jinas and pratyekabuddhas
are not free from tenacious karma?
Ordinary people as well are defined
by the fruits that they have reaped.
The deeds of living beings never die.
The fruit of acts done in this world is one's own;
How then can I speak of this
121 as having been done by others?

"It is I, great king, who have committed an offense, and I who have to live with it. I am the one who did and caused to ripen the deeds that have generated my misfortune."

Swords, lightning, fire,
poisons, snakes—none of these—
can hurt the unchanging sky.[51]
But when the body is set up as the target,
the cruel sufferings of creatures
hit their mark, O king.

But Aśoka [did not listen]. His heart burning with the fire of sorrow, he cried:

Who tore out your eyes my son?
Who is determined to give up this sweet life?
The fearsome fire of sorrow has hit my heart;
Tell me who it was, my son,
and I will swiftly punish him.

At length King Aśoka found out that the whole thing had been Tiṣyarakṣitā's undertaking. He summoned her right away
122 and said:

[51] I here follow P. L. Vaidya's edition of the text in reading "nabhaso'vikāriṇaḥ" instead of "rabhasāpakāriṇaḥ."

How is it, miserable creature,
that you do not sink into the ground?[52]
I shall strike off your head with an axe!
You wicked woman, attached to unrighteousness,
I now disown you the way
a self-possessed sage renounces wealth.

And burning with the fire of anger, glaring at Tiṣyarakṣitā, he went on:

First, I'll tear out her eyes,
and then I think
I'll rip open her body with sharp rakes,
impale her alive on a spit,
cut off her nose with a saw,
cut out her tongue with a razor,
and fill her with poison and kill her.

In this and many other ways, the chief of men spoke of plans for her execution. But the magnanimous compassionate Kunāla hearing his father's words, said somberly:

If Tiṣyarakṣitā's deeds were not honorable,
let your own not be like hers.
Do not kill the woman,
for the reward of loving kindness knows no equal,
123 and forgiveness, my lord, was extolled by the Sugata.

And bowing once again to his father, the prince spoke these words of truth, making an añjali:

O king, I do not feel the slightest pain,
for although it is a severe injury,
there is no suffering in my mind.
If indeed it is true that I
have only kind thoughts for my mother

[52] Great sinners, in the Buddhist tradition, were swallowed up by the earth. See I. B. Horner "The Earth as a Swallower" in *Essays Offered to G. H. Luce*, ed. Ba Shin, Jean Boisselier, and A. B. Griswold, 2 vols. (Ascona: Artibus Asiae, 1966), 1:151:59.

who was directly responsible for my blindness,
then by the power of this statement of truth,[53]
may my eyes be restored at once!

And as soon as he had thus spoken, his sight returned and his eyes regained their former splendor.

Aśoka, however, did not forgive Tiṣyarakṣitā; he threw her into a lacquer house,[54] where she was burned to death, and he had the citizens of Takṣaśilā executed as well.

KUNĀLA'S PAST LIFE

Now a number of monks were unclear about certain points of this story, so they questioned the venerable elder Upagupta, knowing that he could remove all their doubts.

"What deed," they asked, "did Kunāla do that resulted in his eyes being torn out?"

"Listen, venerable sirs," answered the elder. "Long ago, in days gone by, a certain hunter from Vārāṇasī went hunting in the Himālayas. One day, he happened upon five hundred deer who had entered a cave and lain down, and quickly he trapped them all inside the cave with a net. Now it occurred
124 to him that if he killed all the deer immediately, the meat
would get rotten, so instead he put out their eyes, and, thus blinded, they were unable to run away. In this way he was responsible for destroying the eyes of several hundred deer.

"Do you understand, venerable sirs? Kunāla was that hunter. Because he put out the eyes of many hundred deer, as a result of that act, he suffered several hundred thousand years in hell, and then, as the final consequence of his deed, had his own eyes put out in each of five hundred lifetimes."

[53] On the act of truth and its efficacy, see W. Norman Brown, "The Metaphysics of the Truth Act (Satyakriyā)," in *Mélanges d'indianisme à la mémoire de Louis Renou* (Paris: E. de Boccard, 1968), pp 171-77.

[54] Perhaps a reference to the famous lacquer house built by Duryodhana for the execution of the Pāṇḍavas in the *Mahābhārata*. It may be, however, that the text should not be read jatu-gṛha but jantu-gṛha, "a house of jantu," that Edgerton (*Dictionary*, s.v. jantu) interprets as a kind of grass.

"And what deed," the monks asked, "did Kunāla do that resulted in his being born in a prominent family, in his being good-looking, and in his perceiving the Truths?"

"Listen," replied the elder. "Long ago, in days gone by, when men had lifespans of forty thousand years, there appeared in the world a wholly enlightened Buddha named Krakucchanda. When he had finished doing the work of a Buddha, he entered into the state of complete nirvāṇa without any remaining attributes. A king named Aśoka [*sic*] built a stūpa for him made out of four kinds of jewels.

"When this King Aśoka had passed away, a king without faith ascended the throne, and thieves carried off the stūpa's jewels, leaving only the dirt and the wood. A group of people
125 went there, and seeing the ruins, they were filled with sorrow.

"At that time, the son of a guild master happened by, and asked them why they were crying. 'The stūpa of the wholly enlightened Krakucchanda,' they replied, 'was made of four kinds of gems; now it has been broken up.'

"The son of the guild master therefore restored the broken stūpa and set there a life-size image of the completely enlightened Krakucchanda. He then completed this resolute wish: 'May I meet and gratify a master who is just like the Master Krakucchanda, and may I be worthy of him.'

"Do you understand, Venerable sirs? Kunāla was that son of a guild master. Because he rebuilt the stūpa of Krakucchanda, he, as a result of that act, was born into a prominent family. Because he rebuilt the image, he, as a result, became good-looking. And because he made an earnest vow, he met and was worthy of his master Śākyamuni who is just like the wholly enlightened Krakucchanda, and, as a result, he perceived the Truths."

Aśoka's Last Gift

126 One day, after King Aśoka had obtained faith in the Teaching of the Blessed One, he asked the monks who had made

the greatest of all donations to the Buddhist religion. They informed him that it was the householder Anāthapiṇḍada.

"How much did he give?" asked Aśoka.

"He gave," the monks answered, "a gift of one hundred koṭis of gold pieces to the Teaching of the Blessed One."

Aśoka thought about this for a while and then declared: "In the past, this householder gave a total of one hundred koṭis in support of the Buddha's religion; I, therefore, will do likewise."

At that point, Aśoka had already built the eighty-four thousand dharmarājikās, and had made a donation of one hundred thousand pieces of gold to each of them. Then, he had given one hundred thousand to the place of the Buddha's birth, to the Bodhi tree, to the place where he set in motion the Wheel of Dharma, and to the site of his parinirvāṇa. Then he had held a great quinquennial festival and spent four hundred thousand on the entertainment of three hundred thousand monks, a third of whom were arhats, and two-thirds of whom were virtuous ordinary disciples. Also, he had offered to the ārya sangha the whole earth (except for the state treasury), as well as his harem, his state officials, his self, and his son Kunāla, and had redeemed them all with four hundred thousand pieces of gold. Thus, his total gift to the Teaching of the Blessed One amounted to ninety-six koṭis.

Presently, however, Aśoka became ill, and thinking that he would soon pass away [and be unable to complete the balance of his gift], he became despondent. Aśoka's prime minister, Rādhagupta, who had been with him in his previous life at the time of the gift of dirt, noted his depression; falling at his
127 feet, he made an añjali and said:

Your majesty, why is your face—
which your enemies dared not look at
when it shone fiercely like the sun,
which hundreds of lotus-lipped
beauties eagerly kissed—
now covered with tears?

"Rādhagupta," answered the king, "I do not mourn the loss of wealth, the end of sovereignty, or the body that I am leaving, but I do lament the fact that I shall be separated from the āryas." [And he added:]

I shall no more see the community
endowed with every virtue,
honored by men and gods;
I shall no longer be able to honor it
with the finest food and drink.
These thoughts make me shed tears.

"Furthermore, Rādhagupta, it was my wish to give one hundred koṭis of gold pieces to the Teaching of the Blessed One, and I have failed to carry out this intention fully."

Then declaring that he would nevertheless try to complete the gift of four more koṭis, he started sending gold coins to the Kukkuṭārāma.

At that time, Kunāla's son, Sampadin, had become the heir-
apparent. His counsellors said to him: "Prince, King Aśoka
128 will not live much longer, but he keeps sending money to the
Kukkuṭārāma. The power of kings lies in their state treasury;
he should be restrained."

Sampadin, therefore, issued an order prohibiting the treasurer [from disbursing state funds].

But the gold dishes for King Aśoka's meals did not come under this interdiction, and after eating, Aśoka started sending them as offerings to the Kukkuṭārāma. The restriction was then extended to his gold dishes, and he was served his meals on silver plates. But these too he sent to the Kukkuṭārāma. The silver dishes were then restricted, and his food was served on [copper plates. But still he sent these to the Kukkuṭārāma. They were in turn restricted, and finally his food was served on][55] plates of clay.

Eventually, all Aśoka had left was a half of a myrobalan (*āmalaka*) fruit; he took it in his hand, summoned his ministers

[55] The passage in brackets added on the basis of P. L. Vaidya's edition. See Vaidya, *Divyāvadāna*, p. 280.

and the citizens, and, very upset, he said: "Who is presently lord of the earth?"

The ministers got up from their seats, bowed down, made an añjali in King Aśoka's direction, and declared: "Your majesty is lord of the earth!"

But Aśoka, his eyes clouded with tears, replied:

Do you lie in order to indulge me?
I have lost my sovereignty.
The only thing that remains under my rule
is this half of a myrobalan.
Woe! woe! to worthless lordship
that is like the flood waters at the
mouth of a river!
For I too, the Indra of mortals,
129 have fallen into frightful penury.

"Who now could deny the saying of the Blessed One that 'All fortune is the cause of misfortune'? Truth-speaking Gautama asserted that, and indeed he was right! Today, I am no longer obeyed; no matter how many commands I think of issuing, they are all countermanded just like a river that is turned back when it dashes against a mountain cliff." [Again he added:]

Once he ruled the earth
under a single umbrella of sovereignty,
destroyed the haughty enemy hosts,
consoled the distressed and the poor.
But he lost his support,
fell from his position,
and today this wretched king
no longer rules in glory.
Just like an aśoka tree
when its flowers are cut off
and its leaves have shrivelled and fallen,
this king is drying up.

Then King Aśoka called a man to come to him, and said: "My friend, even though I have fallen from power, do this last task for me, out of respect for my past virtues. Take this my half a myrobalan, go to the Kukkuṭārāma, and offer it to the community. Prostrate yourself before the monks on my behalf and say this: 'I give you the present greatness of the king who ruled all of Jambudvīpa.' Then have this my last offering distributed in such a way that it is offered to and enjoyed by the whole community."

130 And he said:

This today is my final offering;
my kingship and identity are gone.
Without good health, doctors, or medicinal herbs,
my only recourse is the assembly of noble ones.
Therefore accept and distribute among yourselves
this last gift that today I make to the sangha.

The man agreed to do as Aśoka asked. He took the half a myrobalan, went to the Kukkuṭārāma, and standing in front of the elders, he made an añjali and offered it to the sangha, saying:

He who previously ruled the earth
over which he had spread his umbrella of sovereignty
and warmed the world like the noonday sun at its
  zenith—
today that king has seen his good fortune cut off.
Deceived by his own karmic acts,
he finds his glory gone
like the setting sun at dusk.

Then the man, with his head bowed devoutly, paid his respects to the sangha and presented the offering of half a myrobalan, as a sign of the fickle nature of prosperity.

The elder of the sangha then spoke to the monks: "Brethren, today it is acceptable for you to show signs of emotion. Why? Because the Blessed One said that the misfortune of others

was an occasion for being upset. Whose heart would not be
131 moved today, for:

A great donor, the lord of men,
the eminent Maurya Aśoka,
has gone from being lord of Jambudvīpa
to being lord of half a myrobalan.
Today this lord of the earth,
his sovereignty stolen by his servants
presents the gift of just half a myrobalan,
as though reproving the common folk
whose hearts are puffed up
with a passion for enjoying great splendor."

Thereupon the myrobalan half was mashed, put in a soup and distributed to the community.

Then Aśoka said to Rādhagupta: "Tell me, Rādhagupta, who is now lord of the earth?"

And Rādhagupta, falling at Aśoka's feet, answered, making an añjali: "Your majesty is lord of the earth."

Then King Aśoka struggled to his feet, gazed around at the points of the compass, and said, making an añjali in the direction of the sangha: "Except for the state treasury, I now present the whole earth, surrounded by the ocean, to the community of the Blessed One's disciples."

And he added:

I give to the sangha this earth,
with its Mandara mountain,
and its dark blue blouse, the ocean,
and its face adorned with many jewel mines.
132 May the community enjoy the fruit.

Furthermore:

With this gift, I do not seek the reward
of rebirth in Indra's abode or Brahma's world;
even less do I want the glory of kingship

that is as unsteady as a choppy sea.
But because I gave it with faith,
I would obtain as the fruit of this gift
something that cannot be stolen,
that is honored by the āryas
and safe from all agitation:
sovereignty over the mind.

Aśoka then had this inscribed on a document and sealed it with his teeth; he had given the great earth to the sangha, and he then passed away.

The ministers carried him off on a blue and yellow bier; they paid their final respects to his body, cremated it, and got ready to install the new king.

Rādhagupta, however, reminded them that King Aśoka had given the whole earth to the sangha.

"What can we do?" asked the ministers.

"It was King Aśoka's wish," replied Rādhagupta, "to give all told one hundred koṭis of gold pieces in support of the Teaching of the Blessed One. He had given ninety-six koṭis when his powers were restricted; but it was with the intention of completing his gift that he gave the great earth away to the sangha."

The ministers therefore gave four koṭis of gold pieces for the Teaching in order to buy back the Earth, and they consecrated Sampadin as king.

Puṣyamitra and the End of the Mauryan Line

133 Sampadin's son was Bṛhaspati who, in turn, had a son named Vṛṣasena, and Vṛṣasena had a son named Puṣyadharman, and Puṣyadharman begot Puṣyamitra.

One day, the latter asked his ministers: "What can I do to make my name renowned forever?"

"In your majesty's lineage," they answered, "there was a

king named Aśoka who built eighty-four thousand dharmarājikās. His fame will endure as long as the Buddhist religion survives. Let your majesty also build eighty-four thousand dharmarājikās, and so be famous like him."

But the king said: "King Aśoka was great and distinguished; is there not some other means?"

Now Puṣyamitra had a Brahmin priest who was a mean and faithless man. He declared: "Your majesty, there are two ways to make a name endure forever. King Aśoka built eighty-four thousand dharmarājikās and is thereby famous. If you, on the other hand, were to destroy those dharmarājikās, your name would endure even longer."

Then King Puṣyamitra equipped a fourfold army, and intending to destroy the Buddhist religion, he went to the Kukkuṭārāma; but at the gate, he heard a lion's roar, and frightened, he retreated to Pāṭaliputra. A second time, and then again a third time, the same thing happened. Finally, he summoned the community and said to the monks: "I am going to destroy the religion of the Blessed One—would you rather keep the stūpas or the saṅghārāma?" The monks decided to
134 keep the stūpas. Puṣyamitra therefore destroyed the saṅghārāma, killed the monks there, and departed.

After some time, he arrived in Śākala, and proclaimed that he would give a hundred dīnāra reward to whomever brought him the head of a Buddhist monk. Now there was a certain arhat there who lived in a dharmarājikā, and he started creating heads by means of his supernatural powers and giving them to the king. When the king learned what was happening, he resolved to have the arhat put to death. The saint then entered the trance of cessation but did not cross over to the other side. The king [unable to kill him] finally gave up and went to Koṣṭhaka.

There the yakṣa Daṃṣṭrānivāsin[56] reasoned: "[If Puṣyamitra is not killed] the Buddhist religion will die out; but I

[56] The name means "He who dwells near the tooth [relic of the Buddha]."

maintain the precepts—it is not possible for me to harm anyone whomsoever!" Now another yakṣa, Kṛmiśa, was seeking the hand of Daṃṣṭrānivāsin's daughter in marriage, but Daṃṣṭrānivāsin had refused him saying "you are an evil-doer!" Now, however, he agreed to give Kṛmiśa his daughter, on the condition that he take appropriate measures for the rescue and continued protection of the Buddhist religion.

Now King Puṣyamitra always had behind him as his body-
guard a very big yakṣa. He was so strong that the king was
135 never beaten. But Daṃṣṭrānivāsin grabbed that yakṣa who
was Puṣyamitra's aide-de-corps, and went for a walk in the
mountains. Puṣyamitra then fled south to the great ocean; but
there the yakṣa Kṛmiśa took up a great mountain and set it
down on top of Puṣyamitra, his troops, and his chariots. He
was then given the name Sunihita ("Well-put-down"). With
the death of Puṣyamitra, the Mauryan lineage came to an end.

APPENDIX

Sanskrit Legends about Aśoka Not Appearing in the *Aśokāvadāna*

There are a number of stories about Aśoka no longer extant in the Sanskrit text of the *Aśokāvadāna* that have been preserved, however, in Chinese translation in various other sources. The following are summaries of some of these, based on a number of different works: the last chapter of the *A-yü wang chuan* translated by Fa-ch'in c. 300 A.D., Aśvaghoṣa's *Sūtrālaṃkara* translated by Kumārajīva in 405 A.D. and the *Chiu tsa pi-yü ching* translated in the 3rd century A.D., probably by K'ang Seng-hui.

(1) Aśoka and the Wish-granting Jewel[1]

Once, long ago, Aśoka was given five precious wish-granting gems by the King of Sri Lanka. He took them and gave one to the stūpa at the birthplace of the Buddha, another to the Bodhi tree, a third to the site of the Buddha's first sermon, and a fourth to the site of the parinirvāṇa. He wanted to give the fifth jewel to one of his wives, but feared that if he did so it would cause jealousy among the others. Nevertheless, he decided to test his wives by declaring that he would give the jewel to the woman who was the best-dressed. All the women of the harem then competed with each other in putting on sumptuous clothes and ornaments, except for a young woman named Sujātā. She reasoned that the Buddha had declared that the eight precepts were the "best of dresses," and so she observed the eight precepts while donning a simple white robe.

When King Aśoka inspected all of his wives, he saw their

[1] See Jean Przyluski, *La légende de l'empereur Açoka* (Paris: Paul Geuthner, 1923), pp. 410-11.

various magnificent garments and ornaments. Then he saw Sujātā. He asked her why she was not dressed like the others, and she replied by repeating her reasoning aloud. Aśoka was filled with respect for her, and declaring her to be truly best-dressed as one dressed in the eight precepts, he gave her the wish-granting jewel. From then on all the women of the harem began to observe the eight precepts.

(2) Aśoka's Concubine and the Monk[2]

When King Aśoka began having faith in the Teaching of the Blessed One, it became his custom to invite monks to the palace where he made offerings to them and listened to their sermons on the Dharma. Occasionally he would set up a curtain behind which his wives could sit and listen to the Dharma, although they were strictly forbidden to approach the monks directly.

One day a bhikṣu was preaching to the women. Since, he reasoned, the women of the harem would be attached to worldly pleasures, he limited himself to a sermon on the practice of dāna and other good works. Upon hearing his words, however, one of the concubines came out from behind the curtain and asked him whether there was not more to the Buddha's Dharma than this. The monk replied that he had not realized he was being heard by someone of penetrating insight, and he then preached to her the Four Noble Truths. The concubine immediately attained the fruit of entering the stream and declared that though she had violated the rule of the king, she had obtained a great reward.

She then went to Aśoka, and offered to kill herself because of her transgression. When, however, he found out that she had done what she had for the sake of the Dharma and thereby become a stream winner, Aśoka forgave her and marvelled greatly at the glory of the Buddha's Teaching.

[2] See Edouard Huber, tr., *Aśvaghoṣa Sūtrālaṃkāra* (Paris: E. Leroux, 1908), pp. 150-57, and Przyluski, *La légende*, pp. 412ff.

(3) Aśoka and the Monk with the Sweet Breath[3]

Once, when Aśoka invited some members of the sangha to his palace for a meal, there came a young monk named Utpala whose breath smelled like the blossom of an utpala lotus. Aśoka noticed this while serving him and was afraid that the perfume might distract the women of his harem. He therefore asked the monk to rinse out his mouth. The monk did so but still his breath smelled sweet. Aśoka marvelled at this, and upon inquiry, the monk then revealed to him the story of his previous life. Long ago, at the time of the Buddha Kāśyapa, he had been a monk who had constantly praised the virtues of the Buddha and preached the Dharma to the crowd. Because of this he was born with a sweet-smelling breath. Aśoka, upon learning this declared: "I have been enlightened today as to the merit that comes from exalting the Buddha. I would only say this therefore: constantly sing the praises of the Blessed One!"

(4) Aśoka and the Young Novice[4]

Once, when Aśoka met a young seven-year-old novice, he waited until they were in a remote, isolated place; then he prostrated himself in front of him, but said "Do not tell anyone that I bowed down before you."

There was a bath-flask nearby; suddenly, by means of his magical powers, the novice entered into it and came out again through the narrow spigot. "O King," he said to Aśoka, "do not tell anyone that I entered this flask and came out again

[3] See Huber, *Sūtrālaṃkāra*, pp. 273-78, and Przyluski, *La légende*, pp. 411f. For a somewhat similar story in the *Avadānaśataka*, see Léon Feer, tr., *Avadāna-çataka: cent légendes (bouddhiques)*, Annales du Musée Guimet, vol. 18 (Paris: E. Leroux, 1891), pp. 238-40.

[4] See Przyluski, *La légende*, pp. 413ff. Compare the beginning to the story of Aśoka and his minister Yaśas. See also Huber, *Sūtrālaṃkāra*, No. 3, where the same story is told but without reference to Aśoka by name.

through the spigot." Aśoka then protested that he could not hide such a marvel, and had to tell others about it.

That is why, the story adds, the scriptures say that there are three things one should never malign: a young king, a young nāga, and a young monk. The first, though young, can put men to death; the second, though very little, can make it rain; and the third, though small, can save mankind.

(5) Aśoka, the Novice, and the Cannibalistic Brahmins[5]

Aśoka had great faith in the Triple Gem and was constantly making offerings to the Buddha, Dharma, and sangha. Some brahmins were very jealous of this and declared that the state would soon come to ruin if the king kept up his liberality. One brahmin, who was endowed with magical power, decided to do something about it. Taking on the form of Maheśvara [Śiva], he flew to Aśoka's palace where, together with five hundred other Brahmins, he demanded to be served by the king.

When Aśoka prepared a sumptuous meal for them, however, they scorned it and declared that they never ate such things; they only ate Buddhist monks. In a quandary as to what course of action to take, Aśoka presented the situation to the members of the sangha; they responded by sending a young novice to the royal palace. There, the novice declared himself willing to serve as a meal for the brahmins but only on condition that he first be fed. He, therefore, was served the meal that had been prepared for the five hundred brahmins; he consumed all of it, but still was not full. He then was served all of the food in the kitchen, and everything in the royal storehouses but still he was not satisified. As there was nothing else left for him to eat the novice then devoured the five hundred brahmins including Maheśvara.

[5] See Przyluski, *La légende*, pp. 414-18.

At this point, Aśoka feared that perhaps he too would be eaten, but the novice reassured him and took him instead to the Kukkuṭārāma; there he saw the monks eating the food that the novice had devoured earlier on, and he also saw the five hundred Brahmins, alive and well, sitting with their heads shaved and ordained as Buddhist monks in the midst of the assembly.

(6) Aśoka and the Servant Girl's Gift[6]

Once, in Aśoka's palace, there was a servant girl who became very depressed, thinking that Aśoka was great because of his meritorious actions in a past life, while she herself was very poor because of her bad karmic past. How, she wondered, would she ever be able to make merit, as destitute as she was?

One day, however, she happened to find a penny in the trash, and, though very poor indeed, she took it and gave it rejoicingly to the sangha. Soon thereafter, she passed away and was promptly reborn in the womb of one of Aśoka's queens. At birth, she had one fist tightly closed. When she was taken to Aśoka, he opened her hand and found therein a gold coin, and every time the coin was removed, another appeared in its place. Wondering about this marvel, Aśoka asked Yaśas what deed the girl had done to merit such a reward, and Yaśas then told him the story of her offering of a penny to the sanghâ in her previous birth.

(7) Aśoka and Ajātaśatru's Gemstone[7]

Once upon a time Aśoka acquired a chipped gemstone that had formerly been a part of King Ajātaśatru's armor, and that

[6] See ibid., pp. 420-21. For a similar story, see Feer, *Avadānaśataka*, pp. 314-18.

[7] See Przyluski, *La légende*, pp. 421-22.

bore an inscription that read: "Bequeathed to the poor King Aśoka who will reign in the future."

The inscription made Aśoka furious: "Ajātaśatru," he declared, "was a petty prince; I rule the whole of Jambudvīpa—how can he call me poor?"

But a wise minister then told Aśoka to put the gemstone to the test, and it was discovered that it had many extraordinary properties. Anyone who held it found himself armed with a mighty and fearsome weapon; anyone who suffered from ulcers found himself cured; in cold weather, the gem was warm and in hot weather, it was cool; anyone who swallowed poisons could easily digest them, if he had the gem.

Aśoka then reflected that although he himself possessed many gems in his treasury, he owned none as great as this one, that had been but a part of Ajātaśatru's armor and was chipped at that! Indeed, he truly was poor in comparison to the men who lived at the time of the Buddha and whose merits were thereby enormous!

(8) Aśoka and Piṇḍola[8]

Once, when Aśoka invited the great arhat Piṇḍola to a meal, he served him water, and then gave him some rice and some fermented milk to go with it. He cautioned him, however, that the fermented milk was very strong and hard to digest, and might give him indigestion. Piṇḍola replied that there was nothing to fear—that he would not get sick for he was used to the food served at the time of the Buddha when plain water was as strong as the fermented milk served nowadays.

Aśoka asked him why this was so. By way of reply, Piṇḍola plunged his hand down into the earth to a depth of forty-two thousand stadii, and brought up a handful of clayey soil. "Today," he said, "men have very little merit and clayey things

[8] See ibid., p. 422.

have all sunken down into the earth." At the time of the Buddha, men's merits were much greater.

(9) Aśoka Exhorts Others to Make Merit[9]

Once, when the court diviner had examined Aśoka's physiognomy, he declared that the king's person bore on it certain inauspicious marks; in order to counter these ill omens, Aśoka should perform meritorious deeds. Aśoka therefore set out to make merit, and built the eighty-four thousand stūpas. He then went back to the diviner, but the inauspicious marks were still there.

The king then asked the elder Yaśas what else he could do to erase these evil signs. The elder replied that so far he had only been acquiring "light" merit for himself; what he needed to do was to acquire "heavy" merit by exhorting others to make merit also.

Aśoka therefore got dressed as a wandering beggar, and started going from door to door, exhorting others to make merit by giving him alms. Soon, he came to the house of a very poor woman who had nothing at all but the single piece of cloth in which she was dressed. Yet, presented with the opportunity of making an offering, she gladly gave up her one robe, and hid, naked behind a wall. Aśoka was profoundly moved by this; he returned to the palace, took a precious necklace and gave it to the woman. He also gave her several villages as a fief.

Then, continuing on his begging round to exhort others to make merit, he arrived at the house of an old and destitute couple who had nothing to give at all. They, however, went to a rich neighbor and borrowed seven gold pieces, declaring that if they did not repay him in a week, they would become his slaves. Then they went and gave the gold to Aśoka. Again, profoundly moved by their action, Aśoka returned to his pal-

[9] See ibid., pp. 423-25.

ace and got some clothes and precious jewels for the couple, and also gave them a village as a fief.

When Aśoka had thus finished exhorting others to give alms, the inauspicious marks on his body disappeared.

(10) Aśoka and the Buddha-relics[10]

When King Aśoka wished to collect the relics of the Buddha that King Ajātaśatru had placed in the Ganges, he went to get them, but found his way blocked by a great wheel armed with sharp swords that spun with the force of the river. Not knowing how to get around it, he asked a monk for advice. The latter told him to throw great quantities of plums into the river in order to gum up the wheel's works. This was successful, but then Aśoka encountered a great nāga king guarding the relics, and again he was at a loss as to how to proceed. The monk then told him that when his merit exceeded that of the nāga, he would be able to pass unharmed and obtain the relics. Their relative merit was then measured by weighing two golden statues of the same size, one of King Aśoka and the other of the nāga. At first, the nāga's statue was heavier. Aśoka therefore performed some meritorious works and again the statues were placed in the balance. They were found to weigh exactly the same amount. Aśoka, therefore, made still more merit; and eventually his statue became heavier and the nāga king let him pass.

Aśoka then went to the relic chamber, opened it up, and took out the relics. At that very moment, the oil lamp that King Ajātaśatru had lit went out. Aśoka marvelled at this and asked the monk how Ajātaśatru had known exactly how much oil to put in the lamp. The monk replied that in those days, the time of the Buddha, there were good calculators who could foresee such things with precision.

[10] See ibid., pp. 425-26.

(11) Aśoka's Son and the Bhikṣus[11]

Once, long ago, King Aśoka, whose custom it was to serve feasts to the Buddhist bhikṣus, ordered his son the prince to do likewise. The heir to the throne resented this and thought to himself "When I become king, I will kill all these monks!" One of the bhikṣus, however, read his thoughts, and making clear to the prince his powers of mind reading, he greatly impressed him. Aśoka's son then changed his mind: "When I become king," he now reflected, "I will make even greater offerings to the monks than my father." His heart thus favorably disposed to the Teaching of the Blessed One, he rejected his evil ways.

(12) Aśoka and the Young Monk[12]

Every day it was Aśoka's practice to feed and entertain one thousand arhats in his palace. One day, a young monk came to the throne room, inspected everything there very closely and especially eyed the king's chief queen. Aśoka, suspicious, asked the elders who this young monk was and what he was doing.

They explained that the monk had come to examine the palace, in order to compare it to the palace of the gods in the Trāyastriṃśa Heaven. He had found the two exactly alike and had reasoned that Aśoka had merited such magnificence because, in a previous life, he had put a handful of dirt into the Buddha's bowl. He had, however, also realized that the chief queen would, in seven days, die, and be reborn in hell.

Aśoka accordingly called his wife, and together they asked the elders what they could do about her impending doom. The elders advised them to go and find the young monk and to get him to preach the Dharma. They did so and the queen, delighting in the doctrine, quickly became a stream winner.

[11] See Edouard Chavannes, *Cinq cents contes et apologues extraits du Tripiṭaka chinois*, 4 vols. (Paris: Imprimerie Nationale, 1934), 1:406-07.
[12] See ibid., pp. 370-71.

Glossary

The following list does not give all the possible meanings for each term, but only those immediately relevant to the text of the *Aśokāvadāna* and our discussion of it.

ĀJÑACAKRA (Pali, *āṇācakka*). The wheel of state or of royal authority in the scheme of the Two Wheels of Buddhism.

ALAKṢAṆAKABUDDHA. A Buddha without the thirty-two marks of the Great Man (Mahāpuruṣa) on his body; an epithet of Upagupta.

ĀMALAKA. A myrobalan; a small, very astringent fruit thought to have medicinal properties.

ANĀTMAN (Pali, *anatta*). The Buddhist doctrine that there is no real, permanent self within individuals.

AÑJALI. A salutation of respect and subservience consisting of cupping the hands and raising them in the direction of the respected person.

APSĀRA. One of a class of heavenly female divinities thought to be very beautiful; sometimes translated as "nymph."

ARHAT. A Buddhist saint, one who has attained enlightenment.

ĀRYA. Literally, a "noble one," and hence, in Buddhism, a respected member of the sangha, a monk.

ASURA. One of a class of supernatural beings whose fate is constantly to wage war against the devas (gods). The asura gaṭi is one of the realms of rebirth.

ĀTMAN. The self as absolute and real; the doctrine of ātman was opposed by the Buddhist notion of anātman (no-self).

AVADĀNA. Often translated as "legend"; a type of Buddhist story usually showing the workings of karma through the deeds of ordinary individuals.

AYAŚCAKRAVARTIN. An iron-wheeled cakravartin ruling over only one of the four continents of the cosmos; also a designation of Aśoka.

BALACAKRAVARTIN. An "armed cakravartin"; a king who needs to use or threaten force in order to establish his rule; an epithet of Aśoka.

BHAKTI. Loving devotion, adoration, generally felt for a divine figure.

BHAVACAKRA. The Wheel of Rebirth or Wheel of Life; a graphic depiction of the five (sometimes six) different realms of rebirth (gaṭi), often painted near the entrance to a monastery.

BHIKṢU (Pali, *bhikkhu*). Literally a "beggar"; a Buddhist monk.

BODHICITTA. The "mind of enlightenment" in all sentient beings which, when awakened and developed, can bring about full enlightenment.

BODHISATTVA. Anyone who is on the way to becoming a Buddha and will successfully attain that goal. In Theravāda Buddhism this refers especially to the Buddha Gotama in his previous existences.

CAITYA. A monument or sanctuary that recalls or brings to mind the person of the Buddha or an event in his life.

CAKRAVARTIN (Pali, *cakkavatti*). A "wheel-turning" monarch; a great king who rules the world according to Dharma.

CATURDVĪPAKACAKRAVARTIN. A cakravartin who rules over all four continents of the cosmos; equivalent to a survarṇacakravartin.

DĀNA. The practice of giving, of making donations, generally to the sangha; one of the principal ways of making merit.

DAṆḌA. Literally, "the stick"; punishment inflicted by a king on his subjects in the maintenance of law and order.

DAŚABALA. The "Ten-powered One"; an epithet of the Buddha.

DEVARĀJA. A divine king; the notion of a monarch embodying the figure of a deity.

DHARMA (Pali, Dhamma). The Teaching of the Buddha, Truth, Law, Righteousness, a basic element of reality (in the latter sense, usually written dharma). The word has many meanings, but they mostly revolve around the notion of anything that is fundamentally true or real.

DHARMACAKRA (Pali, *dhammacakka*). The Wheel of the Teaching or of monastic concerns in the scheme of the Two Wheels of Buddhism.

DHARMACAKṢU. The eye that sees the Truth (Dharma) and is opened when enlightenment is attained.

DHARMADĀYADA. Literally, "an heir to the Dharma"; a kinsman of the Buddha, a monk.

DHARMAKĀYA. The corpus of the Buddha's Teachings, but closely identified with his person. In the context of the fully developed Mahāyāna doctrine of the bodies of the Buddha, the Dharmakāya (generally capitalized) comes to be the Absolute or Truth-body of the Buddha.

DHARMARĀJA. A righteous king who rules according to Dharma; also an epithet of the Buddha.

DHARMARĀJIKĀ. A monument pertaining to a dharmarāja, a stūpa.

DHŪTĀṄGA. A set of ascetic practices not normally expected of Buddhist monks but followed by some individual bhikṣus who are so inclined.

DĪNĀRA. A gold coin of a certain value, sometimes equated with the Roman *denarius*.

DROṆA. A measure of capacity, literally a "bucket." The Buddha's relics were first divided into eight portions of one droṇa each by a Brahmin whose name is also given as Droṇa and were then distributed to eight kings. The stūpas built to enshrine them were thus called droṇa stūpas.

DUḤKHA (Pali, *dukkha*). One of the basic doctrines of Buddhism, often translated as "suffering," "ill," or "unsatisfactoriness." Duḥkha characterizes all existence everywhere.

GANDHARVA. One of a class of heavenly male divinities, often in attendance on other gods, sometimes portrayed as celestial musicians.

GARUḌA. One of a class of bird-like supernatural beings, traditionally held to be an enemy of the nāgas (snakes).

GATI. Literally, "a course," "a way"; a realm of rebirth. There are classically five gati into which a being can be reborn: the realms of the gods, humans, animals, hungry ghosts, and hell-beings. Later a sixth gati, that of the asuras, was added to the scheme.

HĪNAYĀNA. The "lesser vehicle"; one of the major schools of Buddhism, the other being the Māhāyāna or "greater vehicle."

JAMBUDVĪPA. The southern continent in the cosmological scheme of the four continents; usually identified with India.

JĀTAKA. A tale of one of the previous lives of the Buddha; the collection of such stories.

JĀTI. The position one obtains at birth as a result of one's karma; one's caste.

JINA. "The Victor"; an epithet of the Buddha.

JĪVA. In Jainism, the principle of life, the personal soul that eventually can attain liberation.

KALAHAJITA. "Victorious after a quarrel or confrontation"—an epithet of the copper-wheeled cakravartin describing his conquest of the two continents he rules.

KĀMADHĀTU. The realm of desire presided over by Māra; the lowest of the realms in the three-fold world, the others being the rūpadhātu (realm of form), and the arūpadhātu (formless realm).

KARMA. Literally, "action" especially "moral action"; any deed which will bring about certain corresponding effects in this or a future lifetime; also, the law or principle governing these cause and effect relationships.

KAṬHINA. The cloth annually given by laypersons to Buddhist monks for them to dye and make into robes.

KĀYA. A "body"; an assemblage of various parts.

KOṬI. The largest of the numbers in the ancient Indian counting system, usually said to be ten million.

MAHĀPURUṢA. A "Great Man"; one who is endowed with the thirty-two bodily marks and who can be either a Buddha or a cakravartin.

MAHĀSAṄGHIKA. A Hīnayānist sect whose teachings are seen as one of the precursors of the Mahāyāna school of Buddhism.

MAHĀYĀNA. The "greater vehicle"; one of the major schools of Buddhism, the other being the Hīnayāna ("lesser vehicle").

MAITREYA. The next Buddha of this world cycle whose coming is expected in the more or less distant future.

MAṂSACAKṢU. "The eye of flesh"; the everyday physical eye of ordinary persons.

MAṆḌALA. Literally, a "circle"; a structured arrangement, usually of Buddhas or deities, in a cosmologically attuned pattern; a depiction of such a pattern.

MAṆḌALIN. A petty king ruling over a particular region but not over the whole of one of the continents.

NĀGA. A snake; a snake-like supernatural being often thought to live in or control water.

PAÑCAVĀRṢIKA. A quinquennial festival held periodically by kings during which great donations are made to the sangha.

PARINIRVĀṆA. The final nirvāṇa occurring at the death of the Buddha or of any enlightened being, after which there is no more rebirth.

PIṆḌA. A food offering given, in Buddhism, to Buddhist monks, and, in Hinduism, to the deceased ancestors.

PRAKṚTI. "Nature," or "the created world," as distinguished from Puruṣa (the soul or Spirit) in the Sāṃkhya philosophy.

PRAJÑĀCAKṢU. The eye of wisdom which is opened upon enlightenment; equivalent to the dharmacakṣu.

PRAṆIDHĀNA. A vow or resolute wish to attain some form of enlightenment, usually in a future life.

PRATYEKABODHI. The enlightenment attained by a pratyekabuddha.

PRATYEKABUDDHA (Pali, *paccekabuddha*). One who, like the Buddha, attains enlightenment on his own, without the immediate help of a teacher, but who then, unlike the Buddha, does not share his enlightenment with others by teaching or founding a community.

PRATYUDYĀNA. The manner in which the silver-wheeled cakravartin is said to conquer the three continents that he rules—after some sort of "encounter."

PRETA. A hungry ghost whose chief suffering is that of hunger and thirst. The preta gaṭi is one of the realms of rebirth.

PUDGALA. Literally, a "person"; one of the principal tenets of the Personalist school of Buddhism (Pudgalavāda) that was criticized by more strict adherents to the anātman (no-self) doctrine.

PŪJĀ. An act of worship or reverence performed in front of a divinity or great saint or their image.

PUṆYAKṢETRA. A "field of merit" such as the Buddha or the sangha toward whom acts of merit are thought to be most effective.

PURUṢA. Literally, the "Man." In the Sāṃkhya philosophy, the soul or spirit in men and other beings that is caught up in prakṛti (the created world) until it attains salvation and release.

ṚṢI. A seer, a sage, an ascetic.

RŪPA. Form, materiality.

RŪPAKĀYA. The body of form, the physical body of the Buddha.

RŪPYACAKRAVARTIN. A silver-wheeled cakravartin who rules over three of the four continents of the cosmos.

ŚĀKYAPUTRA. A "son" or follower of Śākyamuni (the Buddha—the Sage of the Śākya clan); an epithet for a Buddhist monk.

SĀṂKHYA. A dualistically inclined school of Hindu philosophy, one of whose principal tenets is the doctrine of Puruṣa and prakṛti.

SAṂSĀRA. The flow of rebirth, characterized by suffering, in which all beings are caught.

SANGHA. The Buddhist community; the order of monks and nuns.

SANGHARĀJA. Literally, a "sangha-king"—the supreme patriarch of the monastic community appointed by the king in some Buddhist countries.

SĀRA. Literally, the "pith" or "core"; the essence of anything or person.

SĀRAVADDHI. In the edicts of Aśoka, a term meaning the development and expansion of the essence (sāra).

SARVĀSTIVĀDA. A Hīnayānist sect predominant in Northwest India known for its doctrine that "everything exists" (*sarva asti*) and for its willingness to incorporate avadānas and other legends into its canon.

SĀSANACAKRA (Pali, *sāsanacakka*). The wheel of the Buddhist order, equivalent to the dharmacakra, in the scheme of the Two Wheels of Buddhism.

ŚASTRAJITA. "Victorious by the sword"; an epithet of the iron-wheeled cakravartin describing the way that he conquers the one continent he rules; also, a description of Aśoka.

SKANDHA (Pali, *khandha*). The five "aggregates" that constitute for

Buddhists what is usually thought of as an individual self. The five skandhas are: form (rūpa), feeling (vedanā), perception (saṃjñā), mental formations (saṃskāra), and consciousness (vijñāna).

ŚRADDHĀ. Faith, trust, belief in the Buddha and his Teachings.

ŚRĀMAṆERA. A Buddhist novice who has not yet undergone the full ordination of a monk (bhikṣu).

ŚROTĀPANNA. "Entering the stream"; the first realization of the Truth of the Buddhist path, and hence the first step on the way to enlightenment.

STŪPA. A mound-like monument containing relics of the Buddha or some other object of veneration.

SŪTRA (Pali, *sutta*). Any doctrinal discourse attributed to the Buddha; also one of the major divisions of the Buddhist canon.

SUVARṆACAKRAVARTIN. A golden-wheeled cakravartin who rules over all four continents of the cosmos.

SVAYAṂYĀNA. The way in which a golden-wheeled cakravartin conquers his four continents by his "own going forth."

TĀMRACAKRAVARTIN. A copper-wheeled cakravartin who rules over two of the four continents of the cosmos.

TATHĀGATA. An epithet of the Buddha often used by the Buddha in referring to himself. It literally means the "one who has thus come," the "thus" implying that the Buddha has "come" in just the same way as the Buddhas of the past "came."

THERAVĀDA. Literally, the "Way of the Elders"; a Hīnayānist sect important especially for its preservation of the Pali Canon and its continued existence in South and Southeast Asia up to the present.

TRĀYASTRIṂŚA HEAVEN. The "Heaven of the Thirty-three" gods, of whom Indra is the chief; one of the most important heavens in Hindu and Buddhist mythology. The Buddha is said to have spent a rains retreat there preaching the Dharma to his mother.

UPĀYA. "Expedient means" in teaching the Dharma; good didactic strategy.

ŪRṆĀ. The whorl of hair located between the eyebrows of the Buddha; one of the thirty-two signs of the Great Man (Mahāpuruṣa).

UṢṆĪṢA. The protuberance on top of the Buddha's head; one of the thirty-two signs of the Great Man (Mahāpuruṣa).

VAJRA. Variously translated as "diamond," "thunderbolt," or "adamantine"; an embodiment in material terms of the hardness and sharpness of enlightened wisdom.

VAṂSA. A chronicle or lineage tracing the history of a particular country, monastery, or holy object.

VIDYĀDHARA. One of a class of beings having great magical powers and generally thought to reside in the Himalayas; a sorcerer.

VIHĀRA. A Buddhist monastery, especially the residence halls of its monks.

VINAYA. The discipline or code of conduct for monks; one of the major divisions of the Buddhist canon.

VYĀKARAṆA. A prediction or revelation of the future results (often enlightenment or Buddhahood) of an act of merit. This prediction is generally made by a Buddha.

YAKṢA. One of a class of supernatural beings, sometimes portrayed as demonic, but capable of being tamed and put to work as warriors or helpers.

YANTRA. Any artificial device, especially a diagram of a magical nature.

YOJANA. The distance one can travel without unyoking the oxen. It is variously measured at anywhere between one-and-one-half and nine miles.

Bibliography of Works Cited

Alsdorf, Ludwig. "Aśoka's Schismen-Edikt und das dritte Konzil." *Indo-Iranian Journal* 3 (1959): 161-74.

Andaya, Barbara Watson. "Statecraft in the Reign of Lü Tai of Sukhodaya." In *Religion and Legitimation of Power in Thailand, Laos, and Burma*, edited by Bardwell L. Smith. Chambersburg, Pa.: Anima Books, 1978. Pp. 2-19.

Aṅguttara Nikāya. See Morris, ed., and Woodward and Hare, tr.

Archaimbault, Charles. "La fête du T'at à Luong P'răbang." In *Essays Offered to G. H. Luce*, 2 vols., edited by Ba Shin, Jean Boisselier and A. B. Griswold. Ascona: Artibus Asiae, 1966. Vol. 1, pp. 5-47.

Arthaśāstra. See Kangle.

Āryaśūra, *Jātakamālā*. See Vaidya, ed., and Speyer, tr.

Aśokāvadāna. See Mukhopadhyaya, ed.

Aṣṭasāhasrikāprajñāpāramitā. See Conze, tr.

Aśvaghoṣa. *Buddhacarita*. See Johnston, ed. and tr.

Aśvaghoṣa. *Saundarananda*. See Johnston, ed. and tr.

Aśvaghoṣa. *Sūtrālaṃkāra*. See Huber, tr.

Avadānakalpalatā. See Vaidya, ed.

Avadānaśataka. See Vaidya, ed., and Feer, tr.

Bapat, P. V. and Hirakawa, Akira, trs. *Shan-Chien-P'i-P'o-Sha: A Chinese Version by Saṅghabhadra of the Samantapāsādikā*. Bhandarkar Oriental Series, no. 10. Poona: Bhandarkar Oriental Research Institute, 1970.

Bareau, André. "La jeunesse du Buddha dans les sūtrapiṭaka et les vinayapiṭaka anciens." *Bulletin de l'Ecole Française d'Extrême-Orient* 61 (1974): 199-274.

———. "Le parinirvāṇa du Buddha et la naissance de la religion bouddhique." *Bulletin de l'Ecole Française d'Extrême-Orient* 61 (1974): 275-99.

———. *Les premiers conciles bouddhiques*. Annales du Musée Guimet, vol. 60. Paris, 1955.

———. *Recherches sur la biographie du Buddha dans les sūtrapiṭaka et les vinayapiṭaka anciens*. Publications de l'Ecole Française d'Extrême-Orient, vol. 53. Paris: Ecole Française d'Extrême-Orient, 1963.

Barua, B. M. *Aśoka and His Inscriptions*. 2 vols. Calcutta: New Age Publishers, 1968.

Basham, A. L., ed. *Papers on the Date of Kaniṣka.* Leiden: E. J. Brill, 1968.

Beal, Samuel, tr. *Si-Yu-Ki: Buddhist Records of the Western World.* 2 vols. Reprint ed., New York: Paragon Book Reprint Corp., 1968.

Bechert, Heinz. "Aśoka's 'Schismenedikt' und der Begriff Sanghabheda." *Wiener Zeitschrift für die Kunde Süd-und Ostasiens* 5 (1961): 18-52.

———. "The Beginnings of Buddhist Historiography: Mahāvaṃsa and Political Thinking." In *Religion and Legitimation of Power in Sri Lanka*, edited by Bardwell L. Smith. Chambersburg, Pa.: Anima Books, 1978. Pp. 1-12.

———. *Buddhismus, Staat, und Gesellschaft in den Ländern des Theravāda-Buddhismus.* 3 vols. Wiesbaden: Otto Harrasowitz, 1966-73.

———. "Some Remarks on the Kaṭhina Rite." *Journal of the Bihar Research Society* 54 (1968): 319-29.

Beyer, Stephan. *The Buddhist Experience.* Encino, Calif.: Dickenson, 1974.

Bhandarkar, D. R. *Aśoka.* Calcutta: University of Calcutta Press, 1925.

Birnbaum, Raoul. *The Healing Buddha.* Boulder, Colo.: Shambala, 1974.

Bloch, Jules, ed. and tr. *Les inscriptions d'Aśoka.* Paris: Les Belles Lettres, 1950.

Bloss, Lowell W. "The Taming of Māra: Witnessing to the Buddha's Virtues." *History of Religions* 18 (1979): 156-76.

Bongard-Levin, G. M. "The Historicity of the Ancient Indian Avadānas: A Legend about Aśoka's Deposition and the Queen's Edict." In *Studies in Ancient India and Central Asia.* Soviet Indology Series, no. 7. Calcutta: Indian Studies Past and Present, 1971. Pp. 123-41.

Bongard-Levin, G. M. and Volvoka, O. F. *The Kunāla Legend and an Unpublished Aśokāvadānamālā Manuscript.* Calcutta: Indian Studies Past and Present, 1965.

Brown, W. Norman. "The Metaphysics of the Truth Act (Satyakriyā)." In *Mélanges d'indianisme à la mémoire de Louis Renou.* Paris: E. de Boccard, 1968. Pp. 171-77.

Burnouf, Eugène. *Introduction à l'histoire du buddhisme indien.* Paris: Adrien Maisonneuve, 1876.

Carpenter, J. Estlin, ed. *Dīgha Nikāya.* 3 vols. London: Pali Text Society, 1911.

Carthew, M. "The History of the Thai in Yunnan." In *Journal of the Siam Society, Selected Articles*. 10 vols. Bangkok: The Siam Society, 1954-61. Vol. 3, pp. 133-70.

Chavannes, Edouard. *Cinq cents contes et apologues extraits du Tripiṭaka chinois*. 4 vols. Paris: Imprimerie Nationale, 1934.

Ch'en, Kenneth K. S. *Buddhism in China*. Princeton: Princeton University Press, 1969.

Coedès, Georges. "Les inscriptions malaises de Çrīvijaya." *Bulletin de l'Ecole Française d'Extrême-Orient* 30 (1930): 29-80.

Conze, Edward. *Buddhist Thought in India*. Ann Arbor: University of Michigan Press, 1962.

———. *A Short History of Buddhism*. London: George Allen & Unwin, 1980.

Conze, Edward, tr. *The Perfection of Wisdom in Eight Thousand Lines and its Verse Summary*. Bolinas, Calif: Four Seasons Foundation, 1973.

Conze, Edward, ed. *Buddhist Texts Through the Ages*. New York: Harper and Row, 1964.

Cowell, E. B. and Neil, R. A., eds. *The Divyāvadāna*. Cambridge: The University Press, 1886.

Cūḷavaṃsa. See Geiger, tr.

Dasgupta, Surendranath. *A History of Indian Philosophy*. 5 vols. Delhi: Motilal Banarsidass, 1975.

Davids, C.A.F. Rhys, tr. *The Book of the Kindred Sayings*. 5 vols. Pali Text Society Translation Series, nos. 7, 10, 13, 14, 16. London: Pali Text Society, 1917-30.

Davids, T. W. Rhys. "Aśoka and the Buddha Relics." *Journal of the Royal Asiatic Society*, 1907, pp. 397-410.

———. *Buddhist India*. Orig. pub., 1903; reprint ed., Calcutta: Susil Gupta, 1959.

Davids, T. W. Rhys, tr. *Dialogues of the Buddha*. 3 vols. Sacred Books of the Buddhists, nos. 2-4. London: Pali Text Society, 1899-1921.

———. *The Questions of King Milinda*. 2 vols. Sacred Books of the East, nos. 35-36. Orig. pub. 1890-94; reprint ed., New York: Dover, 1963.

Davids, T. W. Rhys and Oldenberg, Hermann, trs. *Vinaya Texts*. 3 vols. Sacred Books of the East, nos. 13, 17, 20. Orig. pub., 1882-85; reprint ed., Delhi: Motilal Banarsidass, 1975.

Dayal, Har. *The Bodhisattva Doctrine in Buddhist Sanskrit Literature*. Orig. pub., 1932; reprint ed., Delhi: Motilal Banarsidass, 1975.

Demiéville, Paul. "Busshin." In *Hōbōgirin: Dictionnaire encyclopédique du bouddhisme d'après les sources chinoises et japonaises*, edited by Paul Demiéville. Tokyo: Maison Franco-japonaise, 1929- .

Denis, Eugène. "La *Lokapaññatti* et la légende birmane d'Aśoka." *Journal asiatique* 264 (1976): 97-116.

Denis, Eugène, ed. and tr. *La Lokapaññatti et les idées cosmologiques du bouddhisme ancien*. 2 vols. Lille: Atelier Reproduction des thèses, 1977.

Dhammapadaṭṭhakathā. See Norman, ed., and Burlingame, tr.

Dīgha Nikāya. See Carpenter, ed., and Davids, T. W. Rhys, tr.

Dikshitar, V. R. Ramachandra. *The Mauryan Polity*. Madras: The University of Madras, 1932.

Dīpavaṃsa. See Law, ed. and tr.

Divyāvadāna. See Vaidya, ed., and Cowell and Neil, ed.

Douglas, Mary. *Purity and Danger*. London: Routledge and Kegan Paul, 1966.

Drekmeier, Charles. *Kingship and Community in Early India*. Stanford: Stanford University Press, 1962.

Duroiselle, Charles. "Upagutta et Māra." *Bulletin de l'Ecole Française d'Extrême-Orient* 4 (1904): 414-28.

Durt, Hubert. "La version chinoise de l'introduction historique de la Samantapāsākikā." 3 vols. Ph.D. Dissertation, Université Catholique de Louvain, Institut Orientaliste, 1970.

Dutt, Nalinaksha, ed. *Gilgit Manuscripts*, vol. 3, part 1. Srinagar: Research Department, 1947.

Dutt, Nalinaksha and Bajpai, Krishna Datta. *Development of Buddhism in Uttar Pradesh*. Lucknow: Government of Uttar Pradesh Publication Bureau, 1956.

Ecke, Gustav. "Ānanda and Vakula in Early Chinese Carvings." *Sino-Indian Studies* 5 (1957): 40-46.

Eggermont, P.H.L. *The Chronology of the Reign of Asoka Moriya*. Leiden: E. J. Brill, 1956.

Eisenstadt, S. N. *Max Weber on Charisma and Institution Building*. Chicago: University of Chicago Press, 1968.

Eliade, Mircea. *Cosmos and History*. Translated by Willard R. Trask. New York: Harper and Row, 1959.

Emmerick, R. E. *Tibetan Texts Concerning Khotan*. London Oriental Series, vol. 19. London: Oxford University Press, 1967.

Ensink, J. tr. *The Questions of Rāṣṭrapāla*. Zwolle, 1952.

Evans-Wentz, W. Y., ed. *The Tibetan Book of the Great Liberation*. London: Oxford University Press, 1954.

Fa-hsien. *Fo kuo chi.* See Legge, tr. and ed.

Falk, Maryla. *Nama-Rūpa and Dharma-Rūpa.* Calcutta: University of Calcutta Press, 1943.

Feer, Léon, tr. *Avadāna-çataka: cent légendes (bouddhiques).* Annales du Musée Guimet, vol. 18. Paris: E. Leroux, 1891.

Ferguson, John P. "The Quest for Legitimation by Burmese Monks and Kings: The Case of the Shwegyin Sect (19th-20th Centuries)." In *Religion and Legitimation of Power in Thailand, Laos and Burma*, ed. Bardwell L. Smith. Chambersburg, Pa.: Anima Books, 1978. Pp. 66-86.

Filliozat, Jean. "Les deux Aśoka et les conciles bouddhiques." *Journal asiatique* 236 (1948): 189-95.

———. "Les deva d'Aśoka: dieux ou divines majestés." *Journal asiatique* 237 (1949): 225-47.

Forte, Antonino. *Political Propaganda and Ideology in China at the End of the Seventh Century.* Naples: Istituto Universitario Orientale, 1976.

Frauwallner, Erich. "Die ceylonesischen Chroniken und die erste buddhistische Mission nach Hinterindien." In *Actes du IVe Congrès International des Sciences Anthropologiques* (Vienna, 1955). Vol. 2, pp. 192-97.

Frazer, James George. *The Golden Bough.* Abridged ed. London: MacMillan and Co., 1950.

Geiger, Wilhelm, tr. *Cūḷavaṃsa.* 2 vols. London: Pali Text Society, 1973.

———. *The Mahāvaṃsa or the Great Chronicle of Ceylon.* London: Pali Text Society, 1912.

Geiger, Wilhelm, ed. *The Mahāvaṃsa.* Orig. pub., 1908; reprint ed., London: Luzac and Co., 1958.

Gode, P. K. "Indian Science of Cosmetics and Perfumery." *The International Perfumer* 3 (1951): 1-9.

Gokhale, B. G. *Asoka Maurya.* New York: Twayne Publishers, 1966.

———. *Buddhism and Aśoka.* Baroda: Padmaja Publications, 1949.

——— "Dhamiko Dhammarājā: A Study in Buddhist Constitutional Concepts." In *Indica.* The Indian Historical Research Institute Silver Jubilee Commemoration Volume. Bombay: St. Xavier's College, 1953.

———. "Early Buddhist Kingship." *Journal of Asian Studies* 26 (1966): 15-22.

Gombrich, Richard. "The Consecration of a Buddhist Image." *Journal of Asian Studies* 26 (1966): 23-26.

Gombrich, Richard. *Precept and Practice. Traditional Buddhism in the Rural Highlands of Ceylon*. Oxford: Clarendon Press, 1971.

Gonda, Jan. *Ancient Indian Kingship from the Religious Point of View*. Leiden: E. J. Brill, 1966.

Grousset, René. *In the Footsteps of the Buddha*. Translated by J. A. Underwood. New York: Grossman Publishers, 1971.

Handurukande, Ratna, ed. and tr. *Maṇicūḍāvadāna and Lokānanda*. Sacred Books of the Buddhists, 24. London: Luzac and Co., 1967.

Hemacandra. *Sthavirāvalīcarita*. See Jacobi, ed.

Hirakawa, Akira. "The Rise of Mahāyāna Buddhism and its Relationship to the Worship of Stūpas." *Memoirs of the Research Department of the Toyo Bunko* 22 (1963): 57-106.

Hofinger, Marcel. *Le congrès du lac Anavatapta (vies de saints bouddhiques) extrait du Vinaya des Mūlasarvāstivāda Bhaiṣajyavastu*. Bibliothèque du Muséon, vol. 34. Louvain: Institut Orientaliste, 1954.

Hopkins, W. "Two Notes on the Mahābhārata—Religious Intolerance." In *Album Kern*. Leiden: E. J. Brill, 1903. Pp. 249-51.

Horner, I. B. "The Earth as a Swallower." In *Essays Offered to G. H. Luce*, 2 vols., edited by Ba Shin, Jean Boisselier, and A. B. Griswold. Ascona: Artibus Asiae, 1966. Vol. 1, pp. 151-59.

Horner, I. B., tr. *The Middle Length Sayings (Majjhima-Nikāya)*. 3 vols. Pali Text Society Translation Series, nos. 29-31. London: Luzac and Co., 1954-59.

Hsüan-tsang. *Ta-T'ang Hsi-yü chi*. See Beal, tr.

Huber, Edouard. "Etudes de littérature bouddhique: trois contes du *Sūtrālaṃkara* d'Aśvaghoṣa conservés dans le *Divyāvadāna*." *Bulletin de l'Ecole Française d'Extrême-Orient* 4 (1904): 709-26.

———. "Les sources du Divyāvadāna." *Bulletin de l'Ecole Française d'Extrême-Orient* 6 (1906): 1-37.

Huber, Edouard, tr. *Aśvaghoṣa Sūtrālaṃkāra*. Paris: E. Leroux, 1908.

Hurvitz, Leon. " 'Render unto Caesar' in Early Chinese Buddhism." In *Liebenthal Festschrift*, edited by Kshitis Roy. Santiniketan: Visvabharati, 1957. Pp. 80-114.

Itivuttaka. See Woodward, tr.

Jacobi, Hermann, ed. *Sthavirāvalīcharita or Parisishṭaparvan by Hemachandra*. Bibliotheca Indica, n.s. 537. Calcutta: Asiatic Society, 1885.

Jayawickrama, N. A. "A Reference to the Third Council in Aśoka's Edicts?" *University of Ceylon Review* 17 (1959): 61-72.

Jayawickrama, N. A., ed. and tr. *The Chronicle of the Thūpa and the Thūpavaṃsa*. Sacred Books of the Buddhists, 28. London: Luzac and Co., 1971.

———. *The Inception of Discipline and the Vinaya Nidāna*. Sacred Books of the Buddhists, 21. London: Luzac and Co., 1962.

Johnston, E. H., ed. and tr. *The Buddhacarita or Acts of the Buddha*. Orig. pub., 1936; reprint ed., Delhi: Motilal Banarsidass, 1976.

———. *The Saundarananda of Aśvaghoṣa*. Lahore, 1928; reprint ed., Delhi: Motilal Banarsidass, 1975.

Jones, J. J., tr. *The Mahāvastu*. 3 vols. Sacred Books of the Buddhists, nos. 16, 18-19. London: Pali Text Society, 1949-56.

Jones, John Garrett. *Tales and Teachings of the Buddha*. London: George Allen & Unwin, 1979.

Kangle, R. P. *The Kauṭiliya Arthaśāstra*. 3 vols. Bombay: University of Bombay, 1963-65.

Kern, Hendrik. *Histoire du bouddhisme indien*. 2 vols. Translated by J. Huet. Paris: E. Leroux, 1901-03.

Kern, Hendrik, tr. *Saddharma-Puṇḍarīka or the Lotus of the True Law*. Sacred Books of the East, no. 21. Oxford: Clarendon Press, 1884.

Kern, Hendrik and Nanjio, Bunyu, eds. *Saddharmapuṇḍarīka Sūtra*. Bibliotheca Buddhica, no. 10. St. Petersburg, 1912.

Khantipalo Bhikkhu. *The Wheel of Birth and Death*. Wheel Publications nos. 147-49. Kandy: Buddhist Publication Society, 1970.

Kielhorn, F. "Bhagavat, Tatrabhavat, and Devānāmpriya." *Journal of the Royal Asiatic Society* 1908, pp. 502-05.

Kin, Maung, "The Legend of Upagutta." *Buddhism* 1 (1903): 219-42.

Kitagawa, Joseph M. "Some Reflections on the Japanese World of Meaning." *Journal of the Oriental Society of Australia* 11 (1976): 1-16.

Kloppenborg, Ria. *The Paccekabuddha, A Buddhist Ascetic*. Leiden: E. J. Brill, 1974.

Krishna Rao, M. V. *Studies in Kautilya*. Delhi: Munshi Ram Manohar Lal, 1958.

Kumāralāta. *Kalpanāmaṇḍitikā*. See Lüders.

La Vallée Poussin, Louis de. "Appendice iii: Notes sur les corps du Bouddha." In Louis de La Vallée Poussin, tr., *Vijñaptimātratāsiddhi, la siddhi de Hiuan-tsang*. Buddhica, vol. 5. Paris: Paul Geuthner, 1929.

———. *Bouddhisme: études et matériaux*. Brussels, 1898.

———. *L'Inde aux temps des Mauryas*. Paris: E. de Boccard, 1930.

La Vallée Poussin, Louis de, tr. *L'Abhidharmakośa de Vasubandhu*. 6 vols. Paris: Paul Geuthner, 1923-31.

Lafont, Pierre-Bernard. "Le That de Muong-Sing." *Bulletin de la Société des Etudes Indochinoises*, n.s. 32 (1957): 39-57.

Lamotte, Etienne. *Histoire du bouddhisme indien*. Louvain: Institut Orientaliste, 1958.

Lancaster, Lewis R. "An Early Mahāyāna Sermon about the Body of the Buddha and the Making of Images." *Artibus Asiae* 36 (1974): 287-91.

Law, Bimala Churn. *Aśvaghoṣa*. Calcutta: Royal Asiatic Society of Bengal, 1946.

Law, Bimala Churn, ed. and tr. *The Dīpavaṃsa*. *Ceylon Historical Journal* 7 (1957-58).

Lee, Peter H. *Lives of Eminent Korean Monks*. Harvard-Yenching Institute Studies 25. Cambridge, Mass.: Harvard University Press, 1969.

Legge, James, tr. and ed. *A Record of Buddhistic Kingdoms*. Orig. pub., 1886; reprint ed., New York: Paragon Book Co., 1965.

Lessing, Ferdinand D. and Wayman, Alex. *Introduction to the Buddhist Tantrica Systems*, 2nd ed. Delhi: Motilal Banarsidass, 1978.

Lévi, Sylvain. "La Dṛṣṭanta-paṅkti et son auteur." *Journal asiatique* 211 (1927): 95-127.

———. "Eléments de formation du Divyāvadāna." *T'oung pao* 8 (1908): 105-22.

———. "Encore Aśvaghoṣa." *Journal asiatique* 213 (1928): 193-216.

———. "Notes de chronologie indienne—Devānāmpriya, Açoka et Kātyāyana." *Journal asiatique* 18 (1891): 549-53.

———. "Sur la récitation primitive des textes bouddhiques." *Journal asiatique* 5 (1915): 401-47.

———. "Vyuthena 256." *Journal asiatique* 17 (1911): 120-26.

Lévi, Sylvain, ed. and tr. *Mahākarmavibhaṅga et Karmavibhaṅgopadeśa*. Paris: E. Leroux, 1932.

Lévi, Sylvain and Chavannes, Edouard. "Les seize arhat protecteurs de la loi." *Journal asiatique* 8 (1916): 5-48, 189-304.

Lorenzen, David. "The Life of Śankarācārya." In *The Biographical Process*, ed. Frank Reynolds and Donald Capps. The Hague: Mouton, 1976. Pp. 87-107.

Lüders, Heinrich. *Bruchstücke der Kalpanāmaṇḍitikā des Kumāralāta*. Kleinere Sanskrittexte aus den Turfanfunden, no. 2. Leipzig, 1926.

MacPhail, James M. *Aśoka*. London: Oxford University Press, n.d.

Mahābodhivaṃsa. See Strong, S. Arthur, ed.
Mahākarmavibhaṅga. See Lévi, ed. and tr.
Mahāvaṃsa. See Geiger, ed., and Geiger, tr.
Mahāvaṃsaṭīkā. See Malalasekera, ed.
Mahāvastu. See Jones, J. J., tr.
Mahāvyutpatti. See Sakaki, ed.
Majjhima Nikāya. See Horner, tr.
Malalasekera, G. P., ed. *Mahāvaṃsa-ṭīkā*. 2 vols. London: Pali Text Society, 1935-36.
Maṇicūḍāvadāna. See Handurukande, ed. and tr.
Marshall, John. *A Guide to Sāñchī*. 3rd ed. Calcutta: Government of India Press, 1955.
Matisoff, Susan. *The Legend of Semimaru: Blind Musician of Japan*. New York: Columbia University Press, 1978.
Mātṛceṭa. *Śatapañcaśatka*. See Shackleton-Bailey.
Mātṛceṭa. *Sugatapañcatriṃśatstotra*. See Python.
Mātṛceṭa. *Varṇārhavarṇastotra*. See Shackleton-Bailey.
Mauss, Marcel. *A General Theory of Magic*. Translated by Robert Brain. New York: W. W. Norton and Co., 1972.
Milindapañha. See Davids, T. W. Rhys, tr.
Minakata, Kumagusu. "The Wandering Jew." *Notes and Queries* 4 (1899): 121-24.
Mitra, Rajendralal. *The Sanskrit Buddhist Literature of Nepal*. Calcutta: Asiatic Society of Bengal, 1882.
Monier-Williams, Monier. *Buddhism in its Connexion with Brahmanism and Hinduism*. Orig. pub. 1889; reprint ed., Delhi: The Chowkhamba Sanskrit Series Office, 1964.
Mookerji, Radhakumud. *Aśoka*. Orig. pub., 1928; reprint ed. Delhi: Motilal Banarsidass, 1972.
———. *Harsha*. Orig. pub., 1925; reprint ed., Delhi: Motilal Banarsidass, 1965.
Morris, Richard, ed. *The Aṅguttara-Nikāya*. 5 vols. London: Pali Text Society, 1885.
Mukhopadhyaya, Sujitkumar, ed. *The Aśokāvadāna*. New Delhi: Sahitya Akademi, 1963.
Mus, Paul. *Barabuḍur: Esquisse d'une histoire du bouddhisme fondée sur la critique archéologique des textes*. 2 vols. Hanoi: Imprimerie d'Extrême-Orient, 1935.
———. "Barabuḍur, sixième partie: Genèse de la bouddhologie mahāyāniste." *Bulletin de l'Ecole Française d'Extrême-Orient* 34 (1934): 175-400.
———. "Le Buddha paré. Son origine indienne. Çākyamuni dans la

mahāyānisme moyen." *Bulletin de l'Ecole Française d'Extrême-Orient* 28 (1928): 153-278.

———. "Un cinéma solide." *Arts asiatiques* 10 (1964): 21-34.

———. *La lumière sur les six voies*. Travaux et mémoires de l'Institut d'Ethnologie, no. 35. Paris: Institut d'Ethnologie, 1939.

———. "La mythologie primitive et la pensée de l'Inde." *Bulletin de la Société Française de Philosophie* 37 (1937): 83-126.

———. "Où finit Puruṣa?" In *Mélanges d'indianisme à la mémoire de Louis Renou*. Paris: E. de Boccard, 1968. Pp. 539-63.

———. "Le sourire d'Angkor: art, foi et politique bouddhiques sous Jayavarman VII." *Artibus Asiae* 24 (1961): 363-81.

———. "Thousand-Armed Kannon: A Mystery or a Problem?" *Indogaku bukkyōgaku kenkyū/Journal of Indian and Buddhist Studies* 12 (1964): 1-33.

Nagao, Gadgin. "On the Theory of Buddha-Body (Buddha-kāya)." *Eastern Buddhist* 6 (1973): 25-53.

Nikam, N. A. and McKeon, Richard, ed. and tr. *The Edicts of Aśoka*. Chicago: University of Chicago Press, 1959.

Nilakanta Sastri, K. A. *Age of the Nandas and Mauryas*. Delhi: Motilal Banarsidass, 1967.

———. "Cakravartin." *New Indian Antiquary* 3 (1940): 307-21.

———. *Gleanings on Social Life from the Avadānas*. Calcutta: Indian Research Institute, 1945.

Nobel, Johannes. "Kumāralāta und sein Werk." In *Nachrichten von der königlichen Gesellschaft der Wissenschaften, Göttingen, Philol.-histor. Klasse*, 1928, pp. 295ff.

Norman, H. C., ed. *The Commentary on the Dhammapada*. 3 vols. London: Pali Text Society, 1912.

Pelliot, Paul. "Deux itinéraires de Chine en Inde à la fin du VIIIè siècle." *Bulletin de l'Ecole Française d'Extrême-Orient* 4 (1904): 131-413.

Pérez-Rémon, Joaquin. "The Simile of the Pith (Sāra) in the Nikāyas and its Bearing on the Anattavāda." *Boletín de la Asociación Española de Orientalistas* 15 (1979): 71-93.

Prinsep, James. "Interpretation of the Most Ancient of the Inscriptions on the Pillar Called the Lát of Feroz Shah near Delhi, and of the Allahabad, Radhia, and Mattiah Pillar, or Lát, Inscriptions which Agree Therewith." *Journal of the Asiatic Society of Bengal* 6 (1837): 566-609.

Przyluski, Jean. *La légende de l'empereur Açoka*. Paris: Paul Geuthner, 1923.

———. "Le Nord-ouest de l'Inde dans le Vinaya des Mūlasarvāstivādin et les textes apparentés." *Journal asiatique* 4 (1914): 493-568.

———. "Le partage des reliques du Buddha." *Mélanges chinois et bouddhiques* 4 (1936): 341-67.

———. "La ville du cakravartin: influences babyloniennes sur la civilisation de l'Inde." *Rocznik Orjentalistyczny* 5 (1927): 165-85.

Python, P. "Le Sugatapañcatriṃśatstotra de Mātṛceṭa (Louange des trente-cinq Sugata)." In *Etudes tibétaines dédiées à la mémoire de Marcelle Lalou*. Paris: Adrien Maisonneuve, 1971. Pp. 402-10.

Radhakrishnan, S., ed. and tr. *The Principal Upaṇisads*. New York: Harper and Brothers, 1953.

Rāṣṭrapālaparipṛcchā. See Ensink, tr.

Reynolds, Frank E. "Ritual and Social Hierarchy: An Aspect of Traditional Religion in Buddhist Laos." In *Religion and Legitimation of Power in Thailand, Laos, and Burma*, edited by Bardwell L. Smith. Chambersburg, Pa.: Anima Books, 1978. Pp. 166-74.

———. "Sacral Kingship and National Development: The Case of Thailand." In *Religion and Legitimation of Power in Thailand, Laos, and Burma*, edited by Bardwell L. Smith. Chambersburg, Pa.: Anima Books, 1978. Pp. 100-110.

———. "The Several Bodies of the Buddha: Reflections on a Neglected Aspect of Theravāda Tradition." *History of Religions* 16 (1977): 374-89.

———. "The Two Wheels of Dhamma: A Study of Early Buddhism." In *The Two Wheels of Dhamma*, edited by Bardwell L. Smith. Chambersburg, Pa.: American Academy of Religion, 1972. Pp. 6-30.

Reynolds, Frank E. and Reynolds, Mani B., tr. *Three Worlds According to King Ruang*. Berkeley Buddhist Series, vol. 4. Berkeley: Asian Humanities Press, 1982.

Rockhill, W. Woodville. *The Life of the Buddha*. London: Kegan Paul, Trench, Trübner and Co., 1907.

Ruegg, David Seyfort. *La théorie du Tathāgatagarbha et du gotra*. Publications de l'Ecole Française d'Extrême-Orient, vol. 70. Paris: Ecole Française d'Extrême-Orient, 1969.

Saddharmapuṇḍarīka. See Kern, tr., and Kern and Nanjio, ed.

Sakaki, Ryōzaburo, ed. *Mahāvyutpatti*. Kyoto University, Department of Literature, pub. no. 3. Kyoto, 1916.

Saṃyutta Nikāya. See Davids, C.A.F. Rhys, tr.

Sarkisyanz, E. "Buddhist Backgrounds of Burmese Socialism." In *Religion and Legitimation of Power in Thailand, Laos, and Burma*, edited by Bardwell L. Smith. Chambersburg, Pa.: Anima Books, 1978. Pp. 87-99.

Sénart, Emile. *Les inscriptions de Piyadassi.* 2 vols. Paris: Imprimerie Nationale, 1881.

———. "Le manuscript kharosthi du Dhammapada; les fragments Dutreuil de Rhins." *Journal asiatique* 12 (1898): 193-308.

———. "Un roi de l'Inde au IIIe siècle avant notre ère." *Revue des deux mondes* 92 (1889): 67-108.

Shackleton-Bailey, D. R. *The Śatapañcaśatka of Mātṛceṭa.* Cambridge: University Press, 1951.

———. "The Varṇārhavarṇa Stotra of Mātṛceṭa." *Bulletin of the School of Oriental and African Studies* 13 (1950): 671-810; 947-1003.

Shams-i Siraj 'Afif. *Tarikh-i Firoz Shahi*, edited and translated by John Dowson. In *The History of India as Told by its own Historians—The Posthumous Papers of the Late Sir H. M. Elliot.* Vol. 3. Orig. pub., 1871; reprint ed., Allahabad: Kitab Mahal, n.d.

Shorto, H. L. "The Thirty-two Myos in the Medieval Mon Kingdom." *Bulletin of the School of Oriental and African Studies* 26 (1963): 572-91.

Smith, Bardwell L. "The Ideal Social Order as Portrayed in the Chronicles of Ceylon." In *Religion and Legitimation of Power in Sri Lanka*, ed. Bardwell L. Smith. Chambersburg, Pa.: Anima Books, 1978. Pp. 48-72.

Smith, Vincent. *Aśoka, the Buddhist Emperor of India.* Orig. pub., 1909; reprint ed., Delhi: S. Chand & Co., 1964.

———. "Aśoka's Father Confessor." *Indian Antiquary* 32 (1903): 365-66.

Speyer, J. A., tr. *Ārya Śūra's Jātakamālā.* Sacred Books of the Buddhists, vol. 1. London: Henry Frowde, 1895.

Spiro, Melford. *Buddhism and Society.* New York: Harper and Row, 1970.

———. "Reply to Professor Tambiah." *Journal of Asian Studies* 37 (1978): 809-12.

———. [Review of *World Conqueror and World Renouncer.*] *Journal of Asian Studies* 36 (1977): 789-91.

Śrīmālādevīsiṃhanādasūtra. See Wayman and Wayman.

Stevens, Winifred. *Legends of Indian Buddhism.* London: John Murray, 1911.

Strong, John. "Aśoka's Quinquennial Festival and Other Great Acts of Dāna: An Essay on the Nature of Buddhist Giving." Unpublished Manuscript. Lewiston, Maine, 1982.

———. "Buddhism and Filial Piety: The Indian Antecedents to a 'Chinese' Problem." In *Traditions in Contact and Change*, edited by Peter Slater, Maurice Boutin, Harold Coward, and Donald Wiebe. Waterloo, Ontario: Wilfred Laurier University Press, 1983.

———. "The Buddhist Avadānists and the Elder Upagupta." In *Tantric and Taoist Studies in Honour of R. A. Stein*, edited by Michel Strickmann. *Mélanges Chinois et bouddhiques*, vols. 20-22.

———. "Gandhakuṭī: The Perfumed Chamber of the Buddha." *History of Religions* 16 (1977): 390-406.

———. "The Legend of the Lion-Roarer: A Study of the Buddhist Arhat Piṇḍola Bhāradvāja." *Numen* 26 (1979): 50-88.

———. "Making Merit in the *Aśokāvadāna*." Ph.D. Dissertation, University of Chicago, 1977.

———. "The Transforming Gift: An Analysis of Devotional Acts of Offering in Buddhist Avadāna Literature." *History of Religions* 18 (1979): 221-37.

Strong, S. Arthur, ed. *Mahābodhivaṃsa*. London: Pali Text Society, 1891.

Tachibana, Shundo. "Prince Shōtoku, King Aśoka of Japan." *Studies on Buddhism in Japan* 4 (1942): 103-09.

Tagore, Rabindranath. *The Collected Poems and Plays*. New York: MacMillan Co., 1937.

Takakusu, Junjiro, tr. *A Record of the Buddhist Religion as Practised in India and the Malay Archipelago (A.D. 671-694)*. Orig. pub., 1896; reprint ed., Delhi: Munshiran Manoharlal, 1966.

Takasaki, Jikido. *A Study on the Ratnagotravibhāga*. Rome: Istituto Italiano per il Medio ed Estremo Oriente, 1966.

Tambiah, Stanley J. *Buddhism and the Spirit Cults in North-East Thailand*. Cambridge: Cambridge University Press, 1970.

———. "The Buddhist Conception of Kingship and its Historical Manifestations: A Reply to Spiro." *Journal of Asian Studies* 37 (1978): 801-9.

———. *World Conqueror and World Renouncer*. Cambridge: University Press, 1976.

Tāranātha, *History of Buddhism*. Translated by Lama Chimpa and Alaka Chattopadhyaya. Simla: Indian Institute of Advanced Study, 1970.

Thapar, Romila. *Aśoka and the Decline of the Mauryas.* London: Oxford University Press, 1961.

———. *A History of India.* Volume 1. Harmondsworth: Penguin Books, 1966.

Thomas, E. J. "Avadāna and Apadāna." *Indian Historical Quarterly* 9 (1933): 32-36.

———. *The Life of Buddha.* London: Routledge and Kegan Paul, 1927.

Thomas, F. W. "Mahārājakanikalekha." *Indian Antiquary,* 1903, pp. 345ff.

Thūpavaṃsa. See Jayawickrama, ed. and tr.

Tin, Pe Maung, tr. *The Path of Purity.* 2 vols. Pali Text Society Translation Series, nos. 11, 17. London: Pali Text Society, 1923.

Tokiwai, Tsurumatsu. *Studien zum Sumāgadhāvadāna.* Darmstadt: G. Ottos, 1898.

Tsukamoto Zenryū. "Wei Shou on Buddhism and Taoism." Translated by Leon Hurvitz in *Yün-kang, the Buddhist Cave Temples of the 5th Century A.D.,* ed. Mizuno Seiichi and Nagahiro Toshio. Kyoto, 1956. Vol. 16, suppl.

Turnour, George. "Further Notes on the Inscriptions on the Columns at Delhi, Allahabad, Beliah, &c." *Journal of the Asiatic Society of Bengal* 6 (1837): 1049-64.

Vaidya, P. L., ed. *Avadāna-Kalpalatā.* 2 vols. Buddhist Sanskrit Texts, nos. 22-23. Darbhanga, Bihar: Mithila Institute, 1959.

———. *Avadāna-śatakam.* Buddhist Sanskrit Texts, no. 19. Darbhanga, Bihar: Mithila Institute, 1958.

———. *Divyāvadānam.* Buddhist Sanskrit Texts, no. 20. Darbhanga, Bihar: Mithila Institute, 1959.

———. *Jātaka-mālā by Ārya Śūra.* Buddhist Sanskrit Texts, no. 21. Darbhanga, Bihar: Mithila Institute, 1959.

Vasubandhu, *Abhidharmakośa.* See La Vallée Poussin, tr.

Viennot, Odette. *Le culte de l'arbre dans l'Inde ancienne.* Paris: Musée Guimet, 1954.

Vinaya nidāna. See Jayawickrama, ed. and tr.

Vinaya piṭaka. See Davids and Oldenberg, trs.

De Visser, Marinus Willem. "The Arhats in China and Japan." *Ostasiatische Zeitschrift* 7 (1918/19): 87-102, 221-31; 9 (1920/22): 116-44; 10 (1922/23): 60-102.

Visuddhimagga. See Tin, tr.

Waddell, L. A. "The Buddhist Pictorial Wheel of Life." *Journal of the Royal Asiatic Society of Bengal* 61 (1892): 133-55.

———. "Identity of Upagupta, the High Priest of Açoka with Moggaliputta Tisso." *Proceedings of the Asiatic Society of Bengal* 1899, pp. 70-75.

———. "Upagupta, the Fourth Buddhist Patriarch, and High Priest of Açoka." *Journal of the Asiatic Society of Bengal* 66 (1897): 76-84.

Warder, A. K. *Indian Buddhism*. Delhi: Motilal Banarsidass, 1970.

Watters, Thomas. *On Yuan Chwang's Travels in India*. 2 vols. Orig. pub. 1905; reprint ed., Delhi: Munshi Ram Manohar Lal, 1961.

Wayman, Alex. "Notes on the Three Myrobalans." *Phi Theta Annual* 5 (1954): 63-77.

Wayman, Alex and Wayman, Hideko, trs. *The Lion's Roar of Queen Śrīmālā*. New York: Columbia University Press, 1974.

Weber, Max. *The Religion of India*. Translated by Hans H. Gerth and Don Martindale. New York: The Free Press, 1958.

Weeraratne, W. G. "Avadāna." *Encyclopaedia of Buddhism*. Edited by G. P. Malalasekera. Colombo: Government Publications, 1966.

Wells, H. G. *The Outline of History*, 2 vols. New York: MacMillan Co., 1920.

Wieger, Léon, ed. and tr. *Les vies chinoises du Bouddha*. 1st ed., Shanghai, 1913; reprint ed., Paris: Cathasia, 1951.

Windisch, Ernst. *Māra und Buddha*. Leipzig: S. Hirzel, 1895.

Winternitz, Maurice. *A History of Indian Literature*. Translated by S. Ketkar. Calcutta: University of Calcutta Press, 1933. Volume 2.

Woodward, F. L. tr. *Itivuttaka: As It Was Said*. Sacred Books of the Buddhists, vol. 8. London: Oxford University Press, 1948.

Woodward, F. L. and Hare, E. M., tr. *The Book of the Gradual Sayings (Anguttara Nikāya)*. 5 vols. Pali Text Society Translation Series, nos. 22, 24-27. London: Pali Text Society, 1932-36.

Wright, Arthur. "The Formation of Sui Ideology, 581-604." In *Chinese Thought and Institutions*, ed. John K. Fairbank. Chicago: University of Chicago Press, 1957. Pp. 71-104.

Yeshe Tsogyal. *The Life and Liberation of Padmasambhava*. Translated by Kenneth Douglas and Gwendolyn Bays. 2 vols. Emeryville, Cal.: Dharma Publishing, 1978.

Zimmer, Heinrich. *Myths and Symbols in Indian Art and Civilization*. New York: Harper and Row, 1946.

Zürcher, Erik. *The Buddhist Conquest of China*, Leiden: E. J. Brill, 1959.

Index